WITHDRAWN

920
NOT

Notable women in
mathematics.

$49.95

000033843
08/14/1999

DATE			

ALAN N. HOUGHTON LIBRARY
RENBROOK SCHOOL
2865 ALBANY AVENUE
WEST HARTFORD, CT 06117−1899
08/14/1999

BAKER & TAYLOR

NOTABLE WOMEN
IN
MATHEMATICS

NOTABLE WOMEN
IN
MATHEMATICS

A Biographical Dictionary

EDITED BY

Charlene Morrow and Teri Perl

Greenwood Press
Westport, Connecticut • London

Alan N. Houghton Library
Renbrook School
2865 Albany Avenue
West Hartford, CT 06117

Library of Congress Cataloging-in-Publication Data

Notable women in mathematics : a biographical dictionary / edited by
  Charlene Morrow and Teri Perl.
      p.   cm.
    Includes bibliographical references (p.   –   ) and index.
    ISBN 0–313–29131–4 (alk. paper)
    1. Women mathematicians—Biography.   I. Morrow, Charlene, 1948–   .
    II. Perl, Teri.
  QA28.N68   1998
  510'.92'2—dc21
  [B]   97–18598

British Library Cataloguing in Publication Data is available.

Copyright © 1998 by Charlene Morrow and Teri Perl

All rights reserved. No portion of this book may be
reproduced, by any process or technique, without the
express written consent of the publisher.

Library of Congress Catalog Card Number: 97–18598
ISBN: 0–313–29131–4

First published in 1998

Greenwood Press, 88 Post Road West, Westport, CT 06881
An imprint of Greenwood Publishing Group, Inc.

Printed in the United States of America

The paper used in this book complies with the
Permanent Paper Standard issued by the National
Information Standards Organization (Z39.48–1984).

10 9 8 7 6 5 4 3 2

Cover photos courtesy of Fan King Chung, Jean Taylor, Cathleen Synge Morawetz, and
Gloria Conyers Hewitt.

To Hannah, Cassie, and Nadia, who may one day
grow up to be women mathematicians.

To Jim for his expert consultation, support, and excellent computer-side cuisine.

To the wonderful community of colleagues encouraging women's participation in mathematics.

CONTENTS

INTRODUCTION

All fifty-nine women included in this volume have devoted their lives to mathematics. They are recognized leaders in mathematics, including winners of coveted MacArthur "Genius" Fellowships, members of the National Academy of Sciences, winners of prizes given by the mathematical associations, presidents of major professional organizations, and invited speakers at prestigious conferences. A number of younger women are included who show great promise, having won awards early in their careers, but who have not yet (because of their relative youth) amassed as impressive a list of professional credentials. Although more than three-fourths of the mathematicians have worked or are working in the United States, almost half were born in other countries. This work celebrates the lives of minority women in particular, including African American, Latina, and Asian mathematicians.

At the end of the nineteenth century it would have been possible to include a biography of every doctoral-level female mathematician in a fairly slim volume. Because that list is now significantly longer, choices were made in order to obtain a final list of entries to fit the scope of this volume. We began with a comprehensive list, including women whose biographies had appeared in print previously, women who have won major prizes and awards in mathematics, women who have given invited addresses at important conferences, and women who have held leadership positions in key mathematical organizations. In addition to the standard references on women in mathematics and the sciences, a particularly useful reference was the newsletter of the Association of

Women in Mathematics; this publication identifies and celebrates the achievements of women mathematicians as well as providing biographical information. In narrowing down the field of highly successful mathematicians to a reasonable number for this volume, we carefully chose a group representing a variety of backgrounds: those who work at small colleges, at research universities, in industry, and in education; those whose work is theoretical, applied, and crossdisciplinary; those whose work has broad international connections; those of diverse cultural backgrounds; and, finally, those women who always found mathematics engaging and those who came into mathematics much later in their lives.

For many notable women included on our comprehensive list, there was little or no previously published biographical information. Several of these women are included in this work, and their entries are based almost entirely on interviews conducted for this volume, constituting new and unique biographies.

Although the emphasis is on twentieth-century figures, this collection includes both historical and contemporary women who are mathematicians in the traditional sense—those who invent or discover mathematics, add new ideas to the body of material that we call mathematics, or engage in mathematical research. Also included is a smaller group; women who are important to mathematics but not in the traditional sense described above. Although they have not contributed new mathematical knowledge, these women have spent their entire working lives involved with the field. Some are university researchers who study the ways in which children learn mathematics, often pushing the boundaries of what we know about the teaching of mathematics. Women such as Elizabeth Fennema, Gilah Leder, and Leone Burton have international reputations in research on the mathematical education of girls and women. Their work has been most important in pointing toward useful strategies to encourage young women to continue the study of mathematics. They are certainly, in an important sense, "in mathematics." Finally, we have included a group of women who have made nontrivial contributions to mathematics research, at the same time spending much of their professional energy on the mathematical preparation of the upcoming generation. Teaching is not an incidental matter to these women.

The goal of this volume is to provide a collection of biographies that give voice to the richness and diversity of the lives of women in mathematics. Too often, students envision the lives of mathematicians as narrow and dull. Rarely is there an opportunity to be close enough to see the interesting details. There are some wonderful books about mathematicians, but never are enough women included to give full vision to the diversity of their lives. Why is this the case? Women often have less public lives than men, sometimes by design. Their stories appear infrequently in the media; their stories must be searched out.

Most of the biographies in this volume portray women who have strong interests in areas outside of mathematics. Many have families; many have hobbies (such as music, gardening, or running in triathlon events) that they follow passionately. Most stress the value, importance, and enjoyment of working on research with colleagues. Their stories help diminish the misconception that doing good mathematics requires isolation. Independence of mind, however, does emerge as a valued characteristic—as well as the ability to become engaged by an interesting problem and persist in pursuit of a solution. Perhaps this last, persistence, is one of the most outstanding characteristics of the successful research mathematician.

The historical discrimination against women that has existed at the most prestigious research universities and institutions has led to the development of other environments that are strong mathematically and inclusive of women—for instance, liberal arts colleges. At this point there are many women mathematicians who prefer to be based at small, liberal arts colleges, where they usually have a greater number of female colleagues and closer ties to students. It is interesting to note that liberal arts colleges produce a proportionately greater number of women who go on to receive Ph.D.s in mathematics and science than do research universities.

We have noticed that some prestigious institutions seem to attract more than their share of women mathematicians. For instance, the Courant Institute of New York University and Bell Labs (currently split into two entities: AT&T Research, and Lucent Technologies) have historically included many female research mathematicians on staff, perhaps owing to the collaborative working environment that exists at these places—a tough-minded pursuit of problems supported by an atmosphere of encouragement. Another contributing factor may be the presence of a powerful and supportive mentor, often a man. We need to further identify and support the kinds of environments that attract and retain women, as well as continue to work for equal opportunities for men and women at the most prestigious institutions, many of which continue to seem inhospitable to women.

In this volume we have tried to give a sense of the biographees' work in terms that can be understood by the non-mathematician. (An earlier volume of biographies about women in mathematics [Grinstein & Campbell, 1987], delves more deeply into their mathematical work.) This clarification of advanced mathematical concepts has proved to be a formidable task. Many mathematicians say that they simply cannot transmit any idea of their research, even to undergraduates who have already begun to study more advanced mathematics. Unfortunately, this has contributed to a dearth of understanding about what a person pursuing a graduate degree in mathematics actually does—even by those who are advanced undergraduates! In this volume, if mathematical terms are unclear, undefined, or unexplained, the reader is encouraged to use these terms as a starting point for conversations with someone who has greater mathematical training or to seek out reference works, such as mathematical dictionaries. The reader will notice that a few of the bibliographic references included for each entry are works that would not be accessible to individuals who do not have advanced mathematical training. These works, however, do represent the most recent professional work of these eminent women, and we deemed it desirable to give the reader the opportunity to glimpse the language of their mathematical research. Where possible, we have also included references to works that are more accessible to the general reading audience.

Although we celebrate the ever-increasing numbers of women in mathematics, we caution against complacency and self-congratulation. History has a habit of losing track of women. In our own lifetimes the number of women in mathematics, women that we know about, has increased dramatically; however, there are still many "firsts" being accorded to women born in the twentieth century—first woman president of a mathematics organization, first full professor of mathematics at a major university, first to win a prestigious mathematics prize. Even now, as we complete this manuscript, more women who have interesting stories are coming to our attention. Some are in their eighties and nineties, and have never before been written about; many of them may be lost to history in a very short time. Certainly there are still many fewer women than men who are mathematics researchers, and women's stories are far less well known. We must carefully tend this bountiful garden lest the cold winds of social change put an early end to its growing season. We trust that the reader will find these biographies inspirational and will seek out other, yet undiscovered, stories.

The value of writing about the lives of women in mathematics has been underscored by the enthusiasm and dedication of the contributing authors. We wish to thank them. In addition to summarizing a life in a small amount of allotted space, they have worked hard to communicate the nature of the mathematical work in an understandable way. Many of the biographies of contemporary women are based on interviews conducted by the contributors. In several cases the mathematician herself was very involved in the editing of the entry. Most of the contributors have professional careers involving mathematics—some are research mathematicians, most are mathematics educators, and some are scientists.

Not infrequently, the lives of women in mathematics are interconnected, both within and across generations. Names of women that appear in **boldface type** within the text of a biography are included as separate entries in this volume.

We hope this collection will serve not only to encourage more girls to become an integral part of the next generation of mathematicians, but to spark the enthusiasm of all students for a field that is a critical filter for access to a diverse set of careers, an international set of colleagues, and a lifetime of enjoyment and challenge. Although it has proved to be a devilishly difficult task to provide an appreciation of the mathematicians' world to those lacking advanced mathematical training, we hope that the collection of biographies contained here can impart some sense of the excitement, wonder, motivation, and collegiality that is the essential fabric of their lives.

REFERENCES FOR FURTHER READING

Albers, D. G., and Alexanderson, G. L., Eds. (1985). *Mathematical People.* Boston: Birkhäuser.

Albers, D. G., Alexanderson, G. L., and Reid, C., Eds. (1990). *More Mathematical People.* Boston: Harcourt, Brace, Jovanovich.

Association of Women in Mathematics Newsletter. Published bimonthly by AWM, University of Maryland, College Park.

Grinstein, L. S., and Campbell, P. J., Eds. (1987). *Women of Mathematics: A Bibliographic Sourcebook.* Westport, CT: Greenwood Press.

Mark, J. (1996). *Selected Resource Bibliography: Resources for Gender Equity in Mathematics and Technology Published in 1990–1996.* South Hadley, MA: Women and Mathematics Education.

Morrow, C., and Morrow, J. (1995). Connecting Women with Mathematics. In P. Rogers and G. Kaiser, Eds., *Equity in Mathematics Education: Influences of Feminism and Culture.* London: Falmer Press.

Perl, T. (1978). *Math Equals: Biographies of Women Mathematicians + Related Activities.* Menlo Park, CA: Addison-Wesley.

———. (1993). *Women and Numbers.* San Carlos, CA: Worldwide Publishing/ Tetra.

MARIA GAETANA AGNESI
(1718–1799)
Birthplace: Milan, Italy

> ... every Woman ought to exert herself, and endeavor to promote
> the glory of her sex, and to contribute her utmost.
> —Maria Agnesi (1738)

In 1748, when there were almost no women professionals in any field,
Maria Agnesi published a two-volume, 1,020-page manual, *Analytical Institutions*, that clarified, connected, and deepened the work of Leibniz,
Newton, Kepler, Galileo, and L'Hopital—all well-known mathematicians
and scientists of her time. Her clarification of the work of the most brilliant minds of that era was a scientific and social triumph that gained
her acceptance in the Western world as the first major female mathematician and raised doubts about the prevailing notions of male intellectual superiority.

In the early 1700s Italian society operated according to principles that
today would be considered unfair. Only in wealthy, broad-minded families could a girl receive any higher education. Often young women, even
in the upper classes, were not taught to read! Typically, girls were sent
to convents and taught only social graces, dressmaking, etiquette, and
religion. Then they simply awaited marriage as arranged for them by
their families.

On May 16, 1718, in Milan, Italy, Anna Fortunato Brivio Agnesi gave
birth to a baby girl and named her Maria Gaetana Agnesi. We know
little more about Maria's mother. Maria's paternal grandparents came
from wealthy merchant families of Milan. Money and education allowed

Maria Gaetana Agnesi. Photo courtesy of Culver Pictures, Inc.

Pietro Agnesi, Maria's father, to lead the life of a cultured nobleman and scholar. He enjoyed throwing enormous parties to entertain fellow noblemen, scholars, and celebrities from Italy and abroad.

Fortunately, Maria's family was broad-minded as well as wealthy. Pietro recognized that Maria had an excellent memory and noticed how quickly she learned different languages. He also realized that his second daughter, Maria Teresa (herein called Teresa to avoid confusion), had great musical talent. Consequently, Pietro had the two girls tutored to impress his friends and associates.

Even when she was as young as 9 years old Maria, along with Teresa, garnered a reputation that brought visitors from afar to hear them perform. Amid guests dressed in the latest fashion in a lavishly decorated public room, Teresa played harpsichord music she had written herself followed by a very shy and nervous Maria reciting, among other things, a speech advocating higher education for women. Maria herself had translated this speech into Latin and released it for publication.

By age 13 Maria could speak Greek, Hebrew, French, Spanish, and Latin. At her father's parties she conducted debates on mathematical, scientific, and philosophical issues of the day in Latin, the language of scholars. Later, almost two hundred topics she defended at these gatherings appeared in her book *Philosophical Propositions*. One such debate pitted the age-old theories of celestial mechanics against the new theories of universal gravitation. Whereas some scholars supported the celestial mechanics theory that planets moved across the sky because angels pushed them, Maria championed Newton's newly discovered, invisible force called gravity. During the intermission noblemen from distant countries would approach Maria for a waltz, and she would dutifully agree. As they whirled around the dance floor, she spoke with them about the debated topic in the language of their homeland.

Pietro's encouragement and status enabled both his daughters to excel. He promoted Maria's abilities in language and mathematics, and she welcomed the learning he made available. While Teresa became a gifted composer and famous musician, Maria's extraordinary intelligence led her into a realm of accomplishment that was especially unusual for a woman at that time.

To understand the importance of Agnesi's accomplishments, it is necessary to know some of the scientific breakthroughs of the seventeenth and eighteenth centuries. The dawn of modern astronomy took place during the one hundred years ending in the mid-seventeenh century. This new age of scientific astronomy approached the heavens with sober research and calculation. No longer relying solely on ancient philosophical theories, scientists and mathematicians started using experimentation, observation, and mathematics to explain what they saw in the heavens. Copernicus initiated the scientific revolution by stating that the earth revolves around the sun. His theory gained recognition and support and, eventually, overturned the long-standing theories of Aristotle and Ptolemy.

Galileo, one of the first to use experimentation, decided to throw cannonballs of different weights off the Leaning Tower of Pisa to prove his theory that they would land at the same time. He used geometry, particularly the study of conic sections, to analyze his findings. (A conic section is a curve that is formed when a cone is sliced by a plane.) This new study of ballistics helped Galileo and, eventually, other scientists to better understand the motion of the planets. Galileo understood that the same forces that act on flying cannonballs act on the planets. Later, Kepler, also using conic sections, tried to further understand the shapes of planetary orbits. By using mathematics and astronomer Tycho Brahe's detailed observations of the heavens, Kepler discovered three laws that governed the motion of the planets.

Next, Newton and Leibniz, Maria's contemporaries, independently developed calculus. Newton used calculus to demonstrate how gravity altered Kepler's laws of planetary motion. He explained mathematically how gravity causes planets to fall toward the sun in the same way that it causes cannonballs (or apples) to fall toward the earth. This was the state of the science when Agnesi was to make her contributions.

In 1732 Maria's mother died while giving birth to her eighth child, and Maria had to take over the management of her brothers, sisters, and household—an incredible burden for a 14-year-old who had just lost her mother. Despite her new responsibilities she continued to solve problems in analytic geometry and ballistics, essentially following Galileo's trail of cannonballs.

Maria studied mathematics and science under the guidance of several tutors, including Michele Casati (a female tutor who later became a professor at the University of Turin). At age 17, occasionally consulting her tutors, Maria composed a manuscript evaluating the work of two leading mathematicians of the Newtonian era. She reviewed L'Hopital's paper on conic sections and Reyneau's book entitled *Analyse Démontré*. These papers furthered her study of ballistics and planetary motion. Scholars considered her manuscript excellent, but, perhaps because of her gender, no one would publish it.

In the following years her father married two more times and Maria ultimately found herself in charge of twenty brothers and sisters. Because of her shy and modest personality, and her responsibility for this immense family, the social debates scheduled by her father started weighing heavily on her. Maria's health began to decline. Seizures often occurred after physical activity, including the dancing and horseback riding prescribed by her doctor. By the time she was 21 years old, Maria appealed to her father to excuse her from the debates and let her retire to a convent of nuns. Pietro opposed her taking the veil, but he did agree that she could go to church as often as she liked and that he would no longer require her to attend social gatherings. Respectful of her father's wishes, Maria did not push for more.

The Agnesi children grew older and started to marry and move away. Maria, choosing to live a nun-like existence, never married but remained in charge of the Agnesi household. She continued to sharpen her mathematical wits by tutoring her brothers.

While gathering information for a text she was writing for one of her brothers, Maria integrated the work of many mathematicians. She united the calculus of Leibniz and Newton with the analytical geometry of Kepler, the ballistics of Galileo, and the conic sections of L'Hopital. She revised the material considerably in order to make it uniform and coherent. By simultaneously studying their different methods, she discovered hidden connections that no one else had seen. Combining her linguistic and mathematical talents, Maria translated the various works into Italian in order to make the ideas available to Italian youth. In 1748 she published her work in *Analytical Institutions*, a manual modeled after

Reyneau's book that she had critiqued earlier. In the first volume Maria examined mathematical process; in the second, mathematical analysis.

Scientists and mathematicians from abroad recognized the importance of her work and sought to translate it for their own students. The French Academy of Sciences described her work on infinitesimal analysis as "organized, clear, and precise." It authorized the translation of her second volume into French in 1749. When Rev. John Colson, professor of mathematics at Cambridge, heard about Maria's work, he found it so precise and clear that he learned Italian just so he could translate her book into English. Baron Maseres published Colson's translation in 1801.

Her work also drew attention from the highest circles. Maria had dedicated *Analytical Institutions* to the Empress Maria Theresa of Austria (Austria controlled Italy at this time), and in return she received a ring and a crystal jewelry box that were both adorned with diamonds. Pope Benedict XIV, recognizing Maria's expertise in the field, not only sent her jewels but in 1750 named her honorary chair of mathematics and natural philosophy at the University of Bologna. She graciously accepted this great honor but never lectured despite the urging of many scholars.

After centuries of contemplation, mathematicians of our day have finally found physical applications for a curve that Maria reintroduced in the analytic geometry section of her book. She had presented students with the problem of finding a mathematical equation for a geometric curve. Unbeknown to Maria, a mathematician named Fermat had already discovered the equation for the cubic bell-shaped curve almost one hundred years earlier. In 1703 Guido Grandi named Fermat's curve the *versiera*, erroneously now known in English as the Witch of Agnesi. The strange name of Witch probably is Colson's mistranslation of the Italian word *versiera*, or "curve" in English. Because Maria had made several original discoveries in her book, it is odd that her name is widely associated with a concept she did not originate.

Despite her father's remarriages and the hosts of other children, Maria and her father remained quite close. She looked up to him and sought his approval; in turn, he supported her mathematical endeavors. His death in 1752 devastated Maria and apparently made it difficult for her to remain in a field she strongly associated with him. Maria gradually withdrew from mathematical and scientific activities altogether. She had taken pleasure in using her mind and tutoring others, but now she devoted all her time, energy, and money to more pious activities such as studying theology and helping the poor and sick.

In 1759 she moved into a rented house where she sheltered a few poor people. In order to make money when her dowry ran out, Maria taught catechism classes to working-class families. When that did not provide enough, she sold to a rich Englishman the jeweled gifts given to her by the Empress and Pope.

In 1783, Cardinal Pozzobonelli noticed her charitable contributions and appointed Maria director of women for the home of the aged called Pio Albergo Trivulzio. Maria moved into the home (actually a palace donated by Prince Trivulzio in 1771) and spent the rest of her life in devotion to the women who lived there.

After her father's death, Maria's health continued to deteriorate. As she grew older, fainting spells replaced her childhood seizures, leading to a disease known—ironically—as gravitational edema, or dropsy. In her later years Maria gradually grew blind and deaf. On January 9, 1799, she died suddenly when fluids pooled in her chest cavity and caused her heart to stop—a common result of dropsy. She lived 81 years during a time when people generally died much earlier. Despite her fame and importance Maria had no money when she died, and the church buried her in a pauper's grave.

Selected Works by Maria Agnesi

(1738). *Propositiones Philosophicae*. Milan: Publisher unknown.

(1801). *Analytical Institutions* (J. Colson, Trans.). London: Baron Maseres. (Original work published 1748.)

Selected Works about Maria Agnesi

Agnesi Volume. (1994, May–June). *American Women of Mathematics* 24, 8.

Hale, S. J. (1876). *Women's Record: From Creation to A.D. 1869*. New York: Harper & Brothers.

Kennedy, H. (1987). Maria Gaetana Agnesi. In L. Grinstein and P. Campbell, Eds., *Women of Mathematics* (pp. 1–5). Westport, CT: Greenwood.

Kramer, E. A. (1970). Maria Gaetana Agnesi. In C. C. Gillispie, Ed., *Dictionary of Scientific Biography* (Vol. 1, pp. 75–77). New York: Charles Scribner's Sons.

Perl, T. (1978). *Math Equals: Biographies of Women Mathematicians + Related Activities*. Menlo Park, CA: Addison-Wesley.

Reichenbach, H. (1942). *From Copernicus to Einstein* (R. B. Winn, Trans.). New York: Philosophical Library.

Seeds, M. A. (1986). *Foundations of Astronomy*. Belmont, MA: Wadsworth.

CASSONDRA MCDANIEL POWERS

ANDREA BERTOZZI

(1965–   )

Birthplace: Massachusetts

The field of scientific computing has emerged as an important new area for mathematicians, and Andrea Bertozzi, a young mathematician at

Andrea Bertozzi. Photo courtesy of Andrea Bertozzi.

Duke University in North Carolina, has become a leading expert in this field. Her work connects abstract areas of mathematics with applied aspects of physics.

Andrea, born in 1965, grew up in Lexington, Massachusetts. She is the oldest of three daughters of William (a physicist and currently professor at MIT) and Norma Bertozzi. All three children are close in age. Her sister Carolyn, one year younger than Andrea, is now a professor of chemistry at the University of California at Berkeley. Diana, four years younger, is an occupational therapist.

It was always mathematical things that Andrea remembered from her childhood. For example, she recalls that when someone in first grade used blocks to explain the idea of negative numbers, she thought it was the neatest thing she had ever heard. Ordinary computation like long division may have been boring, but Andrea rarely found abstract ideas boring. She knew from a very young age that she liked mathematics. She graduated from high school in 1983 and then attended Princeton

University, where she received a bachelor's degree in 1987, a master's degree in 1988, and a Ph.D. in 1991—all in mathematics.

The 1990s find her married, completing a four-year stint as an instructor at the University of Chicago, and, most recently, a one-year sojourn at Argonne National Laboratory as a recipient of a Fellowship for Women in Science. Now, at age 30, she is in a tenured position as an associate professor of mathematics at Duke University. Andrea's husband, Brad, an engineer, is an international consultant who works with large corporations that own and manage properties such as oil refineries and nuclear power plants.

Most of Andrea's research and writing over the past few years has involved the behaviors of film surfaces (the coating of surfaces with a thin layer of liquid). This work evolved during her first postdoctoral job as an instructor at the University of Chicago. There Andrea became involved with a group of physicists who were trying to understand the basic properties of an equation similar to one that describes or models the behavior of film surfaces. The equation, though simple, had not been studied before. Its properties intrigued her as a mathematician. A few months later the group started focusing on thin films because the same kinds of equations are often used to model thin films. Although the problem of describing liquids flowing around a surface seemed simple, it turned out to be a fundamental problem in physics that people had been thinking about for twenty to thirty years. Andrea found this interplay between mathematics and physics particularly fascinating.

In 1995, Andrea was awarded a fellowship and took a year off from academics to work at Argonne National Laboratory. Again she found herself working with people across disciplines, this time in mathematics and computer science. She was excited by the computer facilities available at the laboratory. With its massive parallel computer workstations— available in few places in the world—Argonne was the perfect place to become involved in scientific computing, which had become her chosen field.

The goal of scientific computing is to understand the complex processes that take place in concrete physical experiments. First the researcher develops a theory or model to explain what's going on, then he or she tries to understand the model itself. Typically the models are too complicated to be analyzed directly. That's where scientific computing comes into play.

Andrea and her coworkers are interested in determining how an initially dry surface may be coated with an even, thin layer of liquid. This is known to be a difficult task. One way to think about this is to compare it to cooking something in a pan on the stove; in the process of trying to get an even layer of oil on the bottom of the pan, you start to tip the pan. But the oil doesn't usually coat evenly. Instead, it runs around in little "fingers." These are the problems involved in coating technology, or fingering technology as it is sometimes called. Coating lots of things evenly—microchips, for example, or photographic film—creates problems that researchers would like to understand. Doing so requires developing a mathematical model, in this case a set of partial differential equations (or an evolution equation, as it is called, because the effect being described is happening over time). Since the model is extremely complicated, researchers must run a computer simulation to get a picture of the film flowing down the surface.

Mathematicians must have expertise in many different areas in order to begin to construct these difficult equations. Assumptions must be made to simplify the mathematics. This involves knowing the physics or finding a collaborator who does. As a result, mathematicians work with physicists; they work with experimentalists; they work with engineers who do modeling. Often the engineers start the modeling before the mathematicians get in on the act. Bertozzi says, "We get in there when they throw up their hands and say, 'I don't know what's going on here.'" Working together, they try to find answers.

Bertozzi has developed a working relationship with another woman mathematician, Mary Pugh, at the University of Chicago. Mary was the first woman she had ever worked with, and Andrea found the dynamics of working with a female colleague somewhat different from working with a man. When Mary moved to New York to work at the Courant Institute, Andrea sometimes visited her and stayed at her apartment. They would be up until one or two in the morning batting around ideas. Out of this work came several joint papers.

Andrea is currently completing a graduate mathematics text co-authored with her former Ph.D. thesis advisor at Princeton, Andy Majda, who is now at the Courant Institute in New York City. The book spans the gap between technical theory and applications in scientific computing, and Andrea sees this interdisciplinary work as potentially useful. It will contain many technical state-of-the-art abstract theorems, examples from numerical simulations to tie things together, and discussions of actual experimental data including descriptive illustrations. She has found the book-writing process to be very different from doing research, and an interesting new professional activity.

Andrea Bertozzi is happy with her career, holding a tenured professorship at a major university at 30 years of age. The one area that has created problems now seems under control. Andrea has been suffering recently from a non–life-threatening but debilitating physical condition known as Ménière's syndrome, a disorder of the inner ear that causes severe dizziness. Andrea's case is caused by allergies. Thus, if the source of the allergic reaction can be identified and eliminated, she can be symptom free with no permanent damage. Although she experienced only infrequent attacks for eight years, some episodes are debilitating. "This kind of problem causes your priorities to change," says Andrea. Although she thoroughly enjoys her research and works very hard, one of her primary goals now is to stay healthy.

Andrea particularly enjoys swimming, which she feels is great for her allergies. That, together with walking and riding her exercise bike, helps support her main goal to keep her health under control and continue her research. Andrea takes comfort in the knowledge that she has been able to work even when Ménière's creates problems. "When it gets really bad I prop myself up in bed with my laptop computer and work away."

Although Andrea can identify many mentors, people from whom she has learned a lot and whom she really admires, she expresses the most admiration for those who are engaged in interdisciplinary work. She believes that people need to break down some of the barriers between fields. In this way, future research will be most productive. As evidence of her accomplishments and her promise, she was chosen to receive a 1996 Presidential Early Career Award for Scientists and Engineers.

Note

This biography is based on an interview that took place in Palo Alto, California, at the time of the Julia Robinson Celebration of Women in Mathematics Conference in Berkeley, California, in July 1996. Professor Bertozzi was a speaker at the conference.

Selected Works by Andrea Bertozzi

(1994). Cancellation Exponents and Fractal Scaling (with Ashvin Chhabra). *Physical Review E: Statistical Physics, Plasmas, Fluids, and Related Interdisciplinary Topics* 49(5), May 1, pp. 4716–19.
(1994). Singularities and Similarities in Interface Flows (with Michael P. Brenner, Todd F. Dupont, and Leo P. Kadanoffl). In L. Sirovich, Ed., *Trends and Perspectives in Applied Mathematics* (Vol. 100, pp. 155–208). *New York*: Springer-Verlag Applied Mathematical Sciences.
(1995). Loss and Gain of Regularity in a Lubrication Equation for Thin Viscous Films. *Free Boundary Problems: Theory and Applications*, Pitman Research Notes in Mathematics Series, Vol. 323. (Proceedings of the International Colloquium on Free Boundary Problems, Toledo, Spain, June 1993.)
(1995, July). Lubrication Approximations for Surface Tension Driven Interfaces: Some Open Problems. *Proceedings of the International Congress on Industrial and Applied Mathematics*, Hamburg, Germany.
(1996). The Lubrication Approximation for Thin Viscous Films: Regularity and Longtime Behavior of Weak Solutions (with Mary Pugh). *Communications on Pure and Applied Mathematics* 49(2), pp. 85–123.

(1996, June). Symmetric Singularity Formation in Lubrication-Type Equations for Interface Motion. *SIAM Journal on Applied Mathematics* 56(3).

TERI PERL

LENORE BLUM
(1942–)
Birthplace: New York

Lenore Epstein Blum—researcher, teacher, and administrator—combines significant contributions to mathematical research, with her work to increase public understanding of mathematics. In the 1970s and 1980s, much of her attention was focused on expanding the participation of women and girls in mathematics and computer science. Her current research focuses on developing concepts that unify the fields of theoretical computer science with the branch of mathematics known as numerical analysis.

Lenore and her family moved to Caracas, Venezuela, when she was 9 years old. Venezuela was very different from New York City, where she had been living. In the United States, Lenore had been part of an extended family surrounded by aunts and uncles and grandparents. In Venezuela, there was only her immediate family: mother, father, and younger sister. School in Caracas was also a shock initially. Having attended progressive schools in the United States, Lenore lasted just two weeks in the extremely structured, Spanish-speaking Venezuelan school. After a period of home schooling, her mother enrolled Lenore and her sister at the private American School. To pay for tuition for both girls, Lenore's mother, a former schoolteacher, arranged to teach at the school.

Throughout school, mathematics and art were Lenore's favorite subjects. Her initial plan was to major in architecture in college; this major seemed to combine the essential elements of both mathematics and art. After applying and being turned down as an undergraduate at the Massachusetts Institute of Technology (MIT), Lenore decided to attend the Carnegie Institute of Technology instead. (The justification for the MIT rejection was that few women were being admitted because of lack of dormitory space—only twenty beds were available in the women's dormitory. Much later Katherine McCormick, the first MIT woman graduate, contributed a large sum of money to the university to build a dormitory for women students.)

Lenore Blum. Photo courtesy of Lenore Blum.

In her second year at Carnegie, Lenore, by then an architecture major, decided that she missed the beauty of "mathematics for its own sake." Whereas architects were interested in mathematics as a tool, using mathematical formulas where necessary, Lenore was more interested in learning where the formulas came from. She decided that mathematics should be her chosen field.

At age 18 Lenore married Manuel Blum, one of four sons of a family that Lenore's family had met shortly after moving to Venezuela. By the time they were married Manuel was a graduate student at MIT, working in Warren McCulloch's neuro-physiology lab there. Electrical engineers, mathematicians, philosophers, biologists, and psychologists from all over the world gathered there to work on a common problem: understanding the human brain.

Now living in Boston and lacking the courage to reapply to MIT, Lenore applied and was accepted as a student at Simmons College, a women's college in Boston. Because the mathematics courses at Simmons were insufficiently advanced, Lenore was allowed to take a course in modern algebra at MIT. "Here was a class with substance, depth, pace—everything I'd imagined a good course to be. It was hard, it was deep, it was abstract. I trusted this guy who was teaching it. He was a top mathematical researcher. The topics were important; they were leading somewhere." The professor who was teaching the course was Isidore Singer. He played a key role in Lenore's career by recommending that his "best student" be admitted to the graduate mathematics program at MIT.

According to plan and with a certain amount of luck, Lenore and Manuel's son Avrim was born on the last day of classes during Lenore's third year in graduate school. As a tiny infant, Avrim spent much time in Manuel's basement office. When he progressed to a more mobile stage, Lenore's mother came to town to care for the toddler, freeing Lenore to work intensively on her graduate thesis.

Lenore was intrigued by the work of several mathematicians who were successfully using new methods of logic to solve old problems in algebra. She taught herself logic and carefully studied these methods and how they were applied. Slowly patterns began to emerge. She began to see common features in the problems she was studying and how one simple but powerful rule could solve them all. This rule and its proof became her first theorem. Later she used this rule to discover new results in algebra, the work that was to become her thesis.

With her Ph.D. successfully completed, Lenore received a postdoctoral fellowship that allowed her to work at any place she chose for one year. The University of California at Berkeley, with one of the strongest mathematics departments in the country, was the obvious place for her to go. A famous logician, **Julia Robinson**, lived in Berkeley, and Lenore's husband, a computer scientist, had a job offer there as well.

In 1971 Lenore was asked to organize a panel on women and mathematics as part of a series of talks on mathematics and social responsibility sponsored by the Berkeley mathematics department. As a result she soon found herself to be the West Coast "expert" on women and mathematics. Meanwhile, on the East Coast, **Mary Gray** of American University formed the Association for Women in Mathematics (AWM). Although reluctant at first to join, Lenore—who wanted very much to be known as a mathematician, not as a *woman* mathematician—soon became convinced that the situation for women in mathematics would not change without the AWM. Lenore ultimately became its third president.

By the middle of the 1970s women mathematicians were becoming more visible. They were invited to present their research results at important professional meetings and were elected to high positions in their professional associations—all important activities for career growth. By the end of the 1970s they were getting better jobs, some in top mathematics departments. Indeed, by its tenth birthday, the AWM had brought about many important changes for women in mathematics.

In the fall of 1973 Lenore was hired to teach a class in college algebra at Mills College, a women's college in Oakland, California. She decided to replace the repetitious and boring high school algebra course with a specially designed precalculus course that could provide a bridge to calculus and higher mathematics. The course was intended to provide students with tools to solve new problems. This class grew into an important program at Mills College, and Lenore became head of the new Department of Mathematics and Computer Science. She continued to serve as head or co-head for thirteen years and in 1979 was awarded the Letts-Villard Research Professorship.

By 1980 more students at Mills were taking classes in mathematics and computer science than in any other subject. They were also getting summer jobs in these technical fields as a result of a strong internship program established by Lenore with companies in the area. Lenore decided to return to her work as a research mathematician. Taking a leave of absence for a year from Mills College, she returned to MIT to immerse herself in research.

In her research Lenore uses mathematics to study why some problems are hard for computers, why some are easy, and why some are completely intractable. For the past few years she has been working with Michael Shub and Steven Smale on a theory of computation and complexity over the real numbers. A major aim of their theory is to unify the intrinsically discrete, binary (i.e., using only 0 and 1) world of theoretical computer science with the more continuous world of numerical analysis.

The classical theory of computation had its origin in the work of logicians such as Gödel and Turing in the 1930s and 1940s. The Turing machine, the model of computation developed during the following decades, became the cornerstone for extraordinarily successful developments in the foundations of theoretical computer science.

The Turing machine is a natural model with which to study discrete algorithms and problems such as those dealing with the integers or with graphs. An example of a discrete algorithm is the Euclidean algorithm for finding the greatest common divisor of two numbers, and an example of a discrete problem is the problem of deciding if a positive integer is a prime. Another example is the famous Traveling Salesman problem. (See the example in the entry on **Joan Feigenbaum**.) However, with its dependence on 0's and 1's, the Turing model is fundamentally inadequate to provide a theoretical foundation for modern scientific computation where most of the algorithms involve computations on real or complex numbers. The Blum-Shub-Smale model of computation expands on the Turing model, yielding a new theory of computation that deals more adequately with issues raised by modern numerical analysis and scientific computation. This research has helped start a new field known as the foundations of computational mathematics, which incorporates a number of areas.

Blum is currently writing a book, *Complexity and Real Computation*, with Shub, Smale, and Felipe Cucker. The first chapter of the book was published in January 1996 under the title "Complexity and Real Computation: A Manifesto" in the journal *Bifurcation and Chaos*. In it, the authors say:

> Finding a natural meeting ground between the highly developed complexity theory of computer science—with its historical roots in logic and the discrete mathematics of the integers—and the traditional domain of real computation, the more eclectic less foundational field of numerical analysis—with its rich history and long-standing traditions in the continuous mathematics of analysis—presents a compelling challenge. Here we illustrate the issues and pose our perspective toward resolution.

Although developing new theories has been the cornerstone of her work in recent years, Lenore has been involved in many other activities as well. The invitation to present a paper at the 1990 International Congress of Mathematicians in Kyoto, Japan, was an honor and recognition of the importance of her work. She became vice-president of the American Mathematics Society. She has been involved in setting up an electronic communication link with African mathematicians. At the twentieth-anniversary celebration of the Association for Women in Mathematics in 1991, Lenore presented a talk summarizing the history of the founding and achievements of AWM. At its twenty-fifth anniversary celebration remembering Julia Robinson, Blum gave a talk drawing parallels between Robinson's work in reducing Hilbert's Tenth Problem (a famous meta-mathematical problem) to a purely number theoretic problem, and her own recent work with Shub and Smale in reducing a famous complexity theory problem to a basic algebraic problem, also formulated by Hilbert.

Since 1988 Lenore has been a research scientist in the theory group of the International Computer Science Institute (ICSI); since 1989 she has been an adjunct professor of computer science at Berkeley. In the fall of 1992 she began a new career in Berkeley as deputy director of the Mathematical Sciences Research Institute (MSRI), one of the foremost mathematics research institutes in the world. Along with MSRI director Bill Thurston, Lenore helped open MSRI to a large cross-section of the mathematical and broader communities, charting new and imaginative directions in public understanding of mathematics.

Ever on the move, she went to Hong Kong for the 1996–1997 academic year to work on her book with coauthor Stephen Smale, a 1996 recipient of the Presidential Medal of Science who is currently building a complexity theory group in the mathematics department at the City University of Hong Kong. While there, she and husband Manuel, the 1996 recipient of the prestigious Turing Award, have enjoyed a productive year of research and teaching in mathematics and theoretical computer science.

Finding interconnections between her work and other projects, and working among creative people who value her work—these have been Lenore's most satisfying rewards as a creative mathematician.

Note

The information included in this biography is based on an interview.

Selected Works by Lenore Blum

(1986, May). A Simple Secure Pseudo-Random Number Generator (with M. Blum and M. Shub). *SIAM Journal of Computing* 15(2), pp. 364–83.

(1988, June). A New Simple Homotopy Algorithm for Linear Programming I. *Journal of Complexity* 4(2), pp. 124–36.

(1989, July). On a Theory of Computation over the Real Numbers; NP-Completeness, Recursive Functions and Universal Machines (with M. Shub and S. Smale). *Bulletin of the AMS* 21(1), pp. 1–46.

(1990). Lectures on a Theory of Computation and Complexity over the Reals (or an Arbitrary Ring)." In *Lectures in the Sciences of Complexity* (pp. 1–47). Menlo Park, CA: Addison-Wesley.

(1991, September). A Brief History of the Association for Women in Mathematics: The Presidents' Perspectives. *Notices of the American Mathematical Society* 38(7). Reprinted in *AWM Newsletter* 21(6), November–December 1991.

(1996, January). Complexity and Real Computation: A Manifesto (with M. Shub and S. Smale). *Bifurcation and Chaos* 6(1).

Selected Work about Lenore Blum

Perl, T. (1993). Lenore Blum. In *Women and Numbers* (pp. 76–93). San Carlos, CA: Wide World Publishing/Tetra.

TERI PERL

SYLVIA BOZEMAN

(1947–)

Birthplace: Alabama

The journey from being a student at a high school that did not offer a trigonometry course to working as a successful Ph.D. mathematician has been fascinating for Sylvia Bozeman, currently professor of mathematics at Spelman College in Atlanta, Georgia.

She was born Sylvia Trimble in 1947 in central Alabama. It was in Camp Hill, a small town near the Georgia border, that she attended Edward Bell High School. Sylvia always had a love for mathematics, and by the time she was in high school she was ready to take trigonometry, but there was virtually no interest in the subject among the other students. Fortunately, there was one teacher in the school who realized the importance of trigonometry for college mathematics courses, so Sylvia and four other students were tutored in trigonometry at night. During the day she took a mathematics reading course in advanced geometry. Here she had the opportunity to explore mathematical ideas on her own with the guidance of an advisor.

Because she wanted to continue her mathematical studies when she graduated from high school, Sylvia entered Alabama A&M University as a mathematics major in 1964. The more mathematics she encountered, the more she wanted to learn. In college she took no education courses, which was unusual because at that time it was expected that a woman would teach after graduation. Fortunately, the chairman of the physics department at Alabama A&M became a mentor to Sylvia, and he assigned her to work on a project at the National Aeronautics and Space Administration (NASA) using computers.

During the summer before her senior year, Sylvia had a research experience at Harvard University in Cambridge, Massachusetts. Here she had the opportunity to learn FORTRAN (one of the first computer languages) and mathematics for engineers. She also had the opportunity to be tutored in the theory underlying calculus, which led to her determination to become a mathematician.

During her freshman year at college Sylvia had met Robert Bozeman, a fellow mathematics major. They were engaged by Christmas of their senior year and married a few weeks after graduation. In order to continue studying mathematics, Sylvia applied to graduate school. In 1968

Sylvia Bozeman. Photo courtesy of Sylvia Bozeman.

she entered Vanderbilt University in Nashville, Tennessee; her husband became a graduate student in mathematics there as well.

During her first year in graduate school Sylvia Bozeman, who had not been exposed to as many mathematics courses as the other students, had to work harder in her courses and often felt inadequate intellectually in comparison with her classmates. Then she took a higher level mathematics course in an area to which none of the other students had been exposed; thus she was on a more equal basis. Bozeman did very well in this course, her confidence rose, and she knew that she was capable of being a member of the professional mathematics community. In 1970 she received a master's degree in mathematics. Her thesis was in group theory (an area within algebra), particularly groups of prime order.

At this time Bozeman decided to take time off from school to begin a family. While out of graduate school, she taught at Vanderbilt University and in the Upward Bound program based at Tennessee State University. Meanwhile, her husband completed his Ph.D. in mathematics at Vanderbilt. The couple then moved to Atlanta, Georgia, where Sylvia interviewed with **Dr. Etta Falconer**, then chair of the mathematics department at Spelman College, a historically black college. For the next two years

Bozeman taught mathematics to the young black women who attended Spelman and was extremely happy working in this environment. Dr. Falconer became an influential mentor to Bozeman and has continued to be a source of professional support and guidance. However, Bozeman soon realized that she needed a doctoral degree in order to receive all the opportunities and benefits of college teaching.

Spelman College was very supportive of Bozeman's desire to continue graduate school. In 1976 she took a leave of absence from Spelman and began taking courses at Emory University. After passing her preliminary examinations, Bozeman resumed a full-time teaching load at Spelman while continuing dissertation work at Emory in functional analysis, an area of advanced mathematics that combines ideas from algebra and topology (a kind of geometry). In 1980 she received her Ph.D. in mathematics. The title of her dissertation is *Representations of Generalized Inverses of Fredholm Operators*. Two years later, in 1982, Bozeman became chair of the mathematics department at Spelman College, a position she held for eleven years.

In 1993 the Natural Sciences Division at Spelman received a $3 million grant from the W. K. Kellogg Foundation to launch a program involving Spelman students in interdisciplinary research in five scientific disciplines: biology, chemistry, physics, computer science, and mathematics. The Center for the Scientific Application of Mathematics (CSAM) was born, and Bozeman was asked to direct and develop its programs. CSAM supports students and faculty in scientific research during the summer as well as during the academic year. The main goal of the program is to increase the number of African American students pursuing research-oriented scientific careers.

At present Bozeman leads and organizes several programs that focus on encouraging women and underrepresented minorities to pursue careers in the mathematical sciences. CSAM, under her direction, sponsors the Spelman Summer Science and Mathematics Institute (S3MI). For two weeks in the summer, high school teachers of science and mathematics come to Spelman's campus to learn new skills and technologies for the classroom. The goal of this program is to motivate teachers to encourage more high school students to continue their study of science and mathematics in college. Bozeman has also created a partnership with **Dr. Rhonda Hughes** of Bryn Mawr College to form the Spelman–Bryn Mawr Summer Mathematics Program. This program offers a summer research experience in mathematics for approximately ten young women from colleges in Atlanta and Philadelphia.

Bozeman has also continued her mathematical research in several areas, including numerical solutions of non-uniquely solvable integral equations, two-dimensional data compression and restoration, and issues in image processing, especially related to data compression and object recognition.

Bozeman's husband, Dr. Robert Bozeman, is a professor of mathematics at Morehouse College, located just across the street from Spelman. Morehouse is a small liberal arts school that has historically educated young African American men. The couple have two children, a boy and a girl, both in their twenties. The Bozemans are active members of Friendship Baptist Church in Atlanta. Sylvia Bozeman spends a significant amount of her time in church-sponsored activities, such as working with young people and with the hand bell choir.

Throughout her tenure at Spelman, Bozeman has maintained her high commitment to teaching women and minorities. As chair of Spelman's mathematics department, she established goals to attract more students into the field of mathematics. She achieved this goal both by becoming involved in the improvement of mathematics education in grade schools and by encouraging students to be more willing to consider the study of mathematics on entering college. In recognition of her outstanding work she has received several distinguished awards, including the Tenneco UNCF Award for Excellence in Teaching in 1988, the White House Initiative Faculty Award for Excellence in Science and Technology in 1988, and the Mathematical Association of America, Southeastern Section, Distinguished College and University Teaching Award in 1995. Dr. Bozeman continues to facilitate the entry of students into mathematics at the college level by implementing programs that support the students academically, financially, and in planning for the future.

Under Sylvia Bozeman's academic care, students are exposed to the various career paths that mathematicians can travel. They are given opportunities to prepare themselves for graduate studies in mathematics, both academically and socially. Bozeman continues to work hard toward encouraging more minorities in mathematics through lectures, presentations, articles, committee work in professional organizations, and actively creating new opportunities for students.

Note

The information included in this biography is based on an interview.

Selected Works by Sylvia Bozeman

(1981, April). Finite Rank Modification and Generalized Inverses of Fredholm Operators (with Luis Kramarz), *Journal of Mathematical Analysis and Applications*, 80(2).

(1985, February). Approximating Eigenfunctions of Fredholm Operators in Banach Spaces (with Luis Kramarz). *Journal of Mathematical Analysis and Applications* 105(2).

(1989, Fall). Black Women Mathematicians: In Short Supply. *SAGE* 6(2).

(1994). The Role of Mathematics Departments in Minority and Majority Institutions in Recruiting Minority Teachers. In *Attracting Minorities into Teaching Mathematics*, A project of the SUMMA Program of the Mathematical Association of America. Washington, DC.

ULRICA WILSON PARKER

Marjorie Lee Browne
(1914–1979)
Birthplace: Tennessee

What makes a mathematics professor inspire a student to want to achieve? In the case of Dr. Marjorie Lee Browne, one of the first black women to receive a doctorate in mathematics, there were many things. She was motivated by her love of mathematics, her desire to instill in her students the same passion that she had for mathematics, and her desire to see her students achieve not only in the mathematics classroom but also in life.

In 1961 during a mathematics class at North Carolina Central College, a sophomore mathematics major volunteered to place his solution to a problem on the board. Being one of the better students in the class, he was confident that he could explain his solution. He also knew that the professor would challenge him to explain and support his solution. On this day the young student stumbled with his explanation of his solution. The more he stumbled, the more she challenged him. Finally he was allowed to move back to his seat.

After class the professor, who usually left the classroom immediately after class, lingered a while, and so did the student. The student was upset at what had happened, and the professor was concerned that the student may not have understood her persistence. She asked how he felt. The student said he was okay. With no further conversation they both left the room. The next day the student volunteered to solve one of the most difficult problems from the homework. The professor looked at his solution and exclaimed to the class, "It seems that Mr. Smith has redeemed himself."

A remarkable event happened a few days later. The professor called the student to her office and offered him a job as her student assistant. The student was surprised, excited, and deeply moved because he valued and respected the professor. He believed that her desire to have him

Marjorie Lee Browne. Photo courtesy of John Smith
and Laura Smith.

as an assistant was one of the greatest compliments she could give. On
this day, professor and student began a relationship that lasted for eighteen years—the rest of her life.

Browne recognized that this student had the resilience and self-
confidence she believed necessary for success in mathematics. Even more
important, she believed that education was a necessity, that education
was the ticket to a better life. She felt that students had to have confidence in themselves and that they needed to believe in themselves in
order to be successful.

Marjorie Lee was born on September 9, 1914, in Memphis, Tennessee,
the second child of Lawrence Johnson Lee and Mary Taylor Lee. Many
people attribute Marjorie's love and passion for mathematics to her father, who was a railway postal clerk. Lawrence Lee had attended college
for two years and was known as a whiz in mental arithmetic. He inspired
both his children to pursue mathematics as a profession by showing
them the pleasure it could give. Marjorie grew up loving mathematics;
she knew as a small child that mathematics was in her future. In an

interview in 1979 Marjorie explained, "I always, always, always liked mathematics. As a child I was rather introverted, and as far back as I can remember I liked mathematics. . . . I could do it alone."[1]

Because her mother died before she was 2 years old, Marjorie was raised by her father and stepmother, whom she called Auntie Lottie. Marjorie's stepmother agreed to give what Marjorie called "real lessons" at home for her early elementary schooling. After attending public schools in the middle grades, Marjorie was sent to a private school for black students, LeMoyne High School. She was proud of her education and attributed much of her later success in mathematics to her teachers. In that same interview she said, "I was privately educated after eighth grade, and I had excellent teachers."[2]

After high school Marjorie attended Howard University as a mathematics major, graduating cum laude in 1935. She taught at Gilbert Academy in New Orleans for a few years and then entered the University of Michigan to work toward a Master of Science degree in mathematics. Upon completion of the master's degree in 1939, she began her first college teaching position at Wiley College in Marshall, Texas. During her seven years at Wiley she spent the summers working on her doctorate in mathematics at the University of Michigan. In 1947, nearing the end of her work on her doctorate, she took a leave from Wiley College to become a teaching fellow at the University of Michigan. In 1949 Marjorie Lee Browne became one of the first two black women to earn a doctorate in mathematics; the other, who earned her Ph.D. in the same year, is **Evelyn Boyd Granville**.

While Browne was a teaching fellow at the University of Michigan she was elected to Sigma XI, an honorary scientific research society, and was an institutional nominee for the American Mathematical Society. Her dissertation title was *On the One Parameter Subgroups in Certain Topological and Matrix Groups*. After graduation she continued her education, along with her teaching in Durham, North Carolina, at the predominately black North Carolina College, now known as North Carolina Central University (NCCU). In 1952 she was named a Ford Foundation fellow; this took her to Cambridge University in England, where she studied combinational topology. Browne also used her year abroad to travel throughout Western Europe. In 1955 Browne's article based on her interest in group theory, "A Note on the Classical Groups," was published in the *American Mathematical Monthly*. The years 1958 and 1965 respectively found her studying at the University of Los Angeles, University of California at Berkeley, and Columbia University as a National Science Foundation fellow. At UCLA she studied numerical analysis and computing; at Columbia she studied differential topology.

Throughout her thirty-year teaching career at NCCU, Browne was instrumental in keeping the mathematics department abreast of innovations in mathematics and mathematics education. She became chair of the mathematics department of NCCU in 1951 and held that post until 1970. In 1960 and 1961 she directed the installation of a computer laboratory with a grant from the IBM Corporation. Under her leadership NCCU became the first predominantly black college to receive a National Science Foundation grant for the professional development of high school mathematics and science teachers. She directed the mathematics courses in these summer institutes for thirteen years. During the summers, in addition to teaching secondary school teachers, she wrote four sets of lecture notes for their use: *Sets, Logic, and Mathematical Thought* in 1957; *Introduction to Linear Algebra* in 1959; *Elementary Matrix Algebra* in 1969; and *Algebraic Structures* in 1964.

In 1970 Browne stepped down from being chair of the mathematics department at NCCU, and she encouraged and supported a former student as he applied for, and won, the position as chair of the department. From 1970 until her retirement in 1979 she worked closely with the chair and other members of the mathematics department to help students complete undergraduate and graduate degrees in mathematics.

Browne was an extraordinary teacher. She took a personal interest in students who demonstrated the desire to achieve in mathematics. Giving her students her time, support, encouragement, and assistance, Browne's goal was to have them become successful mathematicians who could "give back" to the community. She is described by her former students as exacting, challenging, and caring. They remember her passion for mathematics and her desire to have them share her love of mathematics. One former student said, "She took responsibility for all the mathematics majors. Graduating from college was not in question for us because she would check our grades and advise all of us. She was a person that you could admire." Many former students spoke of her as a hard, challenging teacher, and their fondest memory of Browne was her ability to help them build life skills. She told them, "You appreciate those things in life that you earn. People cannot take those things from you." Browne's legacy is in the great number of black men and women who graduated from NCCU with bachelor's and master's degrees in mathematics and who have pursued successful careers in mathematics and related fields.

Browne's achievements match the memories that people have of her as a teacher, friend, and community member. She was and still is described as a brilliant mathematician by colleagues and students. Samuel Massey, president of North Carolina Central University from 1963 to 1966, describes Browne as a woman who lived and spoke according to her principles. He said, "She was strong enough as a mathematician that she could speak honestly with the president (of the university) without fear of repercussion. Many teachers tell the president what they think he wants to hear; she told the president what she thought he ought to know."

Marjorie Lee Browne retired from teaching at the end of the 1979 school year. During her retirement she planned to write a monograph on the real number system, but this never happened. She died suddenly of a heart attack on October 19, 1979.

After Browne's death her former students at North Carolina Central University established the Marjorie Lee Browne Trust Fund to help the mathematics department award full-tuition scholarships to students majoring in mathematics. She was memorialized by her former students and friends with a tribute that stated, "She was a teacher, scholar, author, leader in her profession, humanitarian, builder of character in young men and women, and friend who first showed us that mathematics could be a delightful, creative pursuit. Her forbearance and encouragement made life challenging and brighter when we were beginning students."

Notes

This biography was written with the help of conversations with several colleagues and family members of Marjorie Lee Browne, including Samuel Massey, John O. Smith, Laura Smith, and Josephine White.

1. From an unpublished interview by Pat Kenschaft, 1979.
2. Ibid.

Selected Works about Marjorie Lee Browne

Giles-Giron, Jacqueline. (1991, January–February). Black Pioneers in Mathematics: Browne, Granville, Cox, Clayton, and Blackwell. In *Focus* (p. 18). Washington, DC: Mathematical Association of America.
Kenschaft, Pat. (1980). Marjorie Lee Browne: In Memoriam. *Newsletter of the Association for Women in Mathematics* 10(5).

CAROL E. MALLOY

LEONE BURTON
(1936–   )
Birthplace: Sydney, Australia

Leone Burton, professor of education in mathematics and science at the University of Birmingham, England, has written widely about the gender-based aspects of mathematics education. She has been a leader in developing teaching approaches that promote mathematical thinking

Leone Burton. Photo courtesy of Charlene Morrow.

in students and has an international set of colleagues with whom she has investigated the commonalities and differences in mathematics teaching across cultures.

Leone was born in Sydney, Australia, in 1936 to Scottish parents who had emigrated to Australia in order to seek a safer place to live, especially fearing a spread of the overt anti-Semitism already prevalent in Germany. They were part of a growing movement of Jewish families emigrating from Europe at that time, many of whom left property and substantial belongings behind.

Growing up in Sydney, Leone attended all-female schools, the norm for that time. She also had all female teachers. Although she was quite good academically and did not have to work particularly hard, she felt disconnected from her studies. She had no real relationship with math—"It was just there," she says—and her English teachers despaired of her writing. She finished school and began an arts program at the university but soon became ill and could not continue. When she was well enough she worked as hard as she could to save money to travel, something she had always longed to do. When she had enough saved she left for North America, traveling across the entire United States and staying for a while in New York. Eventually Leone traveled to London, where she moved in with a favorite uncle and aunt.

Leone's temperament was not well suited to doing things in a conventional fashion, but fortunately her new living arrangement in London allowed her plenty of space to think about what she wanted to do and how she wanted to do it. In fact, this time proved to be very influential in Leone's life. The household was stimulating. Her maternal uncle, Hyman Levy, was a well-known, retired mathematician and was involved in leftist politics. Her aunt, an "upright Scottish Protestant" and one of eight children herself, was someone Leone became very fond of. Leone thrived in this environment of care, concern, ideas, and space to explore.

As she discussed political ideas with the many associates of her family, and eventually with her own friends, Leone realized that more education would serve her well. Although she had been a good student, she lacked the advanced work required for entrance into the university. She completed this work in history and mathematics by going to school part-time for two years while also working at any jobs whatsoever to earn money. Mathematics still did not "grab" her; history seemed more appealing. She was invited to study history at the London School of Economics, but around this time she became very interested in teaching so she decided to attend the University of London instead. Leone also decided that her focus for teaching would be mathematics, a decision that has shaped much of her subsequent career path.

At that time, Burton was particularly interested in the philosophical aspects of mathematics. In fact, in earlier centuries philosophy and mathematics were highly related and often thought of as the same discipline. In preparation for her first course in mathematics, she read the classic volume by Russell and Whitehead, *Principia Mathematica*. During the first week she (one of two women in a class of twenty-five students) asked a question to which the reply was, "You are here to study mathematics, not philosophy!" The professor then slammed his book closed and left the class. Burton nearly changed her area of study but decided not to allow herself to be intimidated. She became even more committed to participating in mathematics, earned a degree in mathematics in 1963, and developed an interest in the social and cultural bases of the discipline. During her entire undergraduate university education she was not taught by even one woman!

By now Burton was eager to begin her teaching career, which she did at the secondary level. Although she loved working directly with students, she disliked the educational structures at the secondary level— emphasis on rote memorization of material and passing tests, and lack of opportunity to actively explore ideas with teachers and peers—which interfered with meeting the needs of the children. She found that she did not want to work within these structures; feeling that she could not effect sufficient change in her teaching environment, she moved to teaching at the primary level instead.

During this time Burton began the formal study of education, earning a postgraduate certificate in education in 1966 (the same year she was married) and an academic diploma in education in 1968 (the same year that her son was born), both at the University of London. In 1967 she obtained a post as a mathematics education specialist at Battersea College of Education, an institute dedicated to teacher preparation. Here she finally felt she could reshape some of the educational structures that had so disturbed her during her classroom experiences. She soon became head of the department and subsequently held a series of leadership positions in divisions of mathematics education at various English universities.

During the 1970s Burton began to pursue doctoral work at the University of London, and she earned a Ph.D. in 1980. She currently is professor of education in mathematics and science at the University of Birmingham, England, where she teaches at the postgraduate level. Although many people assume that mathematics simply "is what it is," Burton asks fundamental questions about the nature of mathematics and how it came to be what it is. She studies the ways in which society and culture have shaped it; how some aspects of mathematics have come to be known and well researched, whereas other aspects are far less emphasized or known. Burton remains very close to the philosophical questions she had when she began her undergraduate education. The ways in which she explores her ideas are closely tied to a new and developing area in mathematics education research known as ethnomathematics. Ethnomathematicians look at the ways in which mathematics is embedded in the time and culture in which it was developed. They examine similarities and differences in various number systems, concepts of zero and infinity, and more advanced mathematical topics such as symmetry groups.

Leone Burton spends a great deal of her professional life developing ways to promote effective mathematical thinking in children and studying how people come to understand mathematics and engage in mathematical dialogues. As is the case with many people who study mathematics, Leone's professional community is international. She has been a visiting professor at many institutions in Asia and has spoken extensively at conferences worldwide. From 1984 to 1988 she was elected as international convenor for the International Organization of Women and Mathematics Education. She has served on research and advisory groups studying mathematics education worldwide; recently she traveled to China as an invited member of an advance advisory delegation to the Beijing Women's Conference. When she is not working she likes to slip away to her cottage in France to read, write, and relax.

Note

This biography is based on an interview conducted in Birmingham, England in March 1995 by the author.

Selected Works by Leone Burton

(1984). Mathematical Thinking: The Struggle for Meaning. *Journal for Research in Mathematics Education* 15(1).

(1986). *Girls into Maths Can Go* (Ed.). London: Holt, Rinehart, and Winston.

(1987). From Failure to Success: Changing the Experience of Adult Learners of Mathematics. *Educational Studies in Mathematics* 18.

(1988–1989). Women and Mathematics: Is There an Intersection? Parts 1 and 2. *AWM Newsletter*, Nov/Dec 1988, Jan/Feb 1989. (Abridged version of paper originally appearing in French.)

(1989). Mathematics as a Cultural Experience: Whose Experience? In C. Keitel et al., Eds., *Mathematics, Education and Society*. Paris: UNESCO.

(1992). Becoming a Teacher of Mathematics. *Cambridge Journal of Education* 22(3), pp. 377–86.

(1992). From Rhetoric to Reality: Strategies for Developing a Social Justice Approach to Educational Decision-Making (with C. Weiner). In I. Siraj-Blatchford, Ed., *Race, Gender and the Education of Teachers*. Milton Keynes: Open University Press.

(1994). *Children Learning Mathematics: Patterns and Relationships. London*: Simon & Schuster, Hemel Hempstead, 1994.

(1994). *Who Counts? Assessing Mathematics in Europe* (Ed.). Stoke-on-Trent: Trentham Books.

(1995). Assessment of Mathematics: What Is the Agenda? In M. Birenbaum and F. Dochy, Eds., *Current Trends in Achievement Assessment*. Dordrecht: Kluwer.

(1995). Moving towards a Feminist Epistemology of Mathematics. *Educational Studies in Mathematics* 38(3).

CHARLENE MORROW

FAN KING CHUNG
(1949–)
Birthplace: Kaoshiung, Taiwan

Fan Chung, a mathematician who has had a highly successful career in both industry and academia, chose mathematics for its practical value

Fan Chung. Photo courtesy of Fan Chung.

and its intrinsic appeal. Her father, Yuan Shang King, a mechanical engineer, convinced her that mathematics is practical because it can be done anywhere; it does not require spending long hours in a laboratory. Chung also views it as practical because with a solid background in mathematics, one can move into other areas easily. But mathematics has an appeal of its own for Chung as well; it has always been her favorite subject.

Chung was also influenced in her career goals by her mother, Wu Chi King, a former teacher of high school home economics who still receives letters from her former students. Observing her mother's talent and dedication to teaching led Chung to have an interest in this area as well. Chung has a younger brother, Tom King, who is a civil engineer.

In Taiwan, where Chung grew up, elementary schools are coeducational but junior and senior high school education is not. She was successful in all her classes, but mathematics was particularly fascinating to her and she enjoyed studying it in great detail. She attended Kaoshiung

Girls' High School, where she received a fine education. Even as a child Fan loved planar geometry and physics and fondly remembers her physics teacher, a young, energetic, friendly woman. This teacher had a college friend who taught at the boys' high school. When the two teachers gave the same physics test at both the boys' and the girls' high schools, the girls did much better!

At National Taiwan University, Chung pursued a bachelor of science degree in mathematics in a department that was famous for being extremely demanding of students. In her class (1970) the top six graduates were women despite the fact that men outnumbered women two to one. Chung has always considered herself very lucky to have had a close group of friends when she was a mathematics student. They always helped each other and solved problems together, and after graduation they all came to the United States for graduate study. Chung earned a Ph.D. in mathematics with a specialty in combinatorics at the University of Pennsylvania; the others pursued graduate degrees at the University of California at Berkeley. She still sees some of these classmates, now colleagues, at American Mathematical Society (AMS) meetings. They include Alice S. Y. Chang at UCLA, Winnie W. C. Li at Penn State, and Gloria Wu Kaufmann at the University of Illinois.

At the University of Pennsylvania, Chung's thesis adviser was Herbert Wilf, who was impressed by her fearlessness in attacking difficult problems with frequent success. Wilf introduced her to researchers at Bell Laboratories with whom she began a fruitful research collaboration. After receiving her Ph.D. in mathematics in 1974, Chung joined the technical staff of Bell Laboratories in Murray Hill, New Jersey. From 1983 to 1991 she served as head of the Mathematics, Information Sciences, and Operations Research Division at Bellcore.

Henry Pollack, system vice-president for research, supported Chung in the development of her career at Bell Labs and then at Bell Communications Research (Bellcore). At Bellcore she built a new research group in discrete mathematics and was able to hire the best and strongest combinatorics researchers to join the group. There were no boundaries between disciplines; it did not matter what tool was used to solve a problem. Working at Bellcore, where people discussed and solved problems derived from a variety of disciplines, was a broadening experience. During her time there she was the first Bellcore fellow, visiting professor of mathematics at Harvard University, and visiting professor of computer science at Princeton University.

Chung's primary research interest is the study of combinatorics. This branch of mathematics deals with problems important in the binary universe of the information age. Combinatorics provides a bridge between traditional mathematics and computer science. Chung finds it very exciting to capture information about a graph with easily computable numbers; she compares this exploration to the experience of looking at the spectrum of a molecule from a star to discern what that star is made of.

Although Chung works primarily in the areas of graph theory, combinatorics, and algorithmic design, her research interests are widely varied, sometimes extending beyond mathematics to chemistry and engineering. Having a strong mathematics background has enabled her to make contributions in other disciplines. She has written over 180 research papers, half of which are coauthored. At present she is working on a new book on spectral graph theory as part of the Conference Board of Mathematical Sciences lecture series. She has two patents: one on optical codes embedded in systems, and the other on exponential sums routing schemes.

Chung finds research exciting and enjoys working with others. She has coauthored many papers and refers to some of her coauthors as "brilliant." One of her collaborators is the prominent Hungarian mathematician Paul Erdös, with whom she has written twelve papers. She spent ten years working on Erdös's problems and received money for three of her solutions. (Erdös offers financial rewards for proper solutions to problems he has posed.)

Another of Chung's collaborators is Ron Graham, a Bell Labs mathematician to whom she is married. They frequently work on problems together, often solving them more quickly that way. They have produced very interesting results in graph theory. In 1990, Chung and her coauthors Martin Gardner and Ron Graham received the Allendoerfer award from the Mathematical Association of America (MAA) for their article entitled "Steiner Trees on a Checkerboard," which appeared in *Mathematics Magazine* (Volume 62, 1989).

Chung's firm belief that research in mathematics should be viewed in terms of possible connections to other areas is evidenced by her statement that

> Although various fields in mathematics are quite different in scope and methods, the underlying mathematics is often united and connected. In-depth research usually is focused on a specialized area and then leads to new discoveries and new frontiers. If the depth in one particular area can be transplanted to several related areas, then the impact of the work multiplies and the work can evolve and grow.

Currently, Fan Chung is a professor of mathematics and Class of 1965 Professor at the University of Pennsylvania. She works with students in an interdisciplinary course on solving mathematics problems in science and computer science. Through her work in both pure and applied mathematics, she hopes to convey her delight in problem solving to others and to mold them into the problem solvers needed for the next century. Her advice to students on being successful in mathematics is to select problems wisely, to be persistent in pursuing solutions, and to cultivate friends in the discipline. She believes that collaboration and communication among colleagues make doing mathematics more interesting and rewarding. The exchange of ideas can lead to new knowledge and unexpected inspiration.

In addition to her prolific research life, Chung participates in many professional activities. She is a member of the Board of Mathematical Sciences, National Research Council, and has served as editor-in-chief of the *Journal of Graph Theory*. She has also been on the editorial boards of many professional journals. She has served on numerous committees of the AMS, MAA, and SIAM (Society for Industrial and Applied Mathematics). She is currently on the New York Academy of Sciences advisory board and is vice-chair of the Mathematics Section.

Fan Chung has a busy home life as well. Her son, Dean, is studying to become a mathematician at Harvard, and her daughter, Laura, is in the medical program at Stevens Institute. Chung has an interest in painting and has studied piano. Playing ping pong with Paul Erdös is another favorite pastime.

Note

The information included in this biography is based on an interview by the author.

Selected Works by Fan Chung

(1985). (with D. J. Hajela and P. D. Seymour). Self-Organizing Sequential Search and Hilbert's Inequalities, In *Proceedings of the Seventeenth Annual ACM Symposium on Theory of Computing* (pp. 217–23). Also in *Journal of Computer System Science* 36 (1988), pp. 148–57.

(1987). (with F. T. Leighton and A. L. Rosenberg). Embedding Graphs in Books: A Layout Problem with Applications to VLSI Design, *SIAM Journal on Algorithms and Discrete Methods* 8, pp. 33–58.

(1987). (with R. L. Graham and P. Diaconis). Random Walks Arising in Random Number Generations, *Annals of Probability* 15, pp. 1148–65.

(1988). (with R. L. Graham and R. M. Wilson). In Quasi-Random Graphs, *Proceedings of the National Academy of Science USA* (Vol. 85, pp. 969–70). Long version appeared in *Combinatorica* 9 (1989), pp. 345–62.

(1989). (with Martin Gardner and R. L. Graham). Steiner Trees on a Checkerboard, *Mathematics Magazine* 62, pp. 83–96. (Article was awarded MAA Carl B. Allendoerfer award.)

(1991, August). Should You Prepare Differently for a Non-Academic Career? *Notices of the American Mathematical Society* 38(6), pp. 560–61.

(1993). (with Shlomo Sternberg). Mathematics and the Buckyball, *American Scientist.* 81(1), pp. 56–71.

REGINA BARON BRUNNER

INGRID DAUBECHIES
(1954–   )
Birthplace: Houthalen, Belgium

Only one month before she was to finish her postdoctoral fellowship and leave the United States, Ingrid Daubechies was struggling to finish writing her research paper. She had sent a letter about her work to Yves Meyer, a leading scientist in the field who had given a talk about her work. She was flattered that he found her work important enough to mention in his lecture, but she was concerned that Meyer see the outcome of the work before she published the results. Her worries were unfounded; her paper soon became a major document in the mathematics of wavelets and has been widely referenced since its publication.

Ingrid Daubechies was born on August 17, 1954, in Houthalen, a small town in Belgium. The town's major industry was coal mining, and her father was an engineer in the mines. In school she was always the best student in math and science. When she began high school her family moved to Turnhout, where she rode the bus across town to attend the all-girls academic high school. At the time most students in Europe attended single-sex schools. While she rode on the bus, mathematical patterns and problems would often occupy her mind.

There were few occasions for her to study with friends because her teachers expected her to work independently and her school friends did not live nearby. Fortunately, her parents supported her interest in math and science. She spent many evenings working on math problems with her father. Her family had always assumed that she would be educated and have a career.

Ingrid's mother, who had a university education, stayed home to take care of Ingrid and her brother. The mining company where her father worked as an engineer frowned on the wives of engineers working. As Ingrid and her brother grew older and became more independent, her mother became bored and bitter with staying at home. Her mother's feelings reinforced Ingrid's determination to obtain an education that would provide her with a career.

Ingrid Daubechies. Photo courtesy of Ingrid
Daubechies.

About the time that Ingrid and her brother left home to attend the
university, her family moved to a larger town. This gave her mother the
opportunity to return to the university, where she studied criminology.
With this opportunity to study, learn, and work, Ingrid's mother became
noticeably happier. This was the beginning of her successful, fulfilling
career as a social worker helping children from criminally violent homes.
Recently Ingrid's mother retired and is now studying art history at the
university. She is a wonderful role model for life-long learning. Ingrid
dedicated her first book, *Ten Lectures on Wavelets*, to her parents:

To my mother, who gave me the will to be independent.
To my father, who stimulated my interest in science.

Ingrid's university studies began in Brussels, Belgium, at Vrije Universiteit where she studied physics. Her research interests were in the area
of quantum mechanics. Her university studies also marked her first op-

portunity to attend classes with men. By that time she had gained confidence in herself as a mathematician and scientist; as a result, she had no problem competing with men. She never felt that she was studying in an area that was inappropriate for women.

She earned her Ph.D. studying with Alex Grossmann in Marseilles, France, with whom she continued a research collaboration after her graduation. Even while completing her Ph.D., her work was becoming internationally known through her publications in leading research journals and through her presentations at conferences. Following the completion of her Ph.D., Ingrid came to the United States on a postdoctoral fellowship at Princeton University. She intended to stay for only six months, but the work was so rewarding that she stayed for two years. During this time she was also able to build her fluency in English. There were two other positive outcomes of her stay in the United States: She established an ongoing professional relationship with Yves Meyer, and she decided to marry Robert Calderbank.

At the end of the two years Daubechies decided to return to Belgium, assuming a faculty position at Vrije Universiteit. This university setting, where she could continue her research and also teach, was exactly the kind of environment in which she wanted to work. Her research continued to gain international recognition, and in 1984 she won the Louis Enpain prize for her work in Weyl quantization, a mathematical study of classical and quantum mechanics. This prize is awarded every five years by the Belgian National Science Foundation to young people up to 29 years of age. The award honors outstanding achievement in a variety of disciplines.

Daubechies returned to the United States in 1986 as a researcher and visiting professor at New York University. Here she turned her attention to problems in an area of mathematical physics previously introduced to her by Alex Grossmann, her Ph.D. adviser. These problems in the area of wavelets, an area similar to Fourier analysis, intrigued Daubechies. She explored the mathematical properties and looked for solutions that were easy to implement. Based on the success of her work in this field, as well as her earlier research, she was hired at Bell Laboratories in New Jersey, where she and her husband could both pursue their research interests.

Daubechies's most widely cited work is in an area of mathematical physics known as wavelets. Her decision to include a table of coefficients in the paper she published on the subject is what made the paper very useful to engineers. The mathematical objects in this work have become known as "Daubechies wavelets" or "compactly supported Daubechies wavelets."

Wavelets are a mathematical way of dealing with signals (such as sound waves in speech) or images (such as those in computer screen displays). For example, by using wavelets engineers can work with a picture image and store it more efficiently by compressing it first and then re-creating the original from the compressed version. In addition to the storage of pictures on a computer screen, Daubechies's work with wavelets has been used in the storage of FBI fingerprint files. A construction based on the technique of "compactly supported Daubechies wavelets" helps the FBI to store fingerprints using much less space. Wavelets can also be used for speech analysis and speaker identification. Other areas in which Daubechies wavelets can be used are music analysis and medical image analysis (such as EKGs). Detailed discussions of wavelets can be found in her book *Ten Lectures on Wavelets*, published in 1992. One year later the American Mathematical Society awarded her the Steele prize for the book.

From 1991 to 1993 Ingrid worked part-time at Bell Labs and part-time teaching at Rutgers University. In 1993 she was awarded a MacArthur "genius" award for bridging the disciplines of mathematics and engineering through her work on wavelets. The MacArthur fellowship is a prestigious five-year grant that rewards creative work in many disciplines. Daubechies has published over fifty papers and has given numerous presentations on her work. Now a professor of mathematics at Princeton University, she continues her research on wavelets while moving into new areas of research, extensions of her work on wavelets. Daubechies continues to find that working in a university environment is satisfying because she enjoys interacting with students as well as doing research.

Although most of Daubechies's teaching has been in the areas of mathematics and science, she is now planning a course for nonscience majors. As she explains, students can appreciate mathematics without understanding all the mathematical tools, just as students can appreciate music without playing an instrument.

Despite her busy professional life, Daubechies finds time for her family. She and her husband, Robert, have two children, Michael (born in 1988) and Carolyn (born in 1991). With the help of an *au pair* who helps to care for the children, they are being raised to speak both English and Dutch, the language spoken in the Flemish part of Belgium where Daubechies grew up. Although she jokes that part of the secret to successfully combining work and family is choosing your partner carefully, she is not being entirely humorous. She and her husband have a cooperative relationship with regard to both their careers and child care. Daubechies's days are devoted to research, teaching, working with students, and other professional commitments. Both she and her husband devote evenings and weekends to their children. This combination of personal joy and professional success is a pattern that Daubechies has experienced many times in her life. She has found that personal happiness has given her the confidence and positive attitude that have helped inspire her professional achievements.

Daubechies admits that balancing a personal and professional life can be tricky. She very much enjoys her work at the university and with students, but she finds that the other commitments involved with being in a university and research community take much time. She would like to be able to spend more hours each week on her research.

Ingrid does, however, enjoy setting an example for students, showing them that mathematicians do not have to be aloof or socially inept but can be real people who lead full lives. Although it takes an enormous amount of energy to teach, conduct research, do the administrative and committee work that is part of being a member of an academic and research community, and be a parent and spouse, it can be achieved through self-confidence and perseverance. Ingrid Daubechies continues to be an impressive mathematician and role model.

Note

The information included in this biography is based on an interview by the author.

Selected Works by Ingrid Daubechies

(1988). Orthonormal Bases of Compactly Supported Wavelets. *Communications on Pure and Applied Mathematics* 41(7), pp. 909–96. This is a widely cited paper on wavelets.

(1992). *Ten Lectures on Wavelets*. SIAM Regional Conference Series in Applied Mathematics 61 (Philadelphia, PA). This is an award-winning book on wavelets.

(1993). Book Review of *Ondellets* by Yves Meyer. *Science* 262, pp. 1589–91. This review includes a less technical description of wavelets, without mathematical formulas.

(1993). Different Perspectives on Wavelets (Ed.). *Proceedings of Symposia in Applied Mathematics* 47 (San Antonio, Texas).

EDITH KORT

EMILIE DE BRETEUIL DU CHATELET
(1706–1749)
Birthplace: France

Judge me for my own merits, or lack of them, but do not look upon me as a mere appendage to this great general or that renowned

Emilie du Chatelet. Photo courtesy of Stock Montage, Inc.

scholar, this star that shines at the court of France or that famed author. I am in my own right a whole person, responsible to myself alone for all that I am, all that I say, all that I do. It may be that there are metaphysicians and philosophers whose learning is greater than mine, although I have not met them. Yet, they are but frail humans, too, and have their faults; so, when I add the sum total of my graces, I confess that I am inferior to no one.

—Emilie du Chatelet[1]

Emilie du Chatelet, who studied, translated, and extended the work of Newton and other revolutionary scientific theorists of her day, lived in seventeenth-century France. This was an age when women of the aristocracy were expected to be beautiful, charming, and only well educated enough to participate in the sparkling conversation of court society. Girls from wealthy families were sent to school or privately tutored, but their studies consisted only of subjects that prepared them for marriage into nobility; mathematics and the sciences were considered unimportant in this endeavor. In fact, if a woman was too well educated, she generally encountered ridicule and hostility. As a result, many learned women kept their intellectual activities hidden, pretending to know less than they did.

Emilie de Breteuil was born into this society, and had she been considered a conventionally beautiful child, her intelligence may have been neglected in favor of her looks. As it was, her parents thought she was rather unattractive. Her father noted that she was destined to become the homeliest of women in that she was as tall as a girl twice her years, had prodigious strength, and was clumsy beyond belief. Fearing her looks would keep her from marrying, they provided her with a tutor so that she would have a good education, if not a husband, to keep her occupied as a single woman. She proved to be an intelligent and successful student, studying classic works of literature and readily mastering Latin, Italian, and English. It was mathematics, though, that really held her interest, and a family friend who recognized her talent in the subject encouraged her in her studies.

Despite her parents' expectations, she grew into a handsome and ambitious young woman. When she was 19 years old she married the Marquis Florent-Claude du Chatelet-Lomont. A colonel in the military, the Marquis was often away on military business, and the couple's three children were raised by governesses. As such, Emilie du Chatelet had plenty of time to devote not only to her studies but also to reveling and to gambling in the Parisian court. She enjoyed the glamour of society life, and she cultivated many friends who encouraged her to pursue advanced studies in physics and mathematics.

Determined to live according to her own standards, she creatively took advantage of the support she received for her intellectual interests. In the 1730s, cafés became a popular place for the Parisian intellectual community to gather and exchange ideas. However, women were not generally allowed into these establishments—especially not as equals in philosophical discussions. This barrier did not dissuade Chatelet from disguising herself as a man and joining her friends at a café where scientists met to talk about their work. Her clever ploy didn't really fool anyone, but it did allow her to obtain what was unavailable to most women of her time: access to meaningful scientific discussion.

During Chatelet's lifetime, natural forces were not studied in the same way they are today because twentieth-century instruments and technology were unavailable. Thus conclusions about the natural world were largely based on mathematical thought, not on precise physical measurements. This way of viewing the world was supported by the ideas of philosopher and mathematician René Descartes, whose mathematical discoveries greatly influenced scientific thinking in seventeenth-century Europe. Descartes believed that the world had been created with a divine, predetermined mathematical design and as such could be deduced through thought and logic. Newton, on the other hand, believed that laws of nature could be understood by observing and measuring the physical world to determine patterns. This thinking process, called induction, could be used to formulate theories that could predict natural events to a certain extent, allowing humans, not some outside force, to direct their lives. Because a belief in predetermination had dominated scientific and social thinking for hundreds of years, Newton's views were considered radical.

In 1733, Chatelet met writer and philosopher François Voltaire, who was to remain her life-long friend and companion. They shared many interests, including a passionate dedication to furthering the Newtonian system in France. Because Voltaire's writing often severely criticized the French monarchy and aristocracy, he frequently had to leave Paris to escape their wrath. He found himself in this predicament soon after he met Chatelet. Fearing for his safety, Chatelet invited Voltaire to move with her to Cirey-sur-Blaise, a neglected country estate owned by her husband. They transformed the house into a quiet retreat that included a well-stocked scientific laboratory; without a busy social life to distract them, they were able to throw themselves into their work. Cirey soon became a magnet for many well-respected mathematicians and scientists who were also working to advance Newton's philosophies. In addition to receiving instruction from and discussing philosophy with such stimulating guests, Chatelet fostered important connections with scientific academies in Germany, Scandinavia, and Russia.

Chatelet accomplished some of her most significant work in the seventeen years she spent at Cirey. In collaboration with Voltaire, she wrote *Éléments de la philosophie de Newton*, which explained Newton's philosophies to a French audience. Published in 1738, the book was officially attributed to Voltaire, who stressed that Chatelet's contribution to the work and her understanding of Newton's theories were much greater than his own. In 1740, Chatelet published her *Institutions de physique*. Written for her son's instruction, *Institutions* was an introductory physics text that incorporated the philosophies of Newton and of the German mathematician Gottfried Leibniz. More than an interpretation of Newton and Leibniz's ideas, Chatelet's book included a history of seventeenth-century scientific developments, including the most recent developments in physics. The book received much praise, but because many of her ideas further opposed those of Descartes, and even of Newton, it caused some controversy. In addition, one of her tutors, Samuel Koenig, claimed that the book was simply a rehash of the lessons he had given her! Of course, no one believed that *Institutions* was not Chatelet's work, but this fact was not officially recognized until after her death.

Chatelet's final contribution to mathematics and science was her translation of Newton's *Philosophie naturalis principia mathematica*, publishe posthumously in 1759. Of her work, Voltaire wrote: "Born with a of truth, she . . . applied herself to the discoveries of the great Newton; she translated his whole book on the principles of mathematics into French; and when she had afterwards enlarged her knowledge, she added . . . an 'Algebraical Commentary.' "[2] In addition to her commentary on Newton's work, the translation included a partial revision of *Éléments de la philosophie*. The book greatly contributed to the progression of the scientific revolution in France, helping to establish the transition from the scientific system of Descartes to that of Newton. To this day, Chatelet's work remains the only French translation of Newton's *Principia*.

In 1748, Chatelet became pregnant again. Fearing that she might not survive the birth of her fourth child and being anxious to complete her work on Newton, she maintained a heavy work schedule throughout her pregnancy. She wrote: "I get up at nine, sometimes at eight, I work till three; then I take my coffee; I resume work at four; at ten I stop to eat a morsel alone; I talk till midnight with M. de Voltaire, who comes to supper with me, and at midnight I go to work again, and keep on till five in the morning."[3] She was so committed to her pursuits that Voltaire, perhaps only half-jokingly, wrote that the little girl arrived while her mother was scribbling some Newtonian theories at her writing desk and the newborn was placed for a moment on a geometry volume as her mother gathered together her papers and prepared for bed. On September 10, 1749, a few days after her baby was born, Chatelet died of child bed fever.

Emilie du Chatelet's insightful commentaries, thorough translations, and passionate devotion to the progression of scientific thought have had a substantial impact on the development of science and mathematics. Her ability to rise above the prejudices of her time so that she could live her life as she saw fit continues to serve as an inspiration to generations of mathematicians and scientists. Of her work, Voltaire wrote: "The qualities of her style were clearness, precision, and elegance."[4] The same can most certainly be said of her life.

Notes

1. Samuel Edwards. (1970). *The Divine Mistress*. New York: David McKay, p. 1.

2. Frank Hamel. (1910). *An Eighteenth-Century Marquise*. London: Stanley Paul & Company, p. 57.

3. James Parton. (1881). *The Life of Voltaire*. London: Sampson, Low, Marston, Searle, & Rivington, v. 1, p. 562.

4. Frank Hamel. (1910). *An Eighteenth-Century Marquise*. London: Stanley Paul & Company, p. 57.

Selected Works about Emilie du Chatelet

`` `c, Margaret. (1986). *Hypatia's Heritage*. Boston: Beacon Press.

Osen, Lynn. (1984). *Women in Mathematics*. Cambridge, MA: MIT Press.
Perl, Teri. (1978). *Math Equals*. Menlo Park, CA: Addison-Wesley.
Phillips, Patricia. (1990). *The Scientific Lady: A Social History of Women's Scientific Interests 1520–1918*. New York: St. Martin's Press.
Zahm, J. A. (1974). *Woman in Science*. Cambridge, MA: MIT Press.

GREER LLEAUD

ETTA ZUBER FALCONER
(circa 1931–   )
Birthplace: Mississippi

Dr. Etta Falconer has devoted her entire life to increasing the number of highly qualified African Americans in mathematics and mathematics-related careers. She has contributed to her students' successes by maintaining high expectations, building their self-confidence, and creating a nurturing academic environment.

Falconer was born Etta Zuber in Tupelo, Mississippi, where she subsequently graduated from Carver High School in 1949. Thereafter she enrolled at Fisk University in Nashville, Tennessee, as a chemistry major with mathematics as a minor. By her sophomore year she had reversed her major and minor fields, deciding that mathematics was more interesting than chemistry.

Etta's major professional goal, even as an undergraduate, was to teach. She was unaware of other opportunities for someone with a background such as hers. Dr. Lee Lorch, chair of the mathematics department at Fisk during the time Etta was there, was instrumental in encouraging her to refocus her career goal toward becoming a mathematician.

Etta was a precocious student. By the end of her junior year of college she had completed all the requirements for her major. Professor Lorch advised her to take graduate courses during her senior year and suggested she enter graduate school the following year, which she subsequently did. Falconer regards Lorch as one of several significant mentors that have guided her professionally and personally. She was also fortunate that **Dr. Evelyn Boyd Granville**, one of the first black women to earn a Ph.D. in mathematics, was one of her mathematics professors at Fisk. Granville proved to be an excellent role model for Falconer.

In 1953 Falconer graduated summa cum laude from Fisk University. That fall she entered the University of Wisconsin at Madison. Being in Wisconsin was her first experience living and working in a nonsegregated environment. Unlike Fisk University, the mathematics department

Etta Falconer. Photo courtesy of Etta Falconer.

at the University of Wisconsin had no black professors and no female professors. There was one older black student and several older female students in the department, but Falconer had no interaction with them academically. An older Indian woman did make an effort to show kindness toward her. Otherwise, Falconer had very little social interaction with students; academically she was completely isolated. There was no one she could work with outside the classroom. None of her white male classmates took her seriously as a fellow student.

Falconer had been awarded a teaching assistantship upon entering the Wisconsin graduate program. This meant that she taught a class for the mathematics department in exchange for tuition and expenses. She was assigned to teach college algebra to a class of white students. The first time she stood in front of the class, the students laughed and considered her presence a joke. She managed to establish her credibility in the face of their hostility, but she was becoming increasingly unwilling to live and work in such an environment.

After various other jobs, such as working in the agriculture department on campus and grading papers, she was able to finance the remainder of the credits needed to earn her master's degree. Although she had the opportunity to remain at Wisconsin to complete her graduate work and earn her Ph.D., Falconer decided to leave. At that point it seemed more important to do something that would provide her with a social community and increase her marriage prospects.

Falconer returned to Mississippi and spent the next nine years as a mathematics instructor at Okolona Junior College, 30 miles from her hometown of Tupelo. During this time she met her future husband.

In 1957 and 1958, while Falconer was teaching at Okolona, the Soviet Union launched *Sputnik*, the first space satellite. The primary purpose of this launch was to investigate outer space and to discover if living organisms could survive conditions in space. This event marked the beginning of the "space race" between the United States and the Soviet Union. Suddenly the United States saw an urgent need to upgrade science technology, and that meant upgrading science education. As a result, the University of Illinois received a grant from the National Science Foundation to fund a Teacher Training Institute. The goal of the Institute was to strengthen the science curriculum by training college teachers for four consecutive summers. This program, along with many others around the country, stressed the importance of teaching "mathematical proof techniques" in grade school. Emphasis was placed on a theoretical curriculum in mathematics. Falconer was selected to attend the University of Illinois Institute in the summer of 1962.

At the end of the third summer Falconer accepted an offer to direct the Institute and to remain at the University of Illinois to work on her doctorate. In 1964 Falconer, together with her husband and their three children, moved from Mississippi to Illinois. Etta Falconer did very well that year; but when her husband was offered a position at Morris Brown College in Atlanta, after being unable to find employment in Illinois, she chose to leave with him. She was hired by Dr. Shirley McBay to teach mathematics at Spelman College, a historically black liberal arts college for women located in Atlanta.

One year later, though still teaching at Spelman, Falconer enrolled at Emory University in Atlanta to take a graduate mathematics course. Soon she earned a National Science Foundation Faculty Fellowship and was able to study full-time at Emory while continuing her teaching at Spelman on Saturdays. Finally Falconer was able to complete her program and earned her doctorate. Her dissertation title is *Quasigroup Identities Invariant under Isotopy*. Her work is in a special area of algebra known as quasigroups and loops.

Falconer returned to Spelman after receiving her degree. In 1972 she began her ten-year tenure as chair of the mathematics department there. At this time there were very few math and science majors at the college.

To promote the recruitment of mathematics students, Falconer developed summer science programs. These were designed to expose students to the vast opportunities available to young women with mathematics and science backgrounds. The programs also enriched students academically by providing them the opportunity to learn mathematics in a more relaxed environment, uninfluenced by the stresses of the academic school year.

Falconer also implemented programs that gave students opportunities to do research in mathematics. She obtained scholarships for mathematics students from the National Aeronautics and Space Administration (NASA). She started the practice of inviting prominent mathematicians to speak to Spelman students about their research, and in many cases to teach at Spelman for a year or two.

Since her arrival at Spelman College in 1965, Dr. Falconer has been working toward increasing the number of African American women in the mathematical sciences. Essential to the success of implementing these ideals has been her current position as associate provost for science programs and policy, and as Fuller E. Calloway professor of mathematics. Falconer has spent thirty years creating and building not only the mathematics department but the entire Natural Sciences Division housed in Tapley Hall on Spelman's campus. She has received several awards in recognition for her work, including the Presidential Faculty Award for Distinguished Service given by Spelman College in 1994, the Distinguished Service Award given by the National Association of Mathematicians in 1994, and the Louise Hay Award for Contributions to Mathematics Education given by the Association for Women in Mathematics in 1995.

Throughout the years Dr. Falconer has repeatedly proven her commitment to improving mathematics education for her community and students. As a teacher, scholar, and administrator she has demonstrated unrelenting devotion to her students, providing them an educational experience that prepares them for the professional mathematics community in either academia or industry. Her support extends far beyond college, as she continues to serve as role model and mentor to her students long after their graduation.

Note

The information included in this biography is based in part on an interview by the author.

Selected Work by Etta Falconer

(1994, January). Cox-Talbot Invited Address: Challenges and Opportunities for Minorities in Science, Mathematics and Engineering. National Association of Mathematicians Annual Meeting, Cincinnati, Ohio.

Selected Works about Etta Falconer

(1978). Women in Science at Spelman College. *Signs* 4, pp. 176–77.
(1983, April). Dr. Etta Falconer. *Women in Science Careers* 1(3).
(1989) A Story of Success: The Sciences at Spelman College. *SAGE* 6, pp. 36–38.
(1995, May). Hay Award for Contributions to Mathematics Education. *Notices of the American Mathematical Society* 42(5).

ULRICA WILSON PARKER

JOAN FEIGENBAUM
(1958–)
Birthplace: New York

Joan Feigenbaum had no inkling as a Harvard undergraduate that she would become a theoretical computer scientist. When she was in public school in the 1960s and early 1970s her field had barely come into existence. It was not yet routine for schools and homes to contain computers, the objects to which she would devote her working life. Only in the last few decades have computers become the focus of rigorous study in a field known as computer science. The kind of research that underlies computer science has been defined by researchers such as Joan Feigenbaum.

Born in Brooklyn, Joan Feigenbaum grew up in Valley Stream, Long Island, near New York City. Her father, Harry Feigenbaum, was a high school history teacher; her mother, Joyce Gildersleeve, was an architect who gave up her practice to care for Joan, their only child. Joan did well in school and was accepted at Harvard University as an undergraduate. She chose to major in mathematics because it seemed that her smartest classmates were math majors; competing with them would therefore present the greatest possible challenge. Also she found math hard and believed it would be very difficult to learn on her own; therefore, majoring in math was a way to maximize the value of the very costly Harvard tuition. She was surprised to learn in later years that most math majors choose math because it is easy for them.

Joan did not at first think of mathematics as a prelude to a career. As her college years passed, however, and she learned to enjoy doing math, she began to consider becoming an academic mathematician. This worried her parents, as they felt that such a career might leave her with few job options. She took their concern very seriously and was delighted when she found her true vocation in the Summer Research Program at AT&T's famous Bell Labs between her junior and senior years. She loved

Joan Feigenbaum. Photo courtesy of Joan Feigenbaum.

the work environment at Bell and found it both stimulating and fun. She also appreciated that Bell and AT&T attempted to be a socially conscious company. It was especially interested in employing women and minorities in serious research.

It was at Bell Labs that Joan became interested in theoretical computer science. She had taken some computer courses in college, but they mostly involved programming. In her senior year Joan took her first course in theoretical computer science. Here she could use her mathematical talents in a way that was extremely theoretical and at the same time extremely practical, because she knew that Bell Labs was interested in her and would give her summer work throughout her years in graduate school. In fact, she was partly supported by Bell Labs throughout her graduate work at Stanford, where she earned her Ph.D. in computer science. Upon graduating she was offered a job at Bell Labs, which she accepted. She is now at AT&T Labs, formerly part of Bell Labs but now a separate company.

Feigenbaum is a theoretical computer scientist, not a programmer. There is a significant difference between the two. She loves to explain the computer science she is doing in a way that helps ordinary people understand it. Computer scientists study the behavior of computers, just as applied mathematicians study the behavior of physical objects. In particular, computer scientists study large classes of problems and try to decide which ones can be solved by computers and which of those that *can* be solved theoretically have solutions that are "efficient" as well.

The Traveling Salesman problem is an example of the kind of problem that is at the very heart of the discipline of theoretical computer science. The problem itself is easy to describe:

> You have a set of cities. The distance between each pair of cities is given, and you can go between every pair of cities directly. The traveling salesman has to visit every city on this map. What is the most efficient way to visit every city exactly once? That is, how can one minimize the total distance traveled?

Finding the most efficient method for devising an optimal route can be expressed in a formal mathematical way. However, the mathematician is not interested in finding the most efficient route for a particular set of cities. Rather, she wants to describe a procedure that will produce an optimum route for *any* set of cities.

Clearly an algorithm, or list of steps, can be stated that will indeed give the shortest route for any given set of cities. For example, two cities A and B can be connected in two ways: A to B, or B to A. For three cities A, B, and C, there are six ways: ABC, BCA, CAB, ACB, BAC, or CBA. For four cities there are twenty-four ways. For "n" cities there are "n" factorial ways; that is, $n(n - 1)(n - 2)(n - 3) \ldots 1$. However, even though one knows how to do so, computing an actual answer takes too long when the number of cities becomes large. This is an example of an "exponential time" problem in computer science where, for a large number of cities, such a computer program will not yield the answer within a human lifetime. Theoretical computer scientists work with problems like these wherein the issue is not the finding of an algorithm that will yield a solution, but rather the search for an *efficient* algorithm—one that will deliver a solution in a *reasonable* amount of time.

Although some problems don't have any algorithmic solution, most research in theoretical computer science involves the search for more *efficient* algorithms for problems that are known to be solvable by some algorithm, although perhaps an inefficient one. Some solutions that may be efficient with respect to time require a huge amount of memory. Theoretical computer scientists consider the resources that a computation requires, such as time and memory space, and try to balance the two.

Another kind of problem that intrigues computer scientists is cryptography, or the study of codes. One particularly clever code is based on a relatively simple idea. Efficient methods are known for multiplying large numbers, a computation that computers can do very quickly. However, the reverse operation—finding the factors of a very large number, say, one that is two hundred digits long—is very, very hard. There *is* a known way of doing so (just try every number less than the given product), but it would take so long as to be impossible in practice. Going back from the product to the factors is something that no one knows how to do rapidly.

This "hardship" turns out to be very important because it enables people to communicate in code. A public message can be sent by using the public domain, but no one can decode the message unless he or she knows the factors on which the code was built. Setting up such a system requires the creation of a pair of keys: a public key and a private key. The private key consists of two large prime numbers. The product of these two primes (the public key) is published, but the original factors are kept secret (or private). The encoder runs the message through a formula that uses the public key. The resulting cryptogram can only be read (decoded) by using the private key. Since the private key is the unpublished prime factors, the scheme is very effective because of the intractability of the factoring problem.

Feigenbaum has found her career path to be very smooth. She says that the overlap between computer science and mathematics has continued to grow. Her mathematics classes had very few women, but she didn't mind that. Her computer science classes had a few more women than the mathematics classes, but not many. Although she has encountered little prejudice against women, she does note that some of her colleagues were surprised when she returned to work one month after the birth of her son, as she had intended. She says that "they had been perfectly accepting of a female mathematician or scientist, but one who was also a mother was weird to them." She is happy that she now has female colleagues, and she is a frequent speaker at symposia on women in mathematics and science.

Feigenbaum lives in New York City with her husband, Jeffrey Nussbaum, and their son, Sam Baum. (Sam's last name was chosen as the greatest common suffix of Joan's last name and her husband's last name, but Joan doesn't recommend this procedure because "it doesn't generalize.") Her husband is a musician and teacher specializing in early wind instruments. He was trained as a modern trumpet player, but he now plays early wind instruments such as the cornetto and natural trumpet. Although Joan is not an avid fan of early music, she does enjoy attending his concerts. Jeffrey is also very much involved in the scholarship of early music. He publishes the journal of the Historic Brass Society, which he founded.

Reading detective fiction is Joan's favorite pastime. She sometimes fantasizes about writing a detective story in which the detective is a mathematician. She exercises regularly, mostly swimming and walking on her treadmill. Raising their son, Sam, is a family affair, shared with her husband and her parents.

Joan Feigenbaum has published many journal articles, has contributed chapters to many books, and has been invited to speak at conferences both nationally and internationally. Though still in the early stages of her career, this young professional is already recognized as a top researcher in her field.

Note

This biography is based on an interview by the author that took place at the Julia Robinson Celebration of Women in Mathematics Conference in Berkeley, California, in July 1996. Professor Feigenbaum was a speaker at the conference.

Selected Works by Joan Feigenbaum

(1985). (with J. Hershberger and A. A. Schaffer). A Polynomial-Time Algorithm for Finding the Prime Factors of Cartesian-Product Graphs, *Discrete Applied Mathematics* 1, pp. 123–38.

(1989). (with M. Abadi and J. Kilian). On Hiding Information from an Oracle, *Journal of Computer and System Sciences* 39, pp. 21–50. (Special issue of selected papers from the 1987 Association for Computing Machinery Symposium on Theory of Computing.)

(1992). (with A. A. Schaffer). Finding the Prime Factors of Strong Direct Product Graphs in Polynomial Time, *Discrete Mathematics* 109, pp. 77–102.

(1992). (with R. Beigel). On being Incoherent without Being Very Hard, *Computational Complexity* 2, pp. 1–17.

(1993). Probabilistic Algorithms for Defeating Adversaries. *Statistical Sciences* 8, pp. 26–30.

(1995). The Use of Coding Theory in Computational Complexity, in Different Aspects of Coding Theory. *Proceedings of Symposia on Applied Mathematics, American Mathematical Society*, Providence, pp. 207–33.

JOAN ROSS

ELIZABETH FENNEMA
(1928–)
Birthplace: Kansas

When Elizabeth Fennema was in elementary school, she "knew she was going to be a musician." She had strong abilities in music and knew that

Elizabeth Fennema. Photo courtesy of Elizabeth
Fennema.

the string bass, which she had begun to play, would be her instrument.
As it turned out she traveled down a different path, but one to which
she has had as much devotion as she originally felt toward music.

Fennema was born Elizabeth Hammer in the small town of Winfield,
Kansas, in 1928, a time when the United States was on the brink of a
disastrous economic depression. In 1929 her father, along with thousands
of other Americans, lost all his money, departed, and left her mother to
fend for her two young children, Elizabeth and her brother. Elizabeth's
mother had been born in 1889 and had overcome familial pressures and
extreme poverty, common in southern states at that time, to attend Val-
paraiso University. She taught in one-room schools and in small city
schools. However, because in the early 1930s schools and most businesses would not hire married women, she took in sewing in order to
earn needed money for family expenses. Fennema describes her mother
as a strong woman who made her children feel secure by not focusing
on the fact that they had little money.

Elizabeth was an excellent student in school and was offered a scholarship to attend the prestigious Eastman School of Music. It was at this

point, when she was actually being offered a chance to realize her dream of a musical career, that she decided she didn't want the life that such a career would entail. In addition, orchestras were almost exclusively all-male, which she did not feel promised a good working atmosphere. Complicating her decision even further was the fact that in high school she had begun to seriously date the man she would eventually marry, Owen Fennema. She did not want to attend school in another state far away from him. She therefore decided to attend a small local Methodist college for the first two years; she then transferred to Kansas State University for her final two years, where she majored in psychology. The Fennemas were married in 1948 when she transferred to Kansas State.

She traveled with her husband to Madison, Wisconsin, where he was to begin graduate school at the University of Wisconsin. Fennema found that jobs for graduates in psychology were scarce, so she decided to enter graduate school at the university herself. She earned a master's degree in education in 1952. At this point the Korean War intervened in their lives, with her husband serving in the military in Texas (where their first child was born) and moving to Minneapolis when he was discharged. Here she had her first experience with designing an educational environment when she opened a private kindergarten in her basement.

After a short time in Minnesota, the Fennemas returned to Madison so that Owen could pursue his Ph.D. in food sciences. The 1950s were a very difficult time for married professional women. Although many women were obtaining advanced degrees, it was virtually impossible for both spouses to obtain positions at the same university—sometimes owing to nepotism rules, sometimes owing to strong but informal traditional practices. During this time Fennema engaged in a patchwork of activities, based both at home and professionally. She had two daughters and a son between 1953 and 1960, and taught part-time.

In 1962 a very interesting movement took place in Madison. Recognizing that there were many talented and educated women in the community who were unemployed or underemployed wives of university professors, Kathryn Clarenbach (a founder of NOW, the National Organization for Women) identified a group of these women and sent out questionnaires asking about their interest in a career. She got a very positive response and began to connect these women with appropriate jobs, advocating for them in the process. As a result of this effort, Fennema was asked to be a supervisor of student teachers. She agreed to do this and was fortunate that her mother moved to Madison to help take care of her children.

As a supervisor of student teachers Fennema worked for Vere DeVault, whom she describes as kind and perceptive. He recognized her abilities and encouraged her to pursue a doctorate in education. She began her studies in 1962 with DeVault as her dissertation adviser, and she received her Ph.D. in curriculum and instruction in mathematics education in 1969. During this time her relationship with mathematics came into play. In 1962 the "new math" movement was in full swing, which meant that lots of educators and mathematicians were thinking hard about how to get students to understand mathematics more deeply. Fennema was intrigued with the research about children's learning of mathematics. She also recognized that a good foundation in mathematics is critical for all students. This perception led her to specialize in mathematics as she began to focus on a topic for her dissertation. In this way she became closely involved in the innovations that were developing in mathematics education.

After finishing her Ph.D. she was hired as a half-time faculty member in a non–tenure track position. In 1970 the University was challenged to create half-time tenure track positions, which it did and thereby became one of the first institutions to have positions of this kind. The decision affected women in particular because they were far more likely to be in part-time faculty slots. Fennema obtained one of these positions, which was ideal as her children were still young and she did not want to work full-time. In this way she was able to split her time between being an active professional and an involved parent, and now she is proud of her children, who are grown and involved in interesting careers of their own. (Her oldest daughter is in charge of information services at a computer firm, her second daughter is a family practice physician, and her son is an organist and computer programmer. She enjoys her grandchildren immensely as well.)

Two events in 1970 helped shape her eventual groundbreaking work in gender and mathematics. First, a professor in the Educational Policy Studies Program, Joan Roberts, wanted to find women who would write about their academic disciplines. Roberts approached Fennema, who initially refused, saying she was not a feminist; however, when she looked around her department and saw that there were no tenured women on the faculty and only one assistant professor, she changed her mind. Around this same time she applied to the National Science Foundation for a research grant with a professor in the psychology department, Julia Sherman. They proposed to examine factors in the mathematics classroom that might be associated with gender, and thus launched the well-respected "Fennema-Sherman studies."

For the past quarter-century Fennema and her associates have fostered a vast amount of research on the interactions of girls and young women in mathematics classrooms. She and Julia Sherman devised an attitude questionnaire, the Fennema-Sherman Scales, that enabled researchers to gather data about the attitudes of young women toward mathematics and mathematics learning. With this instrument, results from many different sites could be compared. When educators became aware of the negative attitudes that were held by many girls, they began to devise interventions to change the situation. Now researchers have noticed that although girls have a more positive attitude toward participating in mathematics, the boys around them may still have a negative attitude toward girls' participation. In addition to her gender-related research, Fennema and some of her colleagues have developed an innovative approach to teaching mathematics, Cognitively Guided Instruction, which promotes deeper thinking about the mathematics that is being learned, particularly in elementary school. In recognition of the importance of her work, she has received a great deal of grant money to further her research in these areas. Many aspiring young professionals have spent a productive year or two at the University of Wisconsin learning and working with her (including one of the editors of this book, Teri Perl).

Fennema, in reflecting on her work—both in the equity area and on innovations in mathematics teaching—worries that reform movements may not be reaching a sufficiently broad audience. She hopes these efforts will reach beyond the privileged communities in which they often begin. Currently there is promise that her hopes may be realized because many more innovative projects are appearing in communities that lack economic resources, such as inner cities.

Elizabeth Fennema has received several awards for her contributions, including the First Annual Award for Outstanding Contribution to Research on Women and Education from the American Educational Research Association, Special Interest Group for Research on Women in Education, in 1985; the Dora Helen Skypek Award from the Association for Women and Mathematics Education (WME) in 1986; and a Doctor of Humane Letters degree from Mount Mary College in 1994. Fennema retired from the faculty of the University of Wisconsin at the end of the 1995–1996 academic year. In June an event was held to honor her work and her career. Colleagues from far and wide—those whom she had mentored, those with whom she had collaborated in research, and those whom she had simply inspired—gathered to celebrate her lifetime of work on behalf of students, especially young women, being better able to learn mathematics. A proclamation sent from WME read, "We are pleased to honor you for your extensive contributions in promoting the mathematics education of girls and women, and in facilitating the awareness of gender inequities in our classrooms. You have effectively inspired and mentored a new generation of researchers and educators. You, a founding member of WME, will always be a member of our community." Many colleagues are looking forward to the continuing leadership of Elizabeth Fennema in her "retirement" years.

Note

This biography is based on an interview that was conducted in Madison, Wisconsin, in October 1995 by the author.

Selected Works by Elizabeth Fennema

(1976). Fennema-Sherman Mathematics Attitude Scales: Instruments Designed to Measure Attitudes toward the Learning of Mathematics by Females and Males (with J. Sherman). *Journal for Research in Mathematics Education* 7(5), pp. 324–26.

(1977). The Study of Mathematics among High School Girls and Boys: Related Factors (with J. Sherman). *American Educational Research Journal* 14(2), pp. 159–68.

(1980). *Multiplying Options and Subtracting Bias: An Intervention Program* (with P. Wolleat, A. Becker, and J. Pedro). Reston, VA: National Council of Teachers of Mathematics.

(1985). Women and Mathematics in the U.S.: The New Mythology. In M. Zweng et al., Eds., *Proceedings of the Fourth International Congress on Mathematical Education* (pp. 669–71). Boston: Burkhauser.

(1987). Sex-Related Differences in Education: Myths, Realities, and Interventions. In V. Koehler, Ed., *Educator's Handbook: A Research Perspective*. New York: Longman.

(1989). Gender, Equity, and Mathematics (with M. R. Meyer). In W. Secada, Ed., *Equity in Education* (pp. 146–58). Philadelphia: Falmer Press.

(1990). *Mathematics and Gender: Influences on Teachers and Students* (with G. Leder, Ed.). New York: Teachers College Press.

(1992). *Rational Numbers: An Integration of Research* (with T. A. Romberg and T. P. Carpenter, Eds.). New York: Academic Press.

(1992). *Integrating Research on the Graphical Representations of Functions* (with T. A. Romberg and T. P. Carpenter, Eds.). Hillsdale, NJ: Lawrence Erlbaum.

(1993). Using Children's Mathematical Knowledge in Instruction (with J. L. Franke, T. P. Carpenter, and D. A. Carey). *American Educational Research Journal* 30(3), pp. 555–83.

CHARLENE MORROW

HERTA TAUSSIG FREITAG
(1908–   )
Birthplace: Vienna, Austria

In 1944, Herta Taussig immigrated to the United States with only ten dollars in her pocket. As the most likely of the passengers on her ship

Herta Taussig Freitag. Photo courtesy of Herta Taussig Freitag.

to be a German spy because of her age and level of education, she was questioned in depth when she arrived at U.S. Customs. Also suspicious was her address book, filled with names from her days in Austria. When the interrogation was finally terminated after extensive grilling, she was told, "I believe you will be quite an asset in the United States." Those words were most prophetic of her subsequent lifelong devotion to the investigation of Fibonacci numbers and to her students.

At age 88, Herta Taussig Freitag looks back at a full and active life. Events that have shaped her life included persecution in Nazi Austria, working as a domestic servant in England at age 30 during World War II, and emigrating to the United States. The lives she touched in pursuit of her lifelong dream to become a good teacher of mathematics are still with her today.

In 1978 Professor Freitag gave a lecture entitled "My Last Lecture." This talk was to mark the end of her professional life. Professor Freitag has been giving "her last lecture" for almost twenty years now and is still professionally active. This comes as no surprise to those who know her.

Herta Taussig was born in Vienna, Austria, in 1908. She credits her wonderful home life for the success that both she and her brother ultimately enjoyed. Evenings were spent with the entire family together—mother, father, brother, and Herta—each doing what they most enjoyed. Her brother Walter would be composing, her mother would be doing needlework, her father would be reading *Die Neue Prexe* (he was managing editor of this Austrian newspaper), and Herta would be doing mathematics.

Herta was 12 years old when she fell in love with mathematics. She liked that it was the one subject that did not require memorization. She decided early that she wanted to be a mathematics teacher—and a good one, at that. After elementary school Herta attended *gymnasium*, which is similar to high school in the United States. Mathematics was considered one of the most important subjects there. In fact the prime time of day was reserved for mathematics instruction. In a five-hour school day, mathematics was not taught from 8 to 9 A.M. because the students might be too sleepy, and it was not taught from 12 noon to 1 P.M. because they might be too hungry.

The Viennese university she attended was also quite different from those in the United States. There were no assignments, no tests, no examinations unless one wanted to receive a diploma. Motivation was left completely up to the student. Herta remembers, "We were exceedingly idealistic at that time. We loved mathematics and were preparing for teaching at *gymnasium*. We all knew that the chance of obtaining a position was practically nil as Vienna was overrun with professionals and mathematics professors were anything but in short supply, but we really wanted to teach mathematics." There were many female students studying mathematics at that time, and they often studied together.

Herta lived at home as a student and tutored others in order to help with expenses. Upon completing her examinations, she was a student teacher for a year and then tutored full-time. Herta's teaching certificate read, "Candidate has extraordinary command of her language to make even complicated mathematics topics easily accessible to the students."

Herta received her degree in 1934; Hitler invaded Austria in 1938. Herta's family found that they did not meet Hitler's criteria for being identified as Aryan, which required seven baptismal certificates going back two generations. She had what was then referred to as a "wrong grandmother." The family began to explore ways to leave Austria. Herta wanted to travel to the United States, where she would be allowed to teach. However, because of the mass exodus of people from Europe to the United States at the time, a sponsor was required in order to be issued a visa. Ultimately a friend of a friend, a surgeon from St. Louis named Taussig, agreed to sponsor Herta. Even with a proper sponsor, however, it was to be a long wait.

Meanwhile, Herta decided to travel to England on a visa to work as a maid. These were the only English visas being issued to foreigners at that time, in order to protect professional jobs for the British population. During her six years in England Herta worked as maid, governess, waitress, and teacher. Her parents were able to follow her to England and managed to survive there under extreme conditions. In spite of the bombs and the war, people generously helped the family. Herta's father died in England, content in the knowledge that his family had escaped Austria and would ultimately be reunited in the United States.

In 1944, having finally received their visas, Herta and her mother set off for the United States, traveling on a freighter that was part of a convoy of ninety-eight boats. They arrived after twenty-one days at sea, prevented by fog from viewing the Statue of Liberty welcoming them to the United States. A little later, however, the lights of Ellis Island were shining in front of them, and the next person that Herta and her mother saw was Walter, her brother, meeting them at the dock.

Through an agency Herta was able to find a teaching position at the Greer School, a private school in upstate New York. Professor Freitag describes the setting at Greer as "very, very, ideal." During the summers she returned to school at Columbia University. She received her master's degree in 1948. During her second year at Greer, Herta met a fellow teacher, Arthur Freitag, whom she would later marry.

Following completion of her master's degree Herta became a mathematics instructor at Hollins College, a private liberal arts college for women in Roanoke, Virginia. Through great perseverance she established a mathematics department, where she was the sole member and taught seven courses in a language that was not her native tongue. At the same time she was working on a Ph.D. at Columbia.

At Columbia, Frietag was mentored by Edward Kasner. One day the students were given a problem on neo-Pythagorean triangles to ponder over the weekend. Freitag remembers her professor saying, "If you're good you might come up with one theorem. If you're very good you might come up with two." She found thirty-two theorems, many of which were original. Dr. Kasner was impressed. From this work Freitag was able to generate her first professional publication, which appeared in *Scripta Mathematica*. The well-known mathematician Howard Eves was another mentor at Columbia; she still corresponds with him. Herta Freitag completed her Ph.D. at Columbia in 1953.

At Hollins, Freitag began as an instructor but rose quickly from instructor to full professor. She served as chair of the department throughout her tenure at Hollins, carrying a full teaching load all the while. She considered her students to be her junior colleagues. Her teaching beliefs have been guided by the premise that experience is essential for comprehension. Owing to her influence, many students completed mathematics majors at Hollins College.

Herta Freitag loves all mathematics, but nothing as much as Fibonacci numbers. The Fibonacci sequence {1, 1, 2, 3, 5, 8, 13, 21, 34, 55, 89, . . . } (formally defined as $F1 = F2 = 1$, and $F(n + 2) = F(n + 1) + Fn$ (for n ≥ 1) was to Professor Freitag a gold mine for mathematical research. She also felt that from an examination of the Fibonacci sequence and the related Lucas sequence, even students could engage in real mathematical research.

In 1971 Freitag retired, but she returned to Hollins College for a year as interim department chair in 1978. She was asked to teach again in 1993. Her return was by invitation of the academic vice-president, who had heard her give a talk. He invited her back to teach a course of her own design in a graduate program for teachers working on a master of arts degree in Liberal Studies. Because she had always been excited about mathematics, she decided to offer her course to the "mathematics haters." She wanted to teach those who had been infected by fear and dislike of mathematics, because she felt she could be the "antibiotic" that would cure their problem. Her dose of mathematical antibiotics contained topics that the students had never encountered before, such as recursive sequences (including her favorite, the Fibonacci sequence), pattern generation, and polygonal numbers.

Freitag is the consummate problem solver. Whereas some people work crossword puzzles or knit for relaxation, she solves problems. Her name is very familiar to anyone who reads the problem section in *School Science and Mathematics*. Rarely is an issue published that does not contain at least one of her problems or solutions. Another journal that regularly features her problems is the *Fibonacci Quarterly*. In fact, in a recent issue—Volume 32(5), 1994—the editor dedicated the entire problem section to Herta Freitag's problems. The caption at the top read, "Nary a month goes by without my receiving a problem proposal from the inveterate problemist, Herta Taussig Freitag. So, as a tribute to Herta, and to reduce my backlog, all the problems in this issue come from her." The November 1996 issue of the *Fibonacci Quarterly* is devoted solely to the life and works of Professor Freitag.

Freitag is also very active in the Fibonacci Society. At the 1996 summer conference in Graz, Austria, she presented two papers, including one that described a new application she had found of the Fibonacci sequence. Her work centers around number theoretic systems with an emphasis on periodicity and problems related to the ramifications of the Fibonacci sequence.

The first Virginia College Mathematics Teacher of the Year award was given to Freitag in 1980. She was the first woman president of the

Virginia-Maryland-Washington, D.C., Chapter of the Mathematical Association of America; and she is listed in *Who's Who of American Men and Women of Science*, among other honors.

One of Freitag's most important characteristics, underlying everything that she does, is her sense of humor (as evidenced in a recent "last lecture" entitled "Spinach, New York, and Mathematics Have Much in Common"). She has kept in touch with people from all phases of her life from her *gymnasium* school friends to her students from Hollins College. She speaks with her older brother Walter every Saturday morning by phone. She is still in touch with mathematics every day, by posing problems for others in journals, by presenting papers, and by continuing to give her "last lecture." She has succeeded in being what she has always aspired to be: a good mathematics teacher and a good mathematician.

Note

The information included in this biography is based in part on an interview by the authors.

Selected Works by Herta Freitag

(1988). On the Representation of {Fkn/Fn}, {Fkn/Ln}, {Lkn/Ln} and {Lkn/Fn} as Zeckendorf Sums. *Applications of Fibonacci Numbers* 3, pp. 107–14.

(1989). On the f-Representation of Integral Sequences. *Fibonacci Quarterly* 27(3).

(1990). Conversion of Fibonacci Identities into Hyperbolic Identities Valid from an Arbitrary Argument. *Applications of Fibonacci Numbers* 4, pp. 91–98.

(1990). On Correlated Sequences Involving Generalized Fibonacci Numbers (with G. M. Phillips). *Applications of Fibonacci Numbers* 4, pp. 121–25.

(1991). Thoughts on the Art of Teaching. *Educational Forum*, Winter.

(1992). Co-Related Sequences Satisfying the General Second Order Recurrence Relation. *Applications of Fibonacci Numbers* 5, pp. 257–62.

(1992). The Zeckendorf Representation of {Fkn/Fn} (with Piero Filipponi). *Applications of Fibonacci Numbers* 5, pp. 217–19.

(1994). Fibonacci Autocorrelation Sequences (with Piero Filipponi). *Fibonacci Quarterly* 32(4), pp. 356–68.

Selected Work about Herta Freitag

Johnson, M. A. (1988). *One-Way Ticket: The True Story of Herta Taussig Freitag*. (Published privately by Mary Ann Johnson, ISBN #0-9621465-0-1)
                    LYNAE E. SAKSHAUG and MELFRIED OLSON

SOPHIE GERMAIN
(1776–1831)
Birthplace: Paris, France

> When a person of the sex which, according to our customs and prejudices, must encounter infinitely more difficulties than men to familiarize herself with these thorny researches, succeeds nevertheless in surmounting these obstacles and penetrating the most obscure parts of them, then without a doubt she must have the noblest courage, quite extraordinary talents, and a superior genius.
> —Carl Friedrich Gauss of Sophie Germain[1]

As a child in eighteenth-century Paris, Marie-Sophie Germain was confined to her house during a decade of revolutionary violence, and so spent many hours reading in her father's library. According to one story, at age 13 she came upon the legend of the death of Archimedes in a book about the history of mathematics. In the legend Archimedes was designing a machine to repel the Romans who were attacking the Greek city-state of Syracuse. So engrossed was he in the study of a mathematical figure in the sand that he paid no heed to a Roman soldier ordering him to stop. Consequently he was speared to death. This legend so impressed Germain that she resolved to study mathematics; ultimately she made important contributions to the field of number theory.

Sophie's plan was strongly opposed by her family, who contended that it was improper for women and girls to study mathematics. At that time, even a basic education in mathematics and science was socially acceptable only for girls from aristocratic families. Undaunted, Germain studied differential calculus at night while her family slept. In fact, she studied so much and slept so little that her parents began to fear for her health. To force her to get the rest she needed, they made sure her bedroom was without a light or a fire. They even took her clothes from her after she had retired for the night so that she would have to stay in bed to keep warm! She pretended to comply with her parents' wishes, but when she was sure they were asleep she wrapped herself in her bedding and continued to concentrate on her studies, even when it was so cold that the ink froze in her inkwell. Realizing that their daughter was bound and determined to follow her passion, Germain's parents finally allowed her to study during the day.

When she was 18 years old, Germain wanted to continue her studies at the newly opened École Polytechnique. However, this prestigious school did not accept women students. Undaunted, Germain obtained various professors' lecture notes from students at the Polytech and once

Sophie Germain. Photo courtesy of Stock Montage,
Inc.

again studied on her own. Having become fascinated with the new field
of mathematical analysis being developed by French mathematician Joseph Louis Lagrange, she wrote to Lagrange about his work, using the
pseudonym M. Le Blanc. Lagrange was extremely impressed with her
comments, and upon learning Germain's true identity, he met with her
and commended her observations. Soon the intellectual community of
Paris knew all about this talented young mathematician. She received
many offers from mathematicians who wished to assist her in her education; but because none could offer the advanced instruction she sought,
she continued to work in isolation.

In 1801 Germain became interested in the work of German mathematician Carl Friedrich Gauss in number theory, the study of numbers
and their relation to one another. A few years later she wrote to him,
offering insights and observations related to his publication *Disquisitiotles
Arithmeticae.* Still concerned that he might be prejudiced against a woman
mathematician, she again used the pseudonym M. Le Blanc. As did Lagrange before him, Gauss found her comments to be valuable, and he
initiated a correspondence with "Mr. Le Blanc." After several letters he

discovered Germain's true identity. Although he did not always respond to her letters, he admired her work. In fact, Gauss's esteem for her was so high that shortly after her death in 1831, he was successful in obtaining an honorary degree for her from Germany's University of Göttingen.

Early in the nineteenth century Paris enjoyed the reputation of being the European center of mathematical and scientific discovery. Thus Germain was often exposed to new and stimulating ideas. After having attended a demonstration by German physicist Ernest Chladni, she became excited by something called "mathematical physics" and decided to shift the focus of her work from number theory to this new field. To demonstrate the vibration of elastic surfaces, Chladni had lightly hit a violin bow against a plate covered with a thin layer of sand, producing various patterns. The study of these kinds of vibration patterns, which is used today in the building of skyscrapers, had interested mathematicians for hundreds of years, but no one knew exactly what the vibrations were or how they worked. In 1809, as a result of Chladni's work, French mathematician Pierre-Simon Laplace organized a competition to encourage mathematicians to develop a mathematical theory that explained the vibrations and their patterns.

Although Germain initially had not planned to enter the competition, she spent many months developing a theory and, in September 1811, submitted her work anonymously. As it turned out, hers was the competition's only entry! After two months of evaluation, the judging committee—which knew that Germain was the author of the entry—informed her that her work contained a serious flaw. To allow her time to correct her mistake, the contest was extended until October 1813. She continued to work on her theories, and after another unsuccessful entry and a further extension, the French Academy of Sciences awarded her the competition's grand prize on January 8, 1816. Although her lack of formal mathematical training had proven to be a hindrance, Germain's work in elasticity stimulated considerable interest and was the basis for further study in the subject.

Winning a prize from the prestigious Academy greatly enhanced Germain's reputation, and she was finally able to become a bona fide member of the French scientific community. With the help of her friend Joseph Fourier, permanent secretary of the Academy of Sciences, Germain was allowed to attend sessions of the Institut de France. This was a very high honor, and as the Institut was comprised of four academies, including the Academy of Sciences, it afforded her many important contacts. She began to collaborate with several well-respected mathematicians who worked with her to refine her proofs and her theories.

In the 1820s, Germain resumed her work in number theory. She became particularly interested in developing a proof for Fermat's Last Theorem, a problem that had long intrigued mathematicians. Seventeenth-century French mathematician Pierre de Fermat had written in the margin of a book that he had proved the following theorem: There do not exist positive integers x, y, z, and n such that $x^n + y^n = z^n$ when $n > 2$. Much to the chagrin of future generations of mathematicians, Fermat died without having left a trace of his proof. For years, no one had found positive integers x, y, z, and n that satisfied the conditions stated in the theorem, and no one had been able to prove that there are no positive integers x, y, z, and n that satisfy the equation. Germain developed a theorem showing that for all prime numbers $n < 100$, the equation $x^n + y^n = z^n$ has no solution when x, y, and z are not divisible by n. Although she did not find a general proof of Fermat's Last Theorem—that would require sophisticated computers, which were unavailable in the nineteenth century—her theorem proved to be her most important work in number theory, enabling future mathematicians to progress on the proof's development.

When Germain developed breast cancer she discontinued her work in mathematics, focusing instead on more general philosophical interests. Two years after her death on June 26, 1831, her nephew published an essay she had been writing about intellectual development, the nature of society, and scientific and artistic pursuits.

Despite the fact that Germain had tremendous natural talent, nineteenth-century prejudice against women in the fields of mathematics and science had a great effect on her endeavors. Had she been given access to adequate instruction, she most certainly would not have had to struggle as much as she did to become a recognized, well-respected mathematician. However, her determination to overcome obstacles has served to underscore her important contributions to number theory and mathematical physics. Like the era into which she was born, Sophie Germain's life and work were infused with a revolutionary spirit.

Note

1. Victor J. Katz. (1993). *A History of Mathematics: An Introduction*. New York: HarperCollins College Publishers, p. 591.

Selected Works about Sophie Germain

Alic, Margaret. (1986). *Hypatia's Heritage*. Boston: Beacon Press.
Dash, Joan. (1991). *The Triumph of Discovery*. Westwood, NJ: Silver Burdett and Ginn.
Gray, M. (1987). Sophie Germain. In Louise S. Grinstein and Paul Campbell, *Women of Mathematics: A Bibliographic Sourcebook*. Westport, CT: Greenwood Press.
Osen, Lynn. (1984). *Women in Mathematics*. Cambridge, MA: MIT Press.
Perl, Teri. (1978). *Math Equals: Biographies of Women Mathematicians + Related Activities*. Menlo Park, CA: Addison-Wesley.
———. (1993). *Women and Numbers*. San Carlos, CA: Wide World/Tetra.
Phillips, Patricia. (1990). *The Scientific Lady: A Social History of Women's Scientific Interests 1520–1918*. New York: St. Martin's Press.

Spender, Dale. (1990). *Women of Ideas and What Men Have Done to Them*. London: HarperCollins.

                        SANDERSON M. SMITH and GREER LLEAUD

EVELYN BOYD GRANVILLE
(1924–   )
Birthplace: Washington, DC

What does it take to become a successful mathematician? Although it is difficult to make generalizations, an important factor is the belief that one can do mathematics well. One woman who always believed she could do mathematics well is Evelyn Boyd Granville. She did indeed do mathematics very well, going on to achieve a distinguished career as an applied mathematician in the field of aerospace technology.

Early in her schooling, Evelyn began to pave the way for her own success. She did well in math classes in junior and senior high school; in fact, she did well in all her subjects. At Dunbar High School, Washington, D.C., in the late 1930s, she was fortunate to have several teachers who inspired her academically. Many of these teachers had graduated from top institutions and knew how to challenge their students by holding high expectations for them. Two of her most special and inspiring math teachers were Ulysses Basset and Mary Cromwell. By the time she graduated from high school, Evelyn was first in her class.

Many Dunbar graduates went on to Ivy League colleges. Her mentor, Mary Cromwell, must have guessed that Evelyn was destined for success, for it was the Cromwell family that encouraged her to apply to Smith College, a prestigious women's college in Massachusetts. (Smith College had played a fairly large role in Mary Cromwell's family. A Cromwell niece had graduated from Smith in 1940, and Mary's sister, Otelia Cromwell, had earned a Ph.D. in English from Yale University after graduating from Smith in the early 1900s.)

Evelyn was indeed admitted to Smith and spent the next four years studying there. Before college she had planned to become a teacher. In the African American community, becoming a teacher was highly encouraged and thought to be one of the most honorable professions to which a young person could aspire. When Evelyn got to college, however, she began to expand her options.

Once in college she thought seriously of becoming an astronomer. The subject matter of astronomy was very exciting to her, but the working conditions for astronomers in the 1940s were not quite what Evelyn wanted. In those days being an astronomer often required living in iso-

Evelyn Boyd Granville. Photo courtesy of Evelyn Boyd Granville.

lation in remote observatories for extended periods of time. Understandably, this did not seem a very enticing profession for a bright, cheerful, outgoing young woman like Evelyn. Though she kept in touch with astronomy by taking many physics courses, she decided not to major in astronomy after all. Ultimately, although she did not have a major in physics, she graduated with as many course hours in physics as she had in her major, mathematics.

What had been astronomy's loss turned out to be mathematics' gain. Evelyn's choice of major would become one that led to a long, productive intellectual life. She quickly qualified and was enrolled in the honors mathematics program. Students in the honors program could spend their last two years of college as independent scholars, doing mathematics under the direction of individual professors instead of taking formal classes. Evelyn spent her honors program under the direction of Professor Neal McCoy.

Although sending Evelyn to an expensive private college was a financial challenge for her family—and she received virtually no outside assistance—she was able to reduce her college expenses significantly by living in co-op housing during her last three years at Smith. The main difference between co-op and other housing was that co-op students provided their own maid service and cooked their own meals. Evelyn did not find this work particularly difficult. As it turned out, though, because it was the early 1940s (during World War II), all the maids had left the campus for the defense industry. In fact, all Smith students had to perform their own maid service!

Academically, Evelyn continued to thrive. During the summers she worked in Washington, D.C., at the National Bureau of Standards. In 1945 she graduated summa cum laude and was elected to Phi Beta Kappa, the collegiate honor society.

It was unlikely for a person with so much academic potential to leave school after receiving only a bachelor's degree, so it made sense for Granville to begin graduate school immediately. Success at Smith paid off, and she was admitted to Yale University graduate school. Always ready to outdo herself, she earned an M.A. in both mathematics *and* physics in her first year at Yale. Three years later she completed her Ph.D., writing her dissertation on functional analysis under the direction of Dr. Einar Hille. Considering that many graduate students today take as long as six or seven years to complete doctoral degrees in mathematics, the fact that Granville completed her degree in four years is quite impressive.

Receiving fellowships from Yale and Smith for her first year allowed Granville to start graduate school unencumbered by the need to work to support herself. For the next two years she held a Julius Rosenwald Fellowship designed to further the careers of promising young African American scholars. In her final year she held a fellowship from the Atomic Energy Commission. This fellowship too had no "strings" attached; that is, she could pursue her own work without having to do work that would benefit atomic energy research. Summers were spent working to earn money, including teaching at Morgan College in Baltimore, Maryland.

As at Smith, the quality of dorm life at Yale was influenced by the war. Although the war ended during the summer between Granville's undergraduate and graduate school years, many men had not yet returned from their military service. Thus graduate women at Yale were allowed to live in one of the men's fraternity houses. About forty to sixty graduate women lived in the house with her, and four or five women were first-year mathematics graduate students. This number was higher than it might have been even ten years earlier because women were "getting the breaks," as she says, "since the men had gone off to war." Her own roommate was an African American graduate student in economics.

When she graduated from Yale in 1949, Evelyn Boyd Granville became one of the first two African American women ever to earn a Ph.D. in mathematics. The other was **Marjorie Lee Browne**, who earned her doctorate in the same year.

Evelyn began her postgraduate career with a one-year fellowship at New York University (1949–1950). She spent the next two years (1950–1952) as an associate professor at Fisk University. Although her career there was brief, she did influence two young women who themselves later earned Ph.D.s in mathematics—**Vivienne Malone-Mayes** and **Etta Falconer**. In 1952 she began a career in government and industry research, and she did not return to a university setting until 1967.

Granville's first research position was with the U.S. Army at the Diamond Ordnance Fuse Laboratories, working in the field of celestial mechanics and analyzing mathematical problems related to the development of missile fuses. The following five years were spent doing research at IBM for the Project Vanguard and Project Mercury space probes. These projects were part of the U.S. Space Program. Granville's work involved orbit computations, consulting in numerical analysis and programming for the early IBM 650 and 704 computers. The computer language in which she did her work was S.O.A.P. (Symbolic Optimal Assembly Program). In 1957 she was programming in the computer language Fortran. An ordinary day might find her using numerical analysis to do quick approximations in order to determine where a spacecraft would land. After working for IBM, Granville spent two more years researching orbit computation—this time at the Computation and Data Reduction Center of the U.S. Space Technology Laboratories. Though much of her work with the space industry was of publishable quality, documents issued there were credited to teams rather than individuals; thus only one publication has been credited to her name.

In 1962, with her continually developing expertise as an applied mathematician, Granville became a research specialist providing technical support to the Apollo engineering departments. She continued to work in the area of celestial mechanics, doing orbit and trajectory computations. She also continued her research in the areas of numerical analysis and digital computer techniques. The latter work was done at the North American Aviation Space and Information Systems Division. Granville then returned to IBM for four more years; her new title was senior mathematician.

In 1967 Dr. Granville was divorced from the Reverend Gamaliel Collins, whom she had married in 1960. This life change was partially responsible for her decision to switch to a field of employment that was more settled and would require less moving around. She decided to return to teaching and became a full professor in the mathematics department of California State University at Los Angeles. Her primary area of interest became the mathematics education of prospective elementary school teachers. Being in this field allowed her to teach in many settings outside the university. Under the Miller Mathematics Improvement Program of the State of California, an important innovative math education program of the period, Granville taught half-time in a supplemental mathematics program at an elementary school. She directed an after-school program in mathematics for children in kindergarten through fifth grade, teaching the upper fourth grade classes herself. During this time she was also a senior lecturer at the University of Southern California, and in 1972 she taught in its National Science Foundation Institute for Secondary Teachers of Mathematics.

In addition to her commitment to education, she has been active in the professional community by serving on numerous boards. These include the U.S. Civil Service Panel of Examiners of the Department of Commerce; the Psychology Examining Committee of the Board of Medical Examiners of the State of California; the Advisory Committee of the National Defense Education Act, Title IV, Graduate Fellowship Program of the Office of Education; the Advisory Committee of Project One of the Los Angeles County Schools Mathematics Television Project; the Board of Trustees of the Center for the Improvement of Mathematics Education in San Diego; and the Beverly Hills Branch of the American Association of University Women (for which she served as president from 1968 to 1970).

In 1984 Granville retired and moved with her second husband, Edward V. Granville, a retired real estate broker, to a sixteen-acre ranch in Tyler, Texas. There the couple acquired 800 chickens and went into the business of selling fresh eggs. Though retired, Evelyn Granville continues to work part-time as an instructor at the University of Texas, an upper-division college in Tyler. She continues to teach mathematics to future elementary school teachers and continues to be inspired to create new ways to stimulate a love for mathematics.

Note

The information included in this biography is based in part on an interview by the author.

Selected Work by Evelyn Boyd Granville

(1975). *Theory and Application of Mathematics for Teachers* (with J. Frand). Belmont, CA: Wadsworth Publishing Co.

Selected Works about Evelyn Boyd Granville

Kenschaft, Patricia Clark. (1987). Evelyn Boyd Granville. In Louise Grinstein and Paul Campbell, Eds., *Women of Mathematics* (pp. 57–61). Westport, CT: Greenwood Press.

Perl, Teri. (1993). *Women and Numbers*. San Carlos, CA: Wide World Publishing/
    Tetra.

HANNIA GONZALEZ

MARY GRAY
(1939–   )
Birthplace: Nebraska

Although mathematician Mary Gray is a professor of mathematics at American University in Washington, D.C., she might easily be found in Bosnia, Chile, Israel, or Rwanda. She might be found testifying before congressional committees on Capitol Hill or appearing as an expert witness in California courtrooms. Through her knowledge of law and statistics, and her attention to social justice, she has found many ways to use her professional training to help people around the world.

Gray was born in Nebraska on April 4, 1939, the only child of two native Nebraskans. Mary's father passed on his interest in history by reading to her about the history of Nebraska. Stimulated in this way, Mary was encouraged to study history too. Her mother, a schoolteacher before her marriage, contributed to Mary's knowledge of history by sharing personal stories from her past. For instance, she told Mary about boarding with a family while she taught in a one-room schoolhouse, with American Indian families setting up camp in the fields nearby so that their children could attend school. When Mary was only 5 years old her father was already challenging his daughter with mental arithmetic. During the Depression years he worked as a policeman, later as a truck driver and mechanic, and completed his working years as a traffic manager.

Gray attended Hastings College in Nebraska, where she was an excellent student and was elected to the honorary societies Phi Beta Kappa, Pi Mu Epsilon, and Sigma Xi. She majored in mathematics and physics, and in 1959 graduated summa cum laude. She then spent a year at the J. W. Goethe Institute in Frankfurt, Germany, as a Fulbright fellow.

After returning, Gray entered graduate school at the University of Kansas. She chose to study mathematics primarily because the government made it affordable for her to do so. These were the days following the launching of *Sputnik* when the federal government was pouring funds into the education of scientists. Had this not been the case, she probably would have gone to law school instead. She recalls that the instructor in her first graduate school class asked, "What are you doing

Mary Gray. Photo courtesy of Mary Gray.

here? Why don't you stay home and take care of kids?" This kind of treatment spurred Gray to work even harder.

During the summers, and for several years thereafter, she worked as a physicist at the National Bureau of Standards (now the National Institute of Science and Technology). In 1962 Gray earned her master's degree in mathematics from the University of Kansas and began to work there as an assistant instructor. With the benefit of fellowships from the National Science Foundation and the National Defense Education Act, Gray completed her Ph.D. at the University of Kansas in 1964.

Gray's concern for social justice was already apparent in the 1960s while she was a mathematics graduate student at Kansas. Along with other graduate students, she organized a protest against the local grocery store that refused to hire American Indian students as bag boys. The graduate students simply filled up carts with expensive frozen food and abandoned the carts in the checkout lanes. They did this daily for three or four days. Their protest was duly recognized, and the ban on hiring was dropped.

After earning her doctorate Gray taught for one year at the University of California, Berkeley, and then went on to teach at California State University in Hayward. Here again she was involved in the fight for social justice; this time she joined the struggles of the farm workers in Alameda County. During this year she met and married Alfred Gray, a fellow mathematician on the faculty. Together they moved to the suburbs of Washington, D.C., where Alfred began to teach at the University of Maryland and Mary at American University.

During her years at American University, Mary Gray has served three times as chair of the department and has been active on many committees as well. However, as time went on, her interest in the careers of women professors began to absorb more of her attention. In the early 1970s, together with a few women colleagues who had similar concerns, she worked to establish a new organization to address gender inequity. Gray was the founding president of the Association for Women in Mathematics (AWM). She was concerned that many of her female colleagues were frustrated by the difficulties in getting jobs, the lack of women speakers at American Mathematical Society (AMS) meetings and at conferences, the dearth of women as officers or on committees of the AMS. The AWM membership is comprised mostly of women but also some men. The agenda of AWM was then, and still is, to assist women mathematicians professionally and to encourage more women and girls to study mathematics.

Known for her ability to make a point, Gray once attempted to attend a council meeting of the AMS. When told at the door that the meetings were not open to the membership, Gray, who had previously looked at the by-laws, said that the AMS by-laws did not specify closed meetings. When she was admonished that it was a "gentleman's agreement," Gray said, "I'm no gentleman" and attended the meeting. She subsequently became the first woman to be elected to the council and the first woman to be elected vice-president of the AMS.

Through the efforts of Gray and her fellow activists, influenced by the 1960s civil rights movement, the AMS canceled its reciprocity agreement with the South African Mathematical Society (which had no black members) during the years of apartheid in South Africa.

The AWM, with Gray in the forefront, prepared briefs as friends of the court for testimony on issues affecting women and mathematics. As Gray was asked to appear more and more in court, she determined that a deeper knowledge of the law would be valuable for her activities. She enrolled in the Washington College of Law at American University, graduating summa cum laude with a Juris Doctor (J.D.) degree in 1979. Since then she has been even more active in legal issues, always lending her advice pro bono (for free). She is a member of the District of Columbia Bar; the U.S. Supreme Court Bar; and the Federal District Court Bar. The AWM has taken an active role throughout the world in cases such as those promoting the right of Soviet women mathematicians to emigrate, and the rights of Chinese women imprisoned for pro-democracy activities in 1989.

Armed with a knowledge of the law, a broad knowledge of mathematics and mathematics education, and strong personal convictions, Gray has given testimony to many congressional committees on related topics. She testified about income tax reform to the U.S. House Ways and Means Committee; on affirmative action at the Department of Labor; on pensions and insurance for five U.S. congressional committees as well as in eight states from Maine to Oregon. She has also testified on age discrimination, Social Security, pay equity, women and the military, retirement income security, the constitutional right to travel, and women in science. She has testified in federal courts in nine states.

Gray has been elected to important positions that give her even more platforms for her driving concerns about inequities. She has been a member of the U.S.A. Board of Amnesty International since 1985, acting as treasurer beginning in 1988 and as chair beginning in 1993. She has been treasurer of the Montgomery County section of the American Civil Liberties Union; treasurer and chair of the Women's Equity Action League; and vice-chair of the American–Middle East Education Foundation, where she has been on the board since 1982. Gray's knowledge of statistics and her work as treasurer of Amnesty International brought her talents to the attention of those who are concerned about justice in Rwanda. At the suggestion of the Office of Transition Initiatives, she was asked to help design a plan to facilitate the administration of justice in that country.

Gray has given hundreds of presentations in recent years. With a particular interest in statistics and the law, she has discussed the "Use of statistics and information management in human rights work" in Beijing, China, in 1995 at the Fourth United National Women's Conference; "Statistics and the law" in Oxford, England, in 1994; "Educating the decision makers: The use of statistics in litigation" in Marrakesh, Morocco, at the International Conference on the Teaching of Statistics in 1994; and "Can statistics tell us what we do not want to hear?" for the Palestinian Society of Mathematical Sciences at Bir Seit University in 1993.

Both Gray and her husband, Alfred, travel extensively worldwide to work with their many collaborators in mathematics. Travel also allows Gray to deeply indulge her love of opera, an area in which she has also published papers. Wherever she has a committee meeting, she manages to be head of the entertainment section, to find the opera house, and thus determine which opera will be offered on the meeting schedule. Her love of opera harks back to her high school days in Nebraska when she listened to live Saturday afternoon radio broadcasts from the Metropolitan Opera House in New York City.

Gray has worked closely with her twenty-one Ph.D. students, many of whom have earned their degrees in mathematics education. According to C. J. Houtchens, Gray is credited with "focusing American University's commitment to women and minorities in mathematics." Joan Sterling Langdon, who graduated in 1989, talks of the impression that Gray typically has on her students: "[S]ometimes she gave me a fit, but it was all worth it. She was that way because she wanted me to do well and she wanted me to do my best." Langdon was one of three African American women who earned a Ph.D. in mathematics or mathematics education in the U.S. in 1989. These women are all part of a powerful network explicitly encouraged by Mary Gray.

Note

The information included in this biography is based on an interview by the author.

Selected Works by Mary Gray

(1972). Women in mathematics. *American Mathematical Monthly* 79, pp. 475–79.

(1973). Pawn to Queen 3. *The Sciences* 13, p. 31.

(1981). (with A. Schafer). Sex and Mathematics, *Science* 211, p. 231.

(1981). (with A. Schafer and I. Nichols). The Impact of the 1982 Federal Budget on Women in Higher Education, *Academe* 67, pp. 202–4.

(1985). Legal Perspectives on Sex Equality in Faculty Employment. *Journal of Social Issues* 41, pp. 121–34.

(1987). Sophie Germain. In Louise S. Grinstein and Paul J. Campbell, Eds., *Women of Mathematics*. New York: Greenwood Press.

(1988). Academic Freedom and Non-Discrimination: Enemies or Allies? *University of Texas Law Review* 64, pp. 1591–1615.

(1989). (with M. Awartani). Cultural Influences on Sex Differentials in Mathematics Aptitude and Achievement, *International Journal of Mathematics Education in Science and Technology* 20, pp. 317–20.

(1990). *Achieving Pay Equity*. American Association of University Professors publication. Washington, DC.

(1990). Phantom Universities: West Bank and Gaza. *Academe* 76, pp. 13–16.

(1990). (with L. Hayden). A Successful Intervention Program for High Ability Minority Students, *School Science and Mathematics* 90(4), pp. 323–33.

(1991). Association for Women in Mathematics: A Personal View. *Mathematical Intelligencer* 13, pp. 6–11.

(1991). Sexual Harassment: What Colleges Can Learn from the Thomas Case. *Chronicle of Higher Education*, November 6, p. A60.

(1992). (with K. Sheehan). Sex Bias in the SAT and DTMS, *Journal of General Psychology* 119, pp. 5–14.

(1994). (with S. M. Moore). Next Arena for Genocide? *Washington Post*, August
24.

FLORENCE FASANELLI

GLORIA CONYERS HEWITT
(1935–   )
Birthplace: South Carolina

Black women have always been expected to work. The only question
was, at what?

—Gloria Conyers Hewitt

When Gloria Hewitt, professor of mathematics and department chair at
the University of Montana, graduated from the University of Washington in 1962, she was just the third African American woman to earn a
Ph.D. in mathematics. She was a very talented student who, fortunately,
received some very important mentoring on her way to her doctorate.

Hewitt was born Gloria Conyers in Sumter, South Carolina, into a family of three older brothers: Emmet Jr., John, and James. Her mother, Crenella Clinkscales Conyers, had been born not far away in Levelland and
had moved to Sumter when she was 16 years old to attend Morris College,
a historically black Baptist college. Gloria's father, Emmet Conyers, whose
parents were tenant farmers, was born in Manning, South Carolina, and
also attended Morris College. Although he had earned a degree in education, he preferred to work in the Morris College printing office.

Before Gloria was born, her mother had conducted school for three
years in her own living room and subsequently taught Gloria there
through the first grade. Both Gloria's mother and father worked to get
the city to provide a public school. The land was finally donated and
the building was built, but it was three more years before her mother
received a position to teach there.

Gloria began public school in the second grade and continued through
the eighth grade, walking more than two miles each way. She hated this
school, perhaps in part owing to her first encounter with arithmetic there.
One day, as a second grader, she came to class without having done her arithmetic problems. When she could not recite at the teacher's request, she
had to stand in front of the class with her hands held out. The teacher
"proceeded to slap me on my little hands for what seemed like forever. I
never forgot the incident; I also never forgot to do my arithmetic after
that."

Hewitt quotes her parents as saying that "education was the only sal-

Gloria Conyers Hewitt. Photo courtesy of Gloria Conyers Hewitt.

vation the black man or woman had." Her parents encouraged all their children to believe that they could be anything they wanted. All her brothers went to college: One is a systems analyst, one completed medical school and is a practicing physician, and the third earned a doctorate in sociology.

In 1948, after graduating from the seventh grade and attending the local high school for an additional year, Gloria went off to boarding school. Her mother sacrificed to send her. There, at Mather Academy, a traditionally black co-educational school in Camden, South Carolina, education was taken seriously. However, her experiences in mathematics courses (which included only geometry and intermediate algebra) did not improve. She later wondered if anything she could have learned at this age would have led her to think of mathematics as fun. She did become interested in choir and sports, particularly basketball.

Gloria graduated from high school in 1952 and entered Fisk University, a historically black college where the majority of students were women. Her career choices at that time included nurse, accountant, or teacher. She did not do well on the placement examinations for English and mathematics when she arrived at college and was therefore placed in the "slow" mathematics section, an embarrassment because she had always been an "A" mathematics student in high school. That course proved too easy for her, and she was moved to the middle section, where she still was not challenged. At that point Dr. Lee Lorch, the mathematics department chair, asked her if she was planning to take calculus, a subject he taught. She had no idea what calculus was, and she also did not appreciate who Professor Lorch was when he invited her to enroll in his calculus class. In fact, he was a fervent civil rights activist and had been an important mentor to two African American women who went on to earn doctorates in mathematics: **Vivienne Malone-Mayes** and **Etta Falconer**. Things changed quickly; when Gloria went home for the Christmas holidays, the only book she took with her was the calculus book. She wanted to do those word problems! She worked hard and felt intensely rewarded when she finally solved a problem. That was the beginning of her career in mathematics.

In the early 1950s a very conservative mood predominated in the United States, and those who engaged in human rights activities became suspect. In 1954 Lorch was fired as a result of his civil rights activities. Consequently Gloria Hewitt felt that her early growth in mathematics had abruptly ended. Married and with a son, she dropped out of school before she graduated, withdrawing from classes for a semester. Her parents were crushed; their dream was to educate all their children, including their daughter. Hewitt's father, no longer able to work, offered to take care of her son so that she could return to school. In order to graduate with her class in 1956, Hewitt chose a major in the area in which she had the most credits—mathematics—and graduated with a degree in secondary mathematics education, but her understanding of mathematics did not advance. She was divorced that same year.

Also in 1956 Lorch returned to visit the Fisk campus and spoke with Hewitt about her plans for the future, suggesting that she go to graduate school. She replied, "I don't know." Shortly after this conversation she received offers to be a teaching assistant at the University of Oregon and the University of Washington in Seattle, although she had not applied to either school.

Hewitt chose the University of Washington. There, friendly and outgoing, studying and working hard, Hewitt quickly made friends and admirers. Personally, however, she was painfully aware of the inadequacy of her mathematics background. Through hard work and the encouragement of her fellow students and some faculty—and, of course, her talent—she succeeded. Hewitt felt fortunate to be part of a closely knit, supportive group. Having loved sports since her high school days, she bowled on the mathematics department team and won many games for them.

Hewitt had to work extremely hard to fill in the deficits in her mathematics background but continued with her studies, driven by her pride and a love for mathematics. Professor Edwin Hewitt (no relation) was the first professor to encourage her to pursue a doctorate. For the six years it took her to complete her doctorate, completing a master's degree along the way in 1960, Hewitt's parents took care of her son. When she thought of quitting she also thought of the sacrifices her mother was making; so Hewitt continued.

Just as Hewitt had not applied to graduate school, she did not apply for her first job after graduation. Arthur Livingston, a former professor at the University of Washington, twice offered her a job at the University of Montana—the first time when she was still two years away from completing her doctorate. On the second try, Professor Hewitt convinced her to accept the position. There, in Montana, with her son now in residence, she completed her Ph.D. dissertation, *Direct and Inverse Limits of Abstract Algebras*.

In receiving this degree in 1962 from the University of Washington, Hewitt became the third African American woman to be granted a Ph.D. in mathematics. **Evelyn Boyd Granville** had received her degree from Yale in 1949; **Marjorie Lee Browne** had been awarded her degree from the University of Michigan, also in 1949. Four years after receiving her degree, Hewitt was awarded a prestigious National Science Foundation postdoctoral Science Faculty Fellowship. She spent that year at the University of Oregon, where, again, her reception was one of warmth and friendliness.

Gloria Conyers Hewitt was made chair of the Department of Mathematics at the University of Montana in 1995, the year in which she was elected to the Board of Governors of the Mathematical Association of America. Although she has enjoyed her teaching and her extensive volunteer work within the mathematics community, one disappointment has been that she has not been able to continue an active mathematics research program. Her career, however, has amply demonstrated that women of all races and educational backgrounds can realize their potential talents in mathematics and lead full, rich professional lives. It is also very clear that encouragement, support, and mentorship are important ingredients in working against the obstacles encountered along the way.

Note

The information included in this biography is based on an interview by the author.

Selected Works by Gloria Hewitt

(1963). The Existence of Free Unions in Classes of Abstract Algebras. *Proceedings of the American Mathematical Society*, 14, pp. 417–422.

(1967). Limits in Certain Classes of Abstract Algebras. *Pacific Journal of Mathematics*, 22, 109–115.

(1989). Characterizations of Generalized Noetherian Rings (with Frank Hannick). *Acta Mathematica Hungarica* 53(1–2), pp. 61–73.

FLORENCE FASANELLI

GRACE BREWSTER MURRAY HOPPER
(1906–1992)
Birthplace: New York

Grace Brewster Murray Hopper, born on December 9, 1906, in New York City, became one of the world's foremost pioneers in the field of computer programming, spanning several generations of computers. She developed the base on which one of the most widely used computer languages, COBOL, was built.

Grace's parents, Mary and Walter Murray, headed a closely-knit family that included two younger siblings, Mary and Roger. Grace was quite different from many young girls her age, for she wasn't very interested in "girl-type" activities. She loved to build houses, churches, and other buildings using a variety of building sets. She was most intrigued with building things like motors that had moving parts. Although she had a dollhouse, she didn't really play with it. Instead, she preferred making furniture and other accessories for it.

The Murrays spent their summers in New Hampshire at her grandfather's large lake home. Grace enjoyed the freedom she had there and the games she was able to play with her siblings and cousins. It has been told that one summer in New Hampshire, Grace became very curious about how an alarm clock worked, so she dismantled one. After some time she realized that she could not put it back together. Because her grandparents had put the exact same clock in all seven bedrooms, she tried to figure out how to put the first clock back together by successively taking apart the remaining six clocks. In the end, she was still unable to assemble any of the clocks. She was a researcher even at a young age! Grace also had a passion for reading. She especially liked stories that featured young girls who made an impact on history. However, she also enjoyed stories that involved relationships, such as *The Secret Garden* and those of Rudyard Kipling, such as the *Just So Stories*.

Grace's father had a profound influence on her perseverance to achieve. When she was starting high school, her father had to have both legs amputated. Rather than feeling sorry for himself, he was fitted for wooden legs and used canes to walk. He was able to return to his job as an insurance broker. Because he had a strong belief in the value of education for all children, not just boys, he wanted all his children to go to college. He thought it was especially important that his daughters not only graduate from college but work for at least one year after gradua-

Grace Brewster Murray Hopper.

tion. This was important to him because he was unsure of his own health and wanted his daughters to be able to support themselves.

During her teen years Grace was a good student and participated in numerous activities at school. However, she was such a bright student that she skipped some grades and graduated from high school at age 16. Her parents thought she was too young to begin college, and because she had failed a Latin exam she enrolled in a college preparatory school for a year. At age 17 Grace began her college career at Vassar, which was a women's college at that time. She studied hard, took as many courses as possible, and sat in on many others. Because of her special gift for sharing her knowledge and understanding with others, Grace was asked to tutor other students who had difficulty understanding certain concepts and principles.

Grace graduated from Vassar in 1928 with a bachelor's degree in mathematics and physics, having been elected to Phi Beta Kappa, a national collegiate honor society. Because of her success in college, she earned a fellowship to attend graduate school at Yale. Although she did not meet her father's request of working for a year after graduation, he was delighted with her success and her ability to support herself during graduate school.

In 1930 Grace received a Master of Arts degree in mathematics from Yale. That same year she married Vincent Hopper. Vincent was a teacher of English at New York University's School of Commerce, and Grace began teaching mathematics courses (algebra, trigonometry, and calculus) at Vassar College. Four years later she earned a Ph.D. in mathematics from Yale University. The granting of Ph.D.s in mathematics was not very common for women in the early 1930s.

For generations, Grace's family had served the country by enlisting in the military. One of her ancestors during the Revolutionary War was a Minuteman, and her great-grandfather was a rear admiral during the Civil War. When the United States entered World War II, her husband, Vincent, and her brother, Roger, became members of the U.S. Army Air Corps. Her father, still using wooden legs and canes, worked for the Selective Service Board and her mother served on the Ration Board. Although her sister, Mary, did not work directly for the government, she too played a role by making fuses used to set off bombs as they approached their targets. Grace knew that she had to work for the war effort.

As Hopper attempted to join the Navy, she encountered three obstacles: The government felt she could best serve the country by continuing to teach mathematics; she was too old (she was 35 years old in 1943); and she did not weigh enough (she was 5'6" tall and weighed only 121 pounds). Grace persevered and soon received a special exemption from the age and weight restrictions. In 1943 she became a member of the Naval Reserve and took a leave of absence from her job at Vassar. She went through the rigorous training program and graduated first in her class. In June 1944 she was commissioned as a lieutenant in the U.S. Navy.

Her first assignment in the Navy was to the Bureau of Ordnance Computation Project at Harvard University. There she worked with Commander Howard Aiken, also of the Naval Reserve. For a number of years Aiken had been trying to find a machine that could perform long and complicated calculations. Harvard University and IBM collaborated to build a computer that would do the work Aiken required. The machine (Mark I) was just being finished when the United States entered the war. Hopper and Aiken used the machine to make calculations that would help aim guns to their targets more precisely. Together with several Navy men, Grace Hopper was busy twenty-four hours every day programming and running programs to provide the government with calculations and information needed to win the war.

This first computer, the Mark I, was different from the computers we see today. Most computers today are small desktop machines or even smaller laptops. However, the Mark I was very large, filling an entire room. It weighed about five tons, was very noisy, and was also quite slow by current standards. Hopper loved this machine, for it was the first machine built that could be used to strengthen the mind and not the body.

In 1945 the second computer was built. Called the Mark II, it was five times faster than the Mark I. Also, it had the capacity to run two programs simultaneously. Although this computer seemed superior to the Mark I, one day it stopped dead. As the workmen disassembled part of the computer, they found a dead moth that had been killed by a relay. They saved the moth and told Howard Aiken that they had "debugged the computer." Although it is not certain, many people believe this to be the origin of the computer-related term "debugging."

Hopper left active duty and resigned her teaching position at Vassar in 1946. A year earlier, she and Vincent had been divorced. She was offered a three-year fellowship at Harvard to continue working with Howard Aiken in the Computation Laboratory. In 1949, at the end of the fellowship, she decided to work for the Eckert-Mauchly Computer Corporation in Philadelphia, using her training and experiences as a senior mathematician. After she worked for Eckert-Mauchly for two years, the company introduced the first mass-produced computers. They were considerably smaller than the Mark I or the Mark II.

Hopper's role was to write detailed programs that would tell the computer what to do. Since programs were complex and used mathematical algorithms, only those trained in mathematics or science could effectively write such programs. Although she was very skilled in the writing of computer programs, Grace wanted other people who were not mathematicians and scientists to be able to program. To do this, she knew she would have to develop a computer programming language that could be translated into machine code and then understood by the computer. This translator was called a compiler. She finished her first compiler in 1952.

Hopper continued to work hard and pursue her dream that computers could be programmed by most people and could be used for more than calculations. She developed several other compilers. In 1960, UNIVAC (formerly Eckert-Mauchly, where Grace still worked) and RCA introduced COBOL (Common Business Oriented Language). COBOL was easy to understand because it used English-like sentences. It was also unique because it could be used and understood by different machines. The language became universally accepted, and parts of the U.S. government wanted all companies doing work with the government to use it. Without Hopper's earlier work and her persistence, a universal computer language probably would not have been developed until much later.

In the years since Grace Hopper resigned from active duty until 1986, she continued her connections with the Naval Reserve. Several times she was asked to retire because of her age, then called back into service. Finally, in 1986 she left the Naval Reserve for good. She did so after forty-three years of dedicated service with the rank of rear admiral.

Over the years, for her work, persistence, and creativity, Hopper became affectionately known as "Amazing Grace, Grandmother of the Computer Age." Throughout her life she received high praise, awards, and recognition. She appeared on both *Sixty Minutes* and the *David Letterman Show*; was a grand marshal of the Orange Bowl Parade; was appointed a fellow of the Institute of Electrical and Electronics Engineers; won an Achievement Award by the Society of Women Engineers; was presented with the "Man-of-the-Year" Award by the Data Processing Management Association; and was awarded the National Medal of Technology by President George Bush. To Hopper, however, her most important recognition and highest achievement was "the privilege and honor of serving proudly in the United States Navy" (Tropp 1984, p. 18).

Although she gave up some of her activities and work as she got older, Hopper continued teaching and getting people interested in computers. She believed in the youth of America and was confident that they would be able to take on the challenges that would face them in the future. She knew they would need to take risks to do so. One of her favorite maxims to share with children was: "A ship in port is safe, but that's not what ships are built for" (Tropp, 1984, p. 18).

On a cold January day in Arlington, Virginia, at the age of 85, Grace Brewster Murray Hopper died. However, she left behind an inspiration to all: that we can achieve what we dream if we are willing to take risks and work hard.

Selected Works by Grace Brewster Murray Hopper

(1955). Automatic Coding for Digital Computers. *Computers and Automation* 4(9), pp. 21–24.

(1955). Automatic Programming for Computers. *Systems* 19(5), pp. 3–4.

(1957). Tomorrow—Automatics Programming. *Petroleum Refiner* 36(2), pp. 109–12.

(1959). Education Can Be "Secondary." *Systems for Educators* 6(2), p. 8.

(1967). A Language of Their Own. *Financial Times (London)* 11, Annual Computer Supplement.

(1976). David and Goliath. In Jan Prokop, Ed., *Computers in the Navy*. Annapolis, MD: Naval Institute Press.

(1984). *Understanding Computers* (with Steven L. Mandell). St. Paul, MN: West Publishing.

Selected Works about Grace Brewster Murray Hopper

Clark, Susan E. (1996). Grace Murray Hopper—Computer Pioneer and Admiral. In Miriam P. Cooney, Ed., *Celebrating Women in Mathematics and Science* (pp. 1–5). Reston, VA: National Council of Teachers of Mathematics.

Cushman, John H., Jr. (1986). Admiral Hopper's Farewell. *New York Times*, August 14, p. B-6.

King, Amy C. (with Tina Schalach). (1987). Grace Brewster Murray Hopper. In Louise S. Grinstein and Paul J. Campbell, Eds., *Women of Mathematics* (pp. 67–73). Westport, CT: Greenwood Press.

Smith, Sanderson M. (1996). *Agnesi to Zeno: Over 100 Vignettes for the History of Mathematics* (pp. 179–180). Berkeley, CA: Key Curriculum Press.

Tropp, Henry S. (1984). Grace Hopper: The Youthful Teacher of Us All. *Abacus* 2(1), pp. 7–18.

LAURA COFFIN KOCH

RHONDA HUGHES
(1947–   )
Birthplace: Illinois

Rhonda Hughes is a professor of mathematics at Bryn Mawr College. Although her mathematical talents were not recognized until she was in college, she had the self-motivation to excel in secondary school and recognize her affection for mathematics. Fortunately, she later received the support and recognition necessary to becoming an outstanding mathematics researcher and teacher. In 1997 she received a Distinguished Teaching Award from the Mathematical Association of America.

Hughes, born Rhonda Weisberg on September 28, 1947, in Chicago, Illinois, grew up in a hardworking family. Her mother was a secretary and her father worked for a neckwear company. Although she had no brothers or sisters, her cousins and aunts were part of her extended household. She spent most of her time in her immediate neighborhood on the south side of Chicago. Elementary school was not a very enjoyable experience. The school and her teachers did not offer her much, and she did not attend regularly. However, her spirit and enthusiasm were evident in her love of baseball, and she enjoyed attending White Sox games with her father.

In the sixth grade, life began to change for Rhonda. Her family moved to a different neighborhood with a better school, where she became involved in her studies. Gage Park High school was wonderful. She went to school early and came home late. She was vice-president of her class,

Rhonda Hughes. Photo courtesy of Rhonda Hughes.

a cheerleader, and a participant in club sports. Her high school was similar to many high schools in its emphasis on athletics. Athletic activities seemed to draw more attention and honor than academics, but Rhonda enjoyed learning.

During the sophomore year students were required to choose between two tracks: an academic track including mathematics and physics, or a business track including secretarial courses, shorthand, and typing. Rhonda chose the secretarial track but was miserable and did very poorly. After three weeks she requested to switch to the academic track, where she excelled. She especially enjoyed one English teacher, Mr. Carlin, who was outstanding. Rhonda was valedictorian of her class and made A's in all her courses, but her teachers and counselors still failed to select her as one of the "Ten Outstanding Students." She felt academically invisible.

Despite her outstanding performance in high school and her high scores on the American College Test (ACT), Rhonda was not encouraged to attend college. No one suggested what to study in high school or how to go about applying to colleges. No alumni from famous institutions scoured her neighborhood for talent. Only representatives from local colleges visited the high school, and there was no attempt to match students with a wide range of colleges and universities. In fact, most of her male classmates enlisted in the armed forces and went to Vietnam. Her female friends became part of the work force or began families.

It is not surprising that Rhonda did not initially plan to go to college; but when the time came, and against high odds, she decided to try. Fortunately, the lack of outside encouragement did not stop her; she was persistent, hardworking, and able to find the required strength within herself. She began at the University of Illinois at Urbana, finding college life to be a big change and missing her neighborhood and friends. After one and a half years in an engineering program, she went home to Chicago and took a job. Six months later she earned a scholarship to the University of Illinois at Chicago and was back in college, majoring in mathematics this time.

Mathematics was hard, and perhaps that was part of its appeal. Rhonda's professors were good, but college life in Chicago was not what she had expected. Since there was no campus and students came from all over the Chicago area, it was hard to make friends. However, here she met the first person who encouraged her to pursue a career in mathematics: Dr. Yoram Sagher.

Dr. Sagher, who was from Israel, taught one of Rhonda's advanced mathematics courses. She did not picture herself as a star pupil, but Sagher recognized her spirit and talent. He helped rearrange her schedule so that she would have the courses needed for advanced study in graduate school. His attention and concern had an enormous impact on her. If she had continued taking standard courses for a mathematics major, she would not have been ready for the rigor of graduate mathematics. Having a mentor helped tremendously in setting her on the right course. She recalled several years later, "It took so little to encourage me, but it was so important."

In comparison to her undergraduate experience, Rhonda found graduate school wonderful. There were interesting people who loved to talk about mathematics, and one of these fellow graduate students, Anthony Hughes, became her husband. She did not do as well on her master's degree examination as she had hoped, but she worked hard and retook the exam, posting a much improved score. She continued in graduate school, now working with another Israeli mathematician, Dr. Shmuel Kantorovitz, who became her thesis adviser. She earned her Ph.D. in 1975, thereby opening the door for teaching and mathematical research. Reflecting on her graduate experience, Hughes says, "You do not have to be the best. There is always someone better, but that is not the point. I enjoyed math and felt that there would be a place in the profession for me." She had the self-motivation to keep working and to succeed, but encouragement from her friends and teachers was extremely important.

After beginning her teaching career at Tufts University near Boston, Rhonda Hughes spent a year as a fellow at the Bunting Institute of Radcliffe College. Being in an all-female environment was a powerful experience; she felt extremely supported and consequently was able to do even better work. Subsequently she spent time as a visiting scholar at Harvard University before moving to Bryn Mawr College in 1980, where she remains today. She currently holds the Helen Herrmann professorship at Bryn Mawr. She has been honored for both her scholarship and her teaching excellence. She has traveled throughout the United States giving talks, serving on panels, and organizing programs that encourage women to study mathematics. She has served on key committees of the American Mathematical Society and was president of the Association for Women in Mathematics (AWM) in 1987–1988. She attended the White House Forum on Science in the National Interest in 1994 and is now serving on the Commission on Physical Science, Mathematics, and Applications of the National Research Council.

Hughes makes special note of her term as president of AWM, saying that it was the high point of her professional career so far. Through AWM she has forged a network of colleagues who provide mutual support. Throughout her career she has encouraged women to be mathematicians and to take an active role in the mathematical community, paying special attention to students who might be overlooked as potential mathematicians and giving them extra support. She and **Sylvia Bozeman** (at Spelman College) have organized the Spelman–Bryn Mawr Summer Mathematics Program for female undergraduate students who might be aspiring mathematicians. The National Science Foundation has recognized their work by providing grant money for the program, and they are now designing a program for graduate students.

Rhonda Hughes's research is in the area of analysis, a branch of mathematics that is useful in solving problems in physics (e.g., how heat flows, or why vibrating strings produce musical sounds). The area of mathematical analysis in which she is most interested is related to quantum mechanics, the physical theory developed during this century to explain the mysterious behavior of subatomic particles. Her research has been supported by several grants from the National Science Foundation.

Most recently Hughes has been working in an exciting and relatively new field called wavelet analysis, learning along with her students. A typical problem in wavelet analysis involves transmitting a signal such as a voice or picture as efficiently as possible; that is, transmitting the signal using as little information as possible, yet retaining the important features of the signal. Data compression is the process by which this is accomplished. Wavelet analysis provides a way to break up signals into basic building blocks, discard the blocks that do not contribute much, and reassemble the signal for transmission. Wavelets are being used to analyze fingerprints, to make better compact discs, and to detect signs of the onset of seizures in the electroencephalograms of epileptic patients. Hughes is not discouraged that there will always be more to learn and more parts to add to the puzzle, because it is the unfinished nature of mathematics that she finds most exciting.

In addition to her busy professional life as a professor, mathematical researcher, and consultant, Hughes spends time with her two children: Sarah, a student at Skidmore College, and Jeremy. Hughes is now married to Michael Reed, a mathematician on the faculty at Duke University. She enjoys aerobics, movies, visiting with friends, and occasional cooking. She is still a sports fan as well.

Hughes credits much of her success to hard work, to those who encouraged her, and to the subject of mathematics itself. Professors Pat Montague (her calculus teacher and her only female mathematics professor) and Louise Hay were supportive and provided inspiration in college. They were strong, kind, and willing to speak out on important issues such as child care and increasing the participation of women in mathematics. Professor Irving Segal of MIT became an important mentor and friend when Hughes moved to Boston. She currently collaborates on research with colleagues Paul Chernoff at Berkeley and Mark Kon at Boston University. Hughes claims that mathematics is the hardest work she has ever done, but she is also quick to note how much pleasure it brings, through both research and teaching.

Note

The information included in this biography is based on an interview by the author.

Selected Works by Rhonda Hughes

(1982). Singular Perturbations in the Interaction Representation, II. *Journal of Functional Analysis* 49, pp. 293–314.

(1987). Calculus for a New Century. In Lynn A. Steen, Ed., *Calculus Reform and Women Undergraduates*. Washington, DC: National Academy of Sciences.

(1988). (with S. Kantorovitz). Spectral Representations of Unbounded Operators with Real Spectrum, *Mathematische Annalen* 282, pp. 535–44.

(1993). (with P. Chernoff). A New Class of Point Interactions in One Dimension, *Journal of Functional Analysis*, 111(1) pp. 97–117.

(1994). Improving the Climate for Women and Minorities in Mathematics and Science. *Association for Women in Mathematics Newsletter* 24(6).

(1995). Renormalization of the Relativistic Delta Potential in One Dimension. *Letters in Mathematical Physics* 34, pp. 395–406.

PATRICIA S. WILSON

JOAN HUTCHINSON
(1945–)
Birthplace: Pennsylvania

Professor Joan Hutchinson recently received the distinguished Carl B. Allendoerfer award, which is presented each year by the Mathematical Association of America, and has published numerous scientific papers. These are significant accomplishments—especially for someone who is not yet even 53 years old.

Joan Hutchinson was born in 1945 in Philadelphia, Pennsylvania. Her father was a professor at the University of Pennsylvania. Her mother majored in mathematics in college and later returned to school to get a master's degree in mathematics. Thereafter she started teaching high school mathematics. Her mother truly loved mathematics and spent a great deal of time with Joan working on mathematical puzzles and games. Joan's early dream was to be a high school teacher. Sadly, when Joan was 16 years old her mother died. This loss was very painful.

What remained for Joan was a legacy of reinforcement and support from her mother, and Joan was able to benefit from the guidance and opportunities her parents had provided. They put a great deal of emphasis on school and instilled in her a sense that she could do anything she wanted. She worked hard and had a sense of her own goals. She attributes this to her parents' involvement with her as a child.

In September 1963 Joan entered Smith College in Northhampton, Massachusetts. She knew she was an excellent mathematics student but wanted to try other areas, such as sociology and history. During the second semester of her freshman year she had a teacher, Alice Dickinson, who had a deep knowledge of and love for mathematics. This was a transforming experience for Joan. She adored Dr. Dickinson and admired how she approached her teaching and mathematics. Dickinson made mathematics lively and interesting, and soon became Joan's mentor. Joan had always thought she would follow in her mother's footsteps and become a high school teacher, but now instead she considered following in her father's footsteps by becoming a college teacher and researcher.

Joan and Dr. Dickinson continued their relationship. Joan was amazed to learn that not only did Dickinson teach and do scientific research, but she was also the mother of two children. She remained a vital role model throughout Joan's college career and beyond.

After graduating from Smith in 1967, Joan worked for a year as a

Joan Hutchinson. Photo courtesy of Macalester
College and Greg Helgeson.

computer programmer at Harvard University but then wanted to try
something different. She applied for a Fulbright Fellowship to England,
which she did not receive, but decided to use her savings to attend graduate school for a year in England at the University of Warwick in Cov-
entry. She was also interested in the art of "English change ringing" (the
British practice of ringing church bells according to mathematical patterns) and wanted to learn more about it.

After this two-year break Hutchinson returned to the United States to
begin graduate work at the University of Pennsylvania, where she
earned her Ph.D. in mathematics. She has learned that she most enjoys
combining abstract work with personal interactions. Although much of
it is grounded in reality, mathematics is in fact very abstract. The teaching and coauthoring aspects of doing mathematics provide connections
with other people and reduce the isolation of solitary mathematical re-

search. For Hutchinson, working as a college professor combines the best of both worlds.

Hutchinson loves to collect books, novels, and stories that portray mathematicians—especially female mathematicians. Unfortunately, she has found that there are many negative stereotypes and negative portrayals in works of fiction and biographies, particularly suggesting that these women have problems with personal relationships. Her goal is for the media to present a much more positive picture of women in mathematics.

Frequent travel is part of Hutchinson's life now because she is often invited to give talks about her research. She enjoys her international travels, often combining work and pleasure, and finds them to be great learning experiences about people and cultures. She also enjoys working with colleagues, finding that solving mathematics problems is more effective and more enjoyable in a collaborative environment. Hutchinson is convinced that mathematics offers many opportunities, but it is important to find the area of mathematics that is personally most interesting and appealing if one is going to pursue higher-level study.

Hutchinson has focused her research on graphs and graph theory. She received the Allendoerfer award in recognition of an article she wrote for *Mathematics Magazine* in 1993 entitled "Coloring Ordinary Maps, Maps of Empires and Maps of Moons." The work is an expansion of the famous Four Color Theorem that states that every map drawn in a plane can have one of four colors assigned to each connected region so that for every pair of regions sharing a common border arc, each of those two regions receives a different color. Hutchinson expanded this theorem to include maps drawn on surfaces other than the plane.

Julia Robinson, a well-known mathematician at the University of California at Berkeley, had a profound impact on Hutchinson. Two aspects of Robinson's life made an especially big impression on Joan: first, that Robinson was a mathematician; second, that she faced many difficulties as a female mathematician. Fortunately, despite serious obstacles, Robinson completed her Ph.D. in mathematics and became recognized throughout the world for her work. While Hutchinson was continuing with her own mathematics research, she thought about what Robinson had faced and tried to keep her in mind when she herself encountered problems. As was the case for Robinson, it was more important for Hutchinson to be recognized as a mathematician per se rather than as a female mathematician.

Fortunately for Hutchinson, some of the rules that made it difficult for women to work had changed by the time she completed her Ph.D. in 1973 at the University of Pennsylvania. Joan had many opportunities to work on her own before she married. She was a John Wesley Young research instructor at Dartmouth College in Hanover, New Hampshire, from 1973 to 1975. She also was on the faculty at Tufts University in Massachusetts, Carleton College in Minnesota, and the University of Colorado. After marrying Stan Wagon, also a mathematician, they were able to find a college in which they could share a faculty appointment. This seemed an ideal situation because they both could teach and still have plenty of time to work on their research and travel. Their first shared position was at Smith College in Massachusetts from 1976 to 1990. Subsequently they moved to Macalester College in Minnesota, where they currently are professors of mathematics. In addition to enjoying mathematics and traveling, Joan is an avid hiker and skier.

Hutchinson is dedicated to her work and enjoys it immensely as well, which is very important to her. She believes that mathematics offers numerous possibilities to young people and that it is important to keep this door open when exploring career pathways. A thorough grounding in mathematics can afford opportunities in economics, computer science, social science, business, teaching, and many other areas. Mathematics also need not be a lonely subject, as many people mistakenly believe it is. It can be a field where people work together and benefit from such collaboration, leading to enriched professional and personal lives.

Note

This biography was based in part on a personal interview conducted by the author on March 7, 1995, at Macalester College in St. Paul, Minnesota.

Selected Works by Joan Hutchinson

(1977). Let Me Count the Ways: Women in Combinatorics. *Association for Women in Mathematics Newsletter* 7, pp. 3–7.

(1980). (with P. B. Trow). Some Pigeonhole Principle Results Extended. *American Mathematical Monthly* 87, pp. 648–51.

(1984). A Five Color Theorem for Graphs on Surfaces. *Proceedings of the American Mathematical Society* 90, pp. 497–504.

(1985). (with Stan Wagon). A Forbidden Subgraph Characterization of the Infinite Graphs of Finite Genus. In *Graphs and Applications, Proceedings of the First Colorado Symposium on Graph Theory*. New York: John Wiley and Sons.

(1988). (with M. O. Albertson). *Discrete Mathematics with Algorithms*. New York: John Wiley and Sons.

(1993). Coloring Ordinary Maps, Maps of Empires, and Maps of the Moon. *Mathematics Magazine* 66(4), pp. 211–26.

LAURA COFFIN KOCH

HYPATIA
(circa 360–415)
Birthplace: Alexandria, Egypt

Hypatia was the earliest female mathematician about whom anything is known from the annals of history. She was born in the fourth century in Alexandria, Egypt, which was one of the centers of mathematical thought at that time. It was a city where learning was greatly valued. However, very few people learned or understood mathematics—usually only rich men. One was a well-known mathematician named Theon. Not only did he have great mathematical ability, but he also had a belief that he could raise the perfect child. He was convinced that he could teach his child mathematics, science, languages, arts, and the humanities. In addition, he would make sure that his child was physically strong and could excel in all areas, particularly the intellectual and physical.

Although Theon may have imagined that this child would be a boy, he had a daughter. This did not deter him from fulfilling the dream of raising a perfect person. Theon's daughter, Hypatia, was brought up with the expectation that she could do and achieve anything she wanted—which was very unusual for women, especially in the fourth century. Hypatia was a fast learner and enjoyed the life her father had laid out for her, and she was not afraid to venture into a life that was dominated by men. The exact date of Hypatia's birth is not known. It is believed to be sometime between A.D. 355 and A.D. 370.

Hypatia was raised to seek knowledge and to always be of strong body and mind. Her father made sure she knew about the arts, the sciences, literature, philosophy, swimming, rowing, horseback riding, speech, and mountain climbing. When she quickly surpassed even her own father's mathematical knowledge, he sent her to Athens to study because Athens was known to be the mathematics center of the world. After she finished her studies in Athens, she traveled throughout Europe for about ten years.

Not only was Hypatia an exceptionally bright woman and a good athlete, she was also considered to be very beautiful. Many young men sought her hand in marriage, but she was not interested in sacrificing her career and her love of exploration. In Hypatia's time, wives were subservient and submissive to their husbands; they had few rights of their own. This was a not a role that Hypatia was willing to play.

After returning from Europe to Egypt, she was asked to teach geom-

Hypatia.

etry and astronomy at the University of Alexandria. Her favorite mathematical subject to teach was algebra, which was a very new field. She was a dedicated teacher, and students and scholars came from all over to study with her and to attend her reknowned lectures. She wanted to help her students understand the mathematics she was teaching, so she wrote books that gave explanations that were easier to understand than the original books. These books, called commentaries, are similar to commentaries that are written today for literature courses. Hypatia wrote a commentary on an algebra book that was written by the famous mathematician Diophantus.

In addition, she wrote treatises on algebra in a book entitled *Astronomical Canon of Diophantus and Conics of Apollonius*. In this book Hypatia showed a cone being divided by planes in various positions. The points of intersection of the cuts of the plane through the cone formed the idea of conic sections. These cuts became known as hyperbolas, parabolas, and ellipses. Many centuries later, Hypatia's work became very important because there were many natural phenomena that could only be described through the shapes formed by these intersections of cone and planes. One of these is the path that a comet takes around the sun; it is known as an ellipse. Because Hypatia also loved geometry and wanted her students to learn it well, she and her father wrote a commentary on the famed geometer Euclid's book, *Elements*.

Besides being an intelligent and hardworking mathematician, Hypatia was thought to be a goddess, a genius, an oracle, and a gifted orator. She helped mathematics survive in a very tenuous world. Her work helped not only her own students but also those who lived long past her lifetime. She truly was an influence on early mathematical thought—which was unheard of for a woman, particularly in the fourth and fifth centuries. In this sense it might be said that Hypatia was the "mother of mathematics."

Hypatia was trained not only as a mathematician but as a scientist as well. She is credited with developing a process to distill sea water that is still used today. One of her students, who was serving on ship, wrote to Hypatia of the need for an instrument to determine the altitude of distant stars and planets that could be used to help navigate a ship. She drew plans that could be used to construct such an instrument, which was called an astrolabe. Another instrument, the hydroscope, is also thought to have been designed by Hypatia. It is used to observe objects that lie far below the surface of the water.

During Hypatia's lifetime the world was undergoing tremendous upheavals in the quest for power and control, with much energy focused on scientific discovery and religion. The Roman Empire was taking over the world and spreading Christianity. People were supposed to accept Christianity blindly and not question it. Intellectual thought and inquiry were a threat to the Roman Empire. Unfortunately, this created a decline in the mathematical investigations that were taking place in Greece and elsewhere. The Romans did not appreciate Greek mathematics and in fact thought it was subversive. The Romans had not been greatly involved in the development of mathematics; hence their mathematicians did not compare favorably to the Greeks.

When Christianity took root in Alexandria, Egypt, around A.D. 390, frequent battles and riots broke out between those of opposing religions. Hypatia was a Neoplatonist, which (although not really a religion) allowed her to lead a life of inquiry by questioning ideas and not taking anything on blind faith. She was also able to grow intellectually to seek truth and knowledge without being told what to seek or what the answers were. Because she did not belong to an organized religion or cult, and because of her intellectual stature in the community, she was a marked woman. Many believed that Hypatia was such a great influence that Christianity would not survive as long as she was alive.

Hypatia was not the only target. Many important libraries were burned to the ground. With these fires, many great books and historical documents were lost, including the books written by Hypatia. In Hypatia's time, there was no way to reproduce mass quantities of books.

All books had to written by hand, so at most there were only a few copies of each book. Fortunately, 1,000 years later a few of her books were located in the Vatican Library.

In A.D. 412 Cyril became the patriarch of Alexandria. He opposed Neoplatonists and caused them to be oppressed and brutalized. It is believed that Cyril initiated a rumor that if Hypatia were to be killed or sacrificed, the leaders of the other religions would be able to work together to reach a peaceful agreement. Cyril actually thought that Hypatia might stop the spread of Christianity in Alexandria. In an effort to undermine her influence, rumors were started that she was a witch and used black magic. The intent was to turn the citizens against Hypatia, which ultimately was an effective plot.

One day, in A.D. 415, Hypatia was riding in her chariot when a crowd gathered. The chariot was forced to stop, and Hypatia was pulled from the chariot by her hair. The crowd was huge and frightening. Hypatia was then dragged through the streets and into a church, where she was killed. Her death was painful and terrifying, but it served Cyril's purposes as it marked the end of the formal study of mathematics in Alexandria for the next 1,000 years.

Although Hypatia was relatively young at the time of her death, she had a profound influence on the pursuit of mathematical knowledge. Many years later people such as Descartes, Newton, and Leibniz used her work to build their own mathematical theories.

Selected Works by Hypatia

There are no extant copies of any of Hypatia's works. The works listed below are believed to be written by Hypatia. The only evidence now available is through correspondence between Hypatia and others.
Astronomical Canon of Diophantus and Conics of Apollonius.
Commentary on Diophantus' Arithmetica.

Selected Works about Hypatia

Boyer, Carl B. (1991). *A History of Mathematics*, 2nd ed. (revised by Uta C. Merzbach). New York: John Wiley and Sons, p. 190.
Mueller, I. (1987). Hypatia. In L. S. Grinstein, and P. J. Campbell, Eds., *Women of Mathematics* (pp. 74–79). New York: Greenwood Press.
National Council of Teachers of Mathematics. (1996). *Celebrating Women in Mathematics and Science* (edited by Miriam P. Cooney). Reston, VA, pp. 1–5.
Perl, Teri. (1978). *Math Equals: Biographies of Women Mathematicians + Related Activities.* Menlo Park, CA: Addison-Wesley, pp. 9–27.
Smith, Sanderson M. (1996). *Agnesi to Zeno: Over 100 Vignettes for the History of Mathematics.* Berkeley, CA: Key Curriculum Press, pp. 45–46.

LAURA COFFIN KOCH

Nancy Kopell

(1942–)
Birthplace: New York

Thinking in pictures and relating these pictures to equations—these are the characteristics of mathematics that initially hooked Nancy Kopell. The rest of the development of her career as a mathematician was a series of happy accidents. At least, that is how she describes it.

Kopell, born on November 8, 1942, grew up in New York City and attended the Bronx public schools. She comes from a family in which all the women (Nancy, her mother, and her older sister) were mathematics majors in college. Her father was an accountant. She was the only one in her family, however, to make a profession of mathematics.

After graduating from Christopher Columbus High School in 1959, Nancy went on to Cornell University in Ithaca, New York. At Cornell she was chosen to be in the mathematics honors program. Everyone in that program went on to become a mathematics professor. She remembers being uncomfortable as the only woman in the program. There was some teasing from others, but mostly she had to deal with her own feelings of being a "weird oddball." Kopell graduated from Cornell in 1963 with distinction in all subjects and high honors in mathematics, and was salutatorian of her graduating class.

Even with such a strong undergraduate record, she found the prospect of graduate school daunting. Nevertheless, she attended the University of California at Berkeley, earning a master's degree in 1965 and a doctoral degree in 1967. Her graduate work at Berkeley was in pure mathematics. While still a graduate student, Kopell was assistant director and then director of an enrichment program in mathematics for high school students and teachers. After graduate school she began her first "real job" in 1967 at the Massachusetts Institute of Technology (MIT), where she was the first woman to be the C. L. E. Moore instructor of mathematics. She then went to Northeastern University in Boston, where she was on the faculty for seventeen years. She is now a professor of mathematics at Boston University, where she has been since 1986.

At Boston University, Professor Kopell teaches mainly upper-level mathematics courses and graduate student courses, and conducts seminars on the interface between mathematics and physiology for faculty and graduate students. She particularly appreciates opportunities to interact directly with students. She is interested in using mathematics to

Nancy Kopell. Photo courtesy of Len Rubenstein.

answer questions about problems outside of mathematics itself. For the past decade her research has been at the boundary between mathematics and biology. She works at developing mathematical models to explain the structure and behavior of networks of nerve cells that control rhythmic motor activities in animals, such as walking, swimming, and breathing.

Kopell has worked in areas of chemistry as well as biology. One theme that runs through her work is a fascination with patterns that "self-organize." For example, her work with a colleague, L. N. Howard, dealt with a chemical system that periodically changes color as it is continually stirred. When the fluid is placed in a thin layer and not stirred, bits of fluid communicate with nearby bits via diffusion (the same process by which heat is transferred from a hot part of a metal object to a colder part). Instead of forming a layer with a uniform color, the fluid uses the local interactions to form a complicated and ever-changing pattern of colors. The mathematics done by Kopell and Howard analyzed why these patterns form, and where else they might be expected to appear.

Kopell's research in biology deals with parts of the central nervous system; again, the work is concerned with how interactions among bits of the system (individual neurons or small circuits of neurons) manage to produce output appropriate to coordinated behavior. For example, when a horse walks or trots or gallops, the movements of the limbs are precisely coordinated. When Kopell first became interested in the subject, few biologists understood that the questions could even be conceived of in mathematical language or that mathematics could provide relatively simple answers. There are still significant challenges in working at the interface between mathematics and biology. "The culture of biology stresses detail, differences among species and among individuals with the species," she states. "Mathematics starts from exactly the opposite point of view. The power of mathematics is the ability to find generalizations that span different instances, and the challenge is to do so in ways that preserve the importance of the relevant details."

Within biology, Kopell has worked on questions involving many different species and parts of the nervous system. One of the early projects (which still continues) was a collaboration involving coordination of muscles used in undulatory swimming, the kind of motion made in locomotion by many species of fish and other fish-like organisms. The challenge in this work was that it is very difficult to get "complete" data about the neurons that are involved. Kopell and her collaborators used mathematical theories to show that the undulatory motion, like the patterns in the chemical fluid, is very robust and can be understood without detailed knowledge of all the neurons involved. In more recent work Kopell has been exploring other networks of neurons that have a rhythmic behavior. These include smaller networks (like the ones in lobster and crayfish) that coordinate grinding of food, and large ones, such as the networks in the olfactory (or relating to the sense of smell) portion of the brains of some animals.

During the past several decades, Nancy Kopell's work has taken her far from the Boston area. The twelve to fifteen lectures per year that she is invited to give all over the country and the world provide her with many opportunities for travel.

Kopell has always enjoyed working collaboratively with other researchers. Particularly in her interdisciplinary work, she has actively sought out biologist colleagues. She invests a lot of time in networking, forming groups of researchers, and keeping these groups going. Recently she received a grant to create an interdisciplinary study center in mathematics and biology, involving a group of scientists scattered over two continents, that would operate as a laboratory without walls.

Although the kind of cooperation Kopell encourages is now fairly widely practiced, this was not always the case—especially in mathematics. One of her first collaborations was with Lou Howard, another mathematician who happens to be thirteen years older than Kopell. Because of the age difference, many people assumed she was simply his student. She remembers the comment of an anonymous reviewer in response to her National Science Foundation grant application: "She didn't accomplish anything before collaboration with Lou Howard and will not accomplish anything after." Her long list of achievements, both before and after, demonstrate the inaccuracy of this remark. In fact, in 1996 she was elected to the prestigious National Academy of Sciences—one of only six mathematicians from the United States to receive this honor in 1996, and the only woman.

Outside of her professional life in mathematics, Kopell describes herself as a "serial hobbyist." At various times during her adult life she has been involved in playing Renaissance instruments, singing early music, and creating metal sculpture. She has also served an intense stint as trustee ("unpaid manager") of her condominium. She is married to Gabriel Stolzenberg, also a mathematician, whom she met through a reading group. She has two grown stepchildren and two grandchildren. She and her husband live in Cambridge, Massachusetts.

Note

The information included in this biography is based in part on an interview conducted by the author.

Selected Works by Nancy Kopell

(1978). Pattern Formation in Chemistry and Biology: A Mini-Survey of Mechanisms. In G. Miller, Ed., *Psychology and Biology of Language and Thought: Essays in Honor of Eric Lenneberg*. New York: Academic Press.

(1981). (with L. N. Howard). Target Patterns and Horseshoes from Perturbed Central Force Problems: Some Temporally Periodic Solutions to Reaction-Diffusion Equations, *Studies in Applied Mathematics* 64, pp. 1–56.

(1990). (with T. Williams, K. Sigvardt, G. B. Ermentrout, and M. Remler). Forcing of Coupled Nonlinear Oscillators: Studies of Intersegmental Coordination in the Lamprey Locomotor Central Pattern Generator, *Journal of Neurophysiology* 64, pp. 862–71.

(1992). (with A. H. Cohen, G. B. Ermentrout, T. Kiemel, K. Sigvardt, and T. Williams). Modelling of Intersegmental Coordination in the Lamprey Central Pattern Generator for Locomotion, *Trends in the Neurosciences* 15, pp. 434–38.

(1994). (with G. B. Ermentrout). Inhibition-Produced Patterning in Chains of Coupled Nonlinear Oscillators, *SIAM Journal on Applied Mathematics* 54, pp. 478–507.

(1994). (with G. LeMasson). Rhythmogenesis, Amplitude Modulation and Multiplexing in a Cortical Architecture, *Proceedings of the National Academy of Sciences of the USA* 91, p. 1058.

(1994). (with C. Jones). Tracking Invariant Manifolds with Differential Forms in Singularly Perturbed Equations, *Journal of Differential Equations* 108, pp. 64–88.

BONNIE S. WOOD

SOFYA KORVIN-KRUKOVSKAYA KOVALEVSKAYA
(1850–1891)
Birthplace: Moscow, Russia

Sofya Korvin-Krukovskaya[1] was born on January 15, 1850, in Moscow. Although this was a time when higher education was virtually forbidden for women, she became one of the most important mathematicians of her generation. Her career, like that of many other mathematicians, was a long journey that took her to many countries.

Sofya was the second of three children born to General Vasily Korvin-Krukovskaya, an artillery officer, and his young wife, Elizaveta Fyodorovna, granddaughter of the astronomer F. I. Shubert. Sofya's sister, Anyuta, was seven years older; she also had a younger brother, Fedya. In 1858 Sofya's father retired from the army and the family moved from Moscow to Palobino, a country estate where the children were brought up by a nanny until their education was taken over by governesses and tutors. When the 13-year-old Sofya showed an aptitude for mathematics, her father was alarmed. He did not think that young ladies should be highly educated, and Sofya was not allowed to continue her study of mathematics. However, she managed to borrow a copy of Bourdon's *Algebra* from her tutor. She hid the book from her governess and read it secretly after everyone else was asleep.

Sofya received mathematics training from another source—a very surprising one. It is told that the walls of her bedroom were papered with lecture notes on integral and differential calculus. Sofya spent many hours trying to decipher what she was looking at. She was about 11 years old, and although she did not understand what she was seeing, it occupied her thoughts. Sonya was 15 when she took her first lesson in calculus. Her teacher, Professor Alexander Strannolyubsky, was surprised at the ease with which she grasped the concepts; he remarked that she must have studied the material earlier.

About a year later Professor N. N. Tyrtov, a neighbor, presented a

Sofya Korvin-Krukovskaya Kovalevskaya. Photo courtesy of
Culver Pictures, Inc.

copy of his new physics textbook to the family. Sofya began to read it;
and when she reached the section on optics, she encountered a kind of
mathematics she had not seen before. It was trigonometry. She asked her
tutor for help, but he was not able to give her any. Back she went to the
book and tried to figure it out for herself. She constructed what turned
out to be a method for understanding the sine function that was very
close to the one that had been developed historically. When Tyrtov visited, she explained how she had made sense of the material. He was so
impressed that he insisted her father allow her to study mathematics.
Several years later her father consented, and she took private lessons
with Professor A. N. Strannolyubsky in analytical geometry, as well as
differential and integral calculus.

During this period Russian universities were closed to women. Indeed,
women only left their fathers' homes to enter the homes of their husbands. Thus in order to leave their homes to study abroad, women were

entering into marriages of convenience. Sofya entered into such a marriage with Vladimir Kovalevsky in September 1868. Vladimir was a student of geology and a proponent of Darwin's theories. According to all accounts he was smitten with Sofya and was devoted to her.

In April 1869 Vladimir, Sofya, and Anyuta, Sofya's older sister, left for Germany. Anyuta then went on to Paris, Vladimir went to Vienna, and Sofya remained alone in Heidelberg—only to discover that she could not attend classes at the university. With much persistence she was finally able to get permission to attend lectures unofficially, and subsequently she studied with many famous scientists such as Leo Konigsberger, Emil Du Boi-Reymond, Gustav R. Kirchhoff, and Hermann L. F. von Helmholtz. Sofya's mathematical ability was recognized almost immediately, and after two years in Heidelberg she decided to study mathematics at the University of Berlin with Professor Karl Weierstrass. Again Sofya discovered that she was barred from attending classes. However, Weierstrass was so impressed with Sofya that he agreed to teach her privately.

By 1874 Sofya had produced three original works, two in mathematics and one in astronomy. One of the works, *On the Theory of Partial Differential Equations*, addressed a system of differential equations of the first order in n variables. Her second work, *On the Reduction of a Definite Class of Abelian Integrals of the Third Range*, was an extension of work done by Weierstrass. Her third work was *Supplementary Research and Observations on Laplace's Research on the Form of the Saturn Ring*. According to Weierstrass, any one of these papers would have been acceptable as a dissertation. Realizing that the University of Berlin would not accept these works from a woman, Sofya submitted the papers to the University of Göttingen. On the strength of the three works she presented, the University of Göttingen awarded her the degree of Doctor of Philosophy in Mathematics, summa cum laude, without any examination or public defense.

Sofya and Vladimir subsequently returned to Moscow and finally lived together as a married couple. Positions were difficult to obtain, and neither one was offered a situation in a university. Vladimir had obtained his doctorate two years earlier in paleontology from the University of Jena, also with honors. With an inheritance from Sofya's father, the young couple entered into the construction business with the hope of using the profits to pursue their scientific work independently. However, their business plans were too grandiose, far exceeding their capital, and they suffered a financial disaster.

In the six-year period that Sofya spent in Moscow, she was involved in several totally different projects. She spent a two-year period working for a newspaper as a theater reviewer and science reporter. Later she participated in organizing "higher courses for women," which was to be the nucleus of the curriculum for a women's university. Sofya's offer to teach at the women's university without salary was rejected. This rejection was undoubtedly a blow to her self-esteem and probably contributed to her neglect of mathematics work while in Moscow. In October 1878 a daughter, Sofya Vladimirovna, was born. With the same intensity she used when working on her mathematics, Sofya now devoted her time and attention to motherhood. This was her third project.

In January 1880 the Sixth Congress of Natural Scientists was held in Petersburg, and Sofya was encouraged by a friend to give a paper. She finally agreed to do so, choosing to discuss her work on Abelian integrals (one of her two dissertations that had not yet been published). In one evening she translated the dissertation into Russian, then read her paper the next day to an enthusiastic audience. Even though she had written the paper six years prior to the Congress, no new work had been done in the area in the interim.

Within two weeks of the end of the Congress, Sofya Kovalevskaya sold all her possessions and left for Europe, feeling she could once again return to work in her field. She was encouraged by Gosta Mittag-Leffler, professor of mathematics at the Swedish University of Helsingfors, with the possibility of a position. She spent the next two years in Berlin and Paris working on a research project on the refraction of light in crystals while waiting for a teaching position. During this time she came into contact with Charles Hermite and Henri Poincaré, two of the most distinguished mathematicians in France.

Finally, Mittag-Leffler was able to offer her a position at the University of Stockholm, equivalent to assistant professor but without salary. She was, instead, to receive her salary directly from the students. She arrived in Sweden in November 1883 to begin her teaching career. For the first year she taught in German; after that she taught in Swedish, which she studied from the time of her arrival. Within six months, in July 1884, she was given a five-year contract as professor of mathematics. In the same year she became an editor of the new journal *Acta Mathematica*. In 1885 she was given the Chair of Mechanics, and in 1889 she was given a lifetime appointment at the university.

During this time the Prix Bordin, a prize from the French Academy of Sciences, was being offered for substantive contributions to the solution of a long-standing problem in the area of mechanics: the rotation of a solid body about a fixed point. Examples of this phenomenon include the movement of a pendulum and, under certain conditions, the motion of a top or a gyroscope. Mittag-Leffler wanted Sofya to enter the competition because she had been working on this problem. She worked with zeal to put down on paper what she had worked out in her head, and to submit the work by the competition deadline. The rules of the competition specified that the work be submitted anonymously. Of the fifteen papers that had been submitted, the committee in choosing the winner increased the prize from 3,000 to 5,000 francs in view of the significance of the winning work. When the envelope was unsealed, it was Sofya Kovalevskaya who was the winner. On Christmas Eve, 1888, Sofya accepted the Prix Bordin in Paris.

Prior to Kovalevskaya's solution to the problem, only three cases had been found that gave the complete solution of the differential equations involved in the rotation of a solid body about a fixed point. The first case is attributed to Euler (1750) and Poinsot (1851), the second case is attributed to Lagrange (1788) and Poisson (1813), and the third case is that of complete kinetic symmetry. The value of Kovalevskaya's contribution is not only in the result or in the originality of her method, but also in the increased interest in the problem that was aroused.

Kovalevskaya tried repeatedly to obtain a position at a Russian university but was continually refused. However, in 1889 she was honored by Russian scientists by being elected an associate of the Imperial Academy of Sciences. Although they changed the rules so that she, a woman, could be elected, she still could not attend their meetings, which were closed to women.

Sofya Kovalevskaya was not only a talented mathematical researcher but a writer as well. As a young child she wrote poetry. Because her governess frowned on this activity (in fact, she was not allowed to read literature of any sort), she composed and then memorized her poems. Later she wrote two plays in collaboration with her friend Anna Carlotta Leffler, who was the sister of Mittag-Leffler, her Swedish sponsor. One of the plays, a drama in two parts, was called *The Struggle for Happiness: How It Was, How It Might Have Been*. The play, however, did not get good reviews, and the theater canceled its production. She wrote *The Rayevsky Sisters*, a novel about the revolutionary movement from her youth, published in 1889. She also wrote a novel entitled *Vera Votontzoff*, several essays, and her memoir, *A Russian Childhood*. The latter was written in Russian and later translated into Swedish, French, and English. It appeared that her writing was an attempt to connect herself to her past as well as to Russia, which continued to reject her.

Tragically, at the height of her career, Sofya Kovalevskaya died of pneumonia in February 1891 in Stockholm, Sweden. She was only 41 years old. However, her spirit of persistence and her mathematical results, have left a lasting impression on the mathematical community. Presently a series of one-day conferences for high school girls are held in her honor across the United States.

Note

1. There is a wide variation in the spelling of Kovalevskaya's name because of its translation from Russian. It has variously appeared as Sofia Kovalevsky,

Sonia Kovalevsky, Sophia Kovalevsky, Sofya Kovalevsky, Sofia Kovalevskaia, Sonya Kovalevskaia, and Sonia Kovalevskaya. The form of her name used in this essay comes from her book *A Russian Childhood*, as translated by B. Stillman.

Selected Work by Sofya Kovalevskaya

[1978]. *A Russian Childhood* (translated, edited, and introduced by Beatrice Stillman). New York: Springer-Verlag. (Includes an autobiographical sketch, first published in 1891 in *Russkaya starina*, and an analysis of Kovalevskaya's Mathematics by P. Y. Kochina, USSR Academy of Sciences.)

Selected Works about Sofya Kovalevskaya

Koblitz, Ann Hibner. (1983). *A Convergence of Lives. Sofia Kovalevskaia: Scientist, Writer, Revolutionary*. Boston: Birkhauser.
Kramer, Edna E. (1988). *The Main Stream of Mathematics*. Princeton Junction, NJ: The Scholar's Bookshelf.
Lipsey, Sally I. (1987). Sofia Kovalevskaia. In Louise Grinstein and Paul Campbell, Eds., *Women of Mathematics*. Westport, CT: Greenwood Press.
Osen, Lynn M. (1974). *Women in Mathematics*. Cambridge, MA: MIT Press.
Perl, Teri. (1978). *Math Equals: Biographies of Women Mathematicians + Related Activities*. Menlo Park, CA: Addison-Wesley.
———. (1983). *Women and Numbers*. San Carlos, CA: Wide World Publishing/ Tetra.
Reimer, Wilbert, and Luetta Reimer. (1993). *Historical Connections in Mathematics*, Vol. 2. Fresno, CA: AIMS Education Foundation

SUSAN BEAL

CHRISTINE LADD-FRANKLIN
(1847–1930)
Birthplace: Connecticut

In 1926 Christine Ladd-Franklin, an eminent researcher who contributed significantly to both mathematics and psychology, was pleased to be attending the Johns Hopkins University celebration of its fiftieth anniversary. As the university's first woman graduate student, she was to be awarded the Doctor of Philosophy degree. The university was a little late, however—Dr. Ladd-Franklin had completed work for the degree forty-four years earlier. Although Johns Hopkins was the first graduate and research university in the United States when it opened its doors in 1876, it did not initially award degrees to women. Ladd-Franklin's undergraduate alma mater, Vassar College, had meanwhile honored her in

Christine Ladd-Franklin. Photo courtesy of Rare
Book and Manuscript Library, Columbia
University.

1887 with the only honorary degree it ever granted, Doctor of Literary
Letters.

Christine Ladd-Franklin was 78 years old when Johns Hopkins offered
her the degree. She said of the university's offer, "Of course I've been a
doctor for a long time. I was given an LL.D. years ago, but I thought I'd
like to have my Ph.D. now. And I insisted that it should be given for
the work I did at Johns Hopkins, not what I've done since."[1]

Christine Ladd was born on December 1, 1847, in Windsor, Connecticut, a community on the outskirts of Hartford. Her childhood was spent
there and in New York City, where her father was a merchant for a
number of years. She later attributed her extraordinary energy and pro-
longed vigorous activity to "playing with the boys."[2] Her playmates
were her younger brother Henry and a neighbor boy.

There was exercise for the mind and heart as well as the body. Scarborough and Furumoto (1987) describe how Christine's mother took her

to a lecture by a reformer and women's rights activist, Mrs. Oakes-Smith. The child was not yet 5 years old. In between naps, Christine was pleased with what she heard and told her mother later that she, too, wished to be a lecturer. Unfortunately, Christine's mother died when the child was 12 years old. She went to live with her father's mother in Portsmouth, New Hampshire, for the next four years.

Learning one day that Vassar Female College was soon to open, the 16-year-old Christine became determined to attend. She wrote in her diary, "I am crying for very joy. I have been reading an account of the Vassar Female College that is to be. The glorious emancipation proclamation for women has gone forth and no power can put her back in her former state. . . . Oh! I must go. I must prevail upon my father to send me. . . . Let me study diligently now as preparation."[3] And indeed she did. Sent to a preparatory school in Wilbraham, Massachusetts, about 25 miles from her birthplace, she excelled and was chosen valedictorian of her class upon graduation two years later. Though the school was co-educational, she was the only girl in her Greek class for the two years she studied the subject.

To fulfill her dream of attending Vassar, Christine made no small departure from tradition. To persuade her grandmother that she should go, she had to meet the objection that she would be too old to marry if she spent four years in college.

> I assured her that it would afford me great pleasure to entangle a husband but there was no one [in] the place who would have me or whom I would have and out of this place I was destined never to go, gave her statistics of the great excess of females in New England and proved that as I was decidedly *not* handsome my chances were very small. Therefore since I could not find a husband to support me I must support myself and to do so I needed an education. Grandma succumbed.[4]

With financial support from her maternal aunt, Christine became a member of Vassar's second entering class in the fall of 1866. She was unable to continue after the first year, however, and spent the next year teaching school for a term in Utica, New York, and occupying herself with reading in three or four languages, practicing the piano, making a collection of 150 botanical specimens, solving trigonometry problems, and translating Schiller's poem "Des Mädchens Klage" (The Maiden's Lament) for publication in the *Hartford Courant*. When her aunt was able to renew her aid the next year, Christine returned to Vassar and graduated in 1869 after two academic years there.

At Vassar her favorite professor was Maria Mitchell, an astronomer and the first woman to be elected to the American Academy of Sciences.

As it happens, Mitchell had discovered a comet two months before Christine was born, thereby calling attention to the role of women in science. In addition to astronomy, Christine studied languages and physics. Though she wished to continue work in physics, after graduation she turned her attention to mathematics. She well knew that women were excluded from physics laboratories and thus chose a subject requiring no expensive and restricted apparatus.

For the next nine years she taught science and mathematics in high schools in Massachusetts, New York, and Pennsylvania. She did not much like the work. In Pennsylvania, though, she studied mathematics with Professor George C. Vose of Washington and Jefferson College. In addition to studying, she wrote; she contributed items to the Mathematical Questions section of the *Educational Times* published in London, England. A year later, teaching in Massachusetts, she studied privately with Harvard mathematicians W. E. Byerly and James Mills Pierce. By 1878 she had also published articles in the new American mathematical journal *The Analyst* and at least twenty items in the *Educational Times*.

While Christine Ladd was making ends meet and scraping together further studies in mathematics, eminent citizens of Baltimore, Maryland, were founding a university to be named for their leader, the financier Johns Hopkins. The men were ambitious and assembled a faculty and laboratories to rival those of the German research universities, then considered the best in the world. Christine responded to the news of Johns Hopkins University as she had to the news of Vassar. She wanted to go. The university's policy was to admit only men, but when she applied she wrote directly to Professor James J. Sylvester of the mathematics faculty. Sylvester, an Englishman (and, incidentally, once a teacher of Florence Nightingale), recognized Christine as a contributor of articles to the *Educational Times*. Notwithstanding the university's men-only policy, he obtained permission to allow her to enroll in his classes. After a year, on the strength of her outstanding work, she was permitted to take other courses as well and to receive the stipend of a fellowship. The force of male privilege prevented her from being granted the title of Fellow that normally accompanied the stipend.

At the time, Charles Sanders Peirce was working in government laboratories nearby and teaching a course in logic at Johns Hopkins. Peirce was a person of enormous intellect and many talents who was later recognized as a leader in many fields, among them philosophy, logic, and psychology. When he edited and published a collection of articles by his students and colleagues entitled *Studies in Logic by Members of the Johns Hopkins University* in 1883, it included a dissertation by Christine Ladd entitled "On the Algebra of Logic." Christine had completed the dissertation in 1882. Although she had fulfilled all the requirements for the

Ph.D., and although her work was of publishable quality, the university would not grant her a degree.

In 1883 Christine married Fabian Franklin, a junior faculty member and recent Johns Hopkins Ph.D. in mathematics. As Christine Ladd-Franklin she continued conducting research in mathematics and symbolic logic and maintained a steady stream of academic publications, all without holding an academic position. By 1887 she had also become interested in visual research, publishing a mathematical study of binocular vision in that year. Her dissertation and subsequent publications represented the first work in logic by an American woman. Her paper on vision, accompanied by several reviews of other people's vision research, was published in the first issue of the *American Journal of Psychology* and constitutes the first American work in psychology by a woman.

In 1891 Fabian was granted a sabbatical. He and Christine traveled to Europe, where she was able to study and carry on vision experiments in Germany with G. E. Müller, Hermann Helmholtz, and Arthur König. Müller advocated Ewald Hering's two-color theory of color perception, whereas Helmholtz and König supported the three-color theory originally proposed by Thomas Young and updated by Helmholtz, then a prominent physicist and psychologist. Christine, the visiting American scientist, set to work to resolve the competing theories.

Her paper, "A New Theory of Light Sensation," was presented in London at the International Congress of Experimental Psychology in 1892. After the presentation, her husband overheard Helmholtz discussing the two vision papers that had been delivered at the meeting. He dismissed the one by Hermann Ebbinghaus (now regarded as one of the founders of modern psychology) as unimportant but said of Christine's, "*Ach, Frau Franklin, die versteht die Sache.*" [Ah, Mrs. Franklin, *she* understands the subject.][5]—this notwithstanding the fact that her theory directly opposed Helmholtz's own view.

Johns Hopkins University had been unwilling to honor Christine's work in logic with a doctoral degree, yet the institution was happy to have her teach its students. Each year from 1904 to 1909 she lectured on logic in one semester and on psychology in the other. The Franklins then moved to New York City, where Fabian, now a journalist, was appointed associate editor of the *New York Evening Post*. Christine began a twenty-year career of research and lecturing at Columbia University, although the Columbia personnel records indicate that her service was "without salary."[6]

Christine was 62 years old when she moved to New York. She continued to publish an impressive volume of material. By the end of her life in 1930 she had written 31 papers of five or more pages in length, 33 smaller papers, 28 notes, 57 reviews, and at least 77 items for the *Edu-*

cational Times. Her contribution to symbolic logic and her work on color vision were widely recognized as outstanding.

In addition to the total of at least 245 professional items, she authored 49 contributions to *The Nation* magazine, a companion publication to the *Evening Post*, and many more in the *New York Times*. In *The Nation* and the *Times* she expressed herself on issues of justice for women and other topics of the day. In a letter to the *Times* in 1921, for example, she castigated the American Academy of Arts and Letters for its policy of excluding women. "Isn't it rather absurd that Edith Wharton, for instance, who is without question the most distinguished American in the realm of letters, should not have been invited to join a self-constituted body of 'immortals'?"[7]

Besides advocacy for women's progress, Ladd-Franklin contributed her energy and some money to increase opportunities for graduate study and faculty positions for women. She was active in the forerunner organization to the American Association of University Women. She carried on a continuing exchange of letters demanding that psychologist E. B. Titchener of Cornell University open his association known as "The Experimentalists" to women, since its avowed purpose was professional advancement. Titchener did not bend, but after his death the group reconstituted itself without the formal exclusion of women.

Christine Ladd-Franklin's work on color theory was published as a book in 1929 when she was 81 years old. A physicist reviewing the book referred to her as "a merciless and indomitable logician . . . whose grasp of the phenomena of color vision is truly remarkable."[8] Merciless in pursuit of just treatment for women; indomitable in the practice of science; fearless in the face of opposition; fortunate to have such teachers as Mitchell, Sylvester, Peirce, Müller, and Helmholtz; ambitious, feisty, courageous—many adjectives are needed to describe this foremother of American mathematics and science. Her course ran against the current of male privilege and before the wind of women's advancement. She was quite a sailor.

Notes

1. Quoted by J. Green in L. S. Grinstein and P. J. Campbell, eds., *Women of Mathematics* (Westport, CT: Greenwood Press, 1987), p. 124.

2. D. Malone, *Dictionary of American Biography*, vol. 5 (1932–1933) (New York: C. Scribners, 1958), p. 529.

3. Quoted in E. Scarborough and L. Furumoto, *Untold Lives: The First Generation of American Women Psychologists* (New York: Columbia University Press, 1987), p. 120.

4. Diary entry for 23 July 1866, in Scarborough and Furumoto, *Untold Lives*, p. 121.

5. Green, in Grinstein and Campbell, *Women of Mathematics*, p. 123. Translation slightly modified.

6. T. C. Cadwaller and J. V. Cadwaller, "Christine Ladd-Franklin (1847–1930)," in A. N. O'Connell and N. F. Russo, eds., *Women in Psychology: A Bibliographic Sourcebook* (Westport, CT: Greenwood Press, 1990), pp. 220–229.

7. Scarborough and Furumoto, *Untold Lives*, p. 109.

8. Green, in Grinstein and Campbell, *Women of Mathematics*, p. 123–124.

Selected Works by Christine Ladd-Franklin

(1879). The Pascal Hexagram. *American Journal of Mathematics* 2, pp. 1–12.

(1911). The Foundations of Philosophy: Explicit Primitives. *Journal of Philosophy, Psychology and Scientific Methods* 8, pp. 708–13.

(1912). Implication and Existence in Logic. *Philosophical Review* 21(6), pp. 641–65.

(1918, November). Bertrand Russell and Symbolic Logic. *Bulletin of the American Mathematical Society* 25, pp. 59–60.

(1928). Some Questions in Logic. *Journal of Philosophy* 25, p. 700.

Selected Works about Christine Ladd-Franklin

Cadwallader, T. C., and Cadwallader, J. V. (1990) Christine Ladd-Franklin (1847–1930). In A. N. O'Connell and N. F. Russo, Eds., *Women in Psychology: A Bibliographic Sourcebook* (pp. 220–29). Westport, CT: Greenwood Press.

Green, J. (1987). Christine Ladd-Franklin (1847–1930). In L. S. Grinstein and P. J. Campbell, Eds., *Women of Mathematics* (pp. 121–28). Westport, CT: Greenwood Press.

Malone, D. (1958). "Christine Ladd-Franklin." In *Dictionary of American Biography*, Vol. 5 (1932–1933). New York: Charles Scribners.

Scarborough, E., and Furumoto, L. (1987). *Untold Lives: The First Generation of American Women Psychologists*. New York: Columbia University Press.

HOMER STAVELY

ANNELI LAX
(1922–)
Birthplace: Upper Silesia, Germany/Poland

Anneli Lax, who has inspired effective mathematical communication in many students and teachers, was born Anneli Cahn on February 23, 1922, in Upper Silesia on the Polish/German border and lived there until she was 9 years old. Her childhood and adolescence were very much influenced by the war raging in Europe—particularly because her family was Jewish, one of the groups Hitler had targeted for extermination. Her

Anneli Lax. Photo courtesy of Anneli Lax.

grandmother and some of her cousins were in fact killed, but her immediate family were among the lucky ones to escape before the war. In
1931 Lax and her family moved from their hometown to Berlin, where
they lived until Hitler came to power in 1933. The family—mother, father, brother, and Anneli—then moved to Paris. After a year there her
father, a physician, was unable to obtain permission to work and went
on to Palestine (now Israel) while Anneli and her mother returned to
Berlin to live with an aunt. In 1935 mother and daughter followed father
to Tel Aviv. Jobs were also scarce for physicians in Palestine; in 1936,
sponsored by a relative, the family emigrated to the United States, where
her father was finally able to practice medicine after taking and passing
the appropriate examinations. Anneli was now 14 years old. Her brother,
five years older, had returned to Germany, where he served as an ap-
prentice in a metal business until joining the family in the United States.
    Lax is embarrassed about the reason for her initial interest in mathe-
matics. She believes she became interested in mathematics for what she

now considers the wrong reasons—"a kind of laziness." It was a subject she could pursue without having to go to libraries or look things up. It was easier and more fun to answer questions by deriving the results herself, from scratch. She fondly remembers a geometry class in Germany that afforded her this kind of experience: The teacher gave students three parts of a triangle (possibly a base, an altitude to that base, and an angle) and then asked the students to construct the triangle. The students had to write out a plan. If the plan was approved, they were assigned to carry out the construction for homework. Lax recalls that it was especially fun when the three parts given were unusual—nothing simple like side, side, side.

Unlike in the United States, in Europe mathematics was not compartmentalized into separate classes such as algebra and geometry. Also, these classes were not electives; everyone took them. Lax's first exposure to the way geometry is taught in the United States, with an emphasis on formal proofs, was in high school in 1936–1938.

After completing high school in the borough of Queens in New York City, Anneli was offered a scholarship to the University of Southern California. However, California was too far away for her parents' comfort, so she accepted a scholarship at Adelphi College instead; it was close by, although at that time it did not have a good mathematics program. After graduating in 1942 at the age of 20, she went on to graduate school at New York University (NYU).

She was the only woman hired by the NYU School of Aeronautics to fill an empty slot left by the drafting into the army of many young men. Among her tasks was the calculation of lift and drag coefficients for model airplanes being tested in the wind tunnel. Although she never got to see the experiments, she had to process the data on the calculating machine, which she found *tremendously* boring. Equally boring was researching and summarizing journal articles for a professor whose pioneering work in rotary aircraft kept him busy consulting for the helicopter industry. While doing this, Anneli began taking graduate mathematics courses at NYU which she describes as especially challenging because she hadn't learned much mathematics at Adelphi, and having graduated in January instead of June she found herself enrolled in the second halves of advanced mathematics courses. It wasn't until much later, when she had time to work hard and prepare herself properly, that Lax felt more comfortable.

Anneli Lax is married to a well-known Hungarian mathematician, Peter Lax, whom she met in graduate school. She recalls an early memory of Peter from one of the first courses she took at NYU, complex variables. "The instructor, perhaps through illness, had become totally incompetent, and Peter Lax was a very young, gangly kind of fellow who seemed to know it all. When the instructor got stuck he asked Mr. Lax about a proof, and Peter would end up proving something." Subsequently Peter was drafted into the army in World War II, and Lax didn't see him again until Courant, her boss, invited her to edit a paper left behind by the young Hungarian. When Peter Lax returned to New York on furlough, she met with him to discuss the paper.

Both of Lax's sons were born while she was heavily involved in working toward her Ph.D. She was pregnant with her first son, John, when she took her comprehensive exam. Jimmy, her second son, was born in 1954 while she was writing her dissertation on Cauchy's problem for partial differential equations. She received her Ph.D. just one year later.

Much of Lax's professional career has been devoted to teaching mathematics. As a graduate student at NYU she started tutoring in the university's adult education program to earn money; then she became a regular teaching assistant in the mathematics department. She noticed that many entering students were having trouble with calculus and wondered why. Many years later an opportunity appeared for doing something about this.

In the 1970s, open admission policies caused colleges to institute remedial courses for the many entering students who were not adequately prepared. NYU mandated courses in writing and mathematics for the many students who could not pass an exam to establish a proficiency. Whereas only very good writers were able to "place out" of a writing course, it was much easier to do so in mathematics. Therefore the students who ended up in the mandatory mathematics course were those who either hadn't taken geometry or algebra in high school at all, or hadn't understood what they were supposed to have learned at that time. Lax designed a Mathematical Thinking course for those students. She was fascinated by the differences between the way *they* thought about mathematics and the way *her colleagues* thought about mathematics. What factors interfered with the learning process for many people? What role did anxiety and the pressure of testing play? The more she thought about it, the clearer it became that the harm had been done years ago and would be very difficult to fix in college. As a result she became increasingly interested in pre-college education.

Working with the writer Erika Duncan, who was teaching in NYU's expository writing program, and intrigued by the Writing across the Curriculum movement, Lax became even more convinced that some of the young peoples' problems and difficulties in mathematics had to do with their understanding of language. She was particularly interested in why people have so much trouble with word problems. She and the writing teacher arranged to co-teach a class of fifteen freshmen. They saw the students four times a week and alternately emphasized writing and mathematics.

This writing and mathematics program led to a series of workshops, funded by the Ford Foundation, for language arts and mathematics teachers from several high schools. Lax comments on the innovative teaching experiments of many of the participating teachers. She recalls an English teacher who, in connection with teaching students how to write letters, gave them a math problem to write about. The assignment was as follows: "Write a letter to Aunt Rosanna, who owns a small spaghetti sauce factory and suddenly can't get ahold of her twelve-ounce jars and has to use eight-ounce jars to make her batch of so many gallons. How many jars will she need? Can you help her out?" Because the focus was on helping, it wasn't considered cheating if the students asked each other for help, which they did. In this way, Lax relates, they came at the problem "through the back door" and didn't have the usual anxieties they would have had in mathematics class. Much of this work is still going on. Lax comments on the difficulty of transmitting what some teachers have learned about teaching to other teachers. Although other people can be inspired, they can't be told to do the same thing. However, Lax herself has been effective in inspiring others to teach well, and in 1976 she received the Mathematical Association of America's Polya Award for Exposition for her article "Linear Algebra, a Potent Tool."

One of Lax's main professional contributions has been as longtime editor of the Mathematical Association of America's prestigious *New Mathematical Library*. Lax is now working on the thirty-eighth volume in this series, which includes works by many well-known mathematicians such as Ivan Niven and W. W. Sawyer. Her work with the *New Mathematical Library* has enabled Anneli Lax to combine her interests in language and mathematics to help more people understand and appreciate the power and beauty of the subject. In 1995 she received the Yueh-Gin Gung and Dr. Charles Y. Hu Award for Distinguished Service to Mathematics from the Mathematical Association of America. The rewards of a life spent so engaged are evident as Professor Lax expresses her belief that she and her colleagues enjoy a rare luxury: spending most of their lives doing things they like to do.

Note

This biography is based on an interview that took place in New York City in May 1996 conducted by the author.

Selected Works by Anneli Lax

(1965). The New Mathematical Library: A Project to Promote Good Elementary Mathematical Exposition. *American Mathematical Monthly* 72(9), 1–014–1017.

(1976). (with Peter Lax and S. Z. Burstein). *Calculus with Applications and Computing.* Vol. 1, New York: Springer-Verlag.

(1976). Linear Algebra, a Potent Tool. *Two Year College Mathematics Journal* 7(1), pp. 3–15.
(1978). (with P. D. Lax). On Sums of Squares, *Linear Algebra and Its Applications* 20, pp. 71–75.
(1989). They Think, Therefore We Are. In P. Connolly and T. Vilardi, Eds., *Writing to Learn Mathematics and Science* (Chapter 19). New York: Teachers College Press.
(1993). (with G. Davidoff). An Inclusion-Exclusion Principle, *UME Trends*, September.
(1993). A Letter and Part I, Survive to Succeed. *UME Trends*, July.
(1996). Drifting into Mathematics. In Bettye Ann Case, Ed., *A Century of Mathematical Meetings* (pp. 179–81). Providence, RI: American Mathematical Society.

Selected Works about Anneli Lax

Albers, D. (1992). Once Upon a Time. *Focus*, June.
Albers, D. J., Alexanderson, G. L., and Reid, C. (1990). *More Mathematical People*. Boston: Harcourt Brace Jovanovich.
MAA Polya Award for Exposition for Linear Algebra, a Potent Tool. (1976). *Two Year College Mathematics Journal* 7(1), pp. 3–15.

TERI PERL

GILAH CHAYA VANDERHOEK LEDER
(1941–   )
Birthplace: Hilversum, The Netherlands

In 1994, when Gilah Leder was appointed professor of education at La Trobe University in Melbourne, Australia, she was the first woman in the history of the Graduate School of Education to hold a position at that level. She received this position as a result of her outstanding contributions in the area of mathematics and gender.

The fact that Gilah was born during the early part of World War II greatly affected the direction of her life. Any Jewish child born in Nazi-occupied Holland was not safe, but Gilah was lucky. She was taken in, hidden, protected, and saved by a Catholic family. Accepted and treated as one of their own, she was affectionately named "Zusje" (little sister, or "sis"). During these dangerous times, circumstances dictated that when visitors came to the house Gilah be kept out of sight and remain silent. She was taught to read and attributes her lifelong love of reading to these early childhood experiences.

Gilah Leder. Photo courtesy of Gilah Leder.

After the war Gilah was reunited with her parents. The family re-mained in The Netherlands, where she attended a small, private, coed-ucational elementary school. Each morning, even when it snowed, Gilah rode her bike to school. In summer, a swim in an unheated pool often started the day. She has happy memories of her school days; she was a good student and enjoyed everything she learned. She liked mathematics and has vivid recollections of a textbook full of problems that she loved doing.

In November 1953 the family moved to Adelaide, Australia. Gilah's parents saw Australia as a young country full of opportunities for their children. At the beginning of the new school year (which starts in Feb-ruary in Australia) Gilah started seventh grade at Woodville High School, a coeducational government school. Although it did not take her long to learn English, mathematics was the subject that gave her the greatest pleasure because the numbers were so familiar.

During her high school years, two mathematics teachers inspired Gilah's interest in mathematics and influenced the direction her research would take many years later. The first, a woman, was very encouraging of Gilah's mathematical talent and had high expectations for her. If Gilah did not perform well on a test, the teacher would take her aside and tell her that she could have done better. Gilah did not want to disappoint this teacher, whom she felt would take it personally if she did not excel. By her final year of high school Gilah was achieving outstanding grades in mathematics. The other teacher, a man, once said, "What a pity you're a girl; you're so good at mathematics, and it seems you won't be able to use it." At this, Gilah was more determined than ever to pursue mathematics at the university level. Some twenty years later she was invited to Adelaide to speak about her research. Her former teacher was in the audience, and Gilah reminded him of his comment. He replied, "Teachers can make a difference even when they don't intend to." He certainly had!

Gilah's undergraduate years were spent at the University of Adelaide. She was passionately committed to gender equity, even at this point in her life. In the late 1950s women had to wear dresses or skirts to the universities if they were enrolled in teacher training courses. Gilah led a successful delegation to the Minister of Education in South Australia to allow women to wear slacks.

Gilah completed a B.A. degree with Honours in mathematics; her thesis was an exploration of Boolean algebra. In the final two years of her undergraduate program, she was the only woman studying mathematics at the Honours level and felt very much on the outside. Gilah also found that in her social circles it was something of a "party stopper" when she told people that she was a mathematics student. These experiences persuaded her to concentrate her energies on mathematics education and not purely in mathematics itself. She wanted to influence how mathematics was taught so that it would be easier for other women to pursue higher-level studies in the field. She went on at the University of Adelaide to complete a Diploma in Education at the secondary level, which qualified her as a high school teacher of mathematics.

Leder began her working life teaching mathematics at a coeducational government high school in Melbourne, where she had moved when she married. Contrary to the beliefs of the times, her husband, a medical practitioner, did not consider it unusual that Gilah should want to work or to study. Early in her career she was recognized as a talented teacher and was recommended to the Melbourne Secondary Teachers College (which is now part of the University of Melbourne) to train mathematics teachers. When offered the position, she was asked how long she would work before having children—a question no employer could ask today, but at that time Australian women not only worked for a lower salary than their male counterparts but also were expected to resign when they were five months pregnant. Only in 1967, the year between the births of her two children, was Gilah not in school herself or working in a school.

After her second child was born, Gilah was awarded a scholarship at Monash University in Melbourne and completed a master's degree in education. At Monash she was awarded another scholarship and earned her Ph.D. as well. For her doctoral research she explored the relationship between gender differences in mathematics achievement and "fear of success" (i.e., avoidance of the achievement of success in order to avoid its consequences).

On the completion of her doctorate, Leder was appointed to a lectureship in the Faculty of Education at Monash University. She soon gained a reputation as an outstanding teacher and as an exemplary researcher of international standing. She rapidly advanced to the position of senior lecturer and was the first woman to be promoted to the level of associate professor. In 1993 Leder was named Monash University's "Supervisor of the Year," an award that recognized her exceptional talent as a supervisor of postgraduate research. Her postgraduate students speak passionately of her genuine interest in their projects and their career development, of her insightful and constructive evaluation of their work, of her care and understanding during periods of personal or academic crisis, and of the self-confidence and motivation she inspires. In 1994 she was appointed professor of education at La Trobe University in Melbourne, the first woman in the history of the Graduate School of Education to hold a position at that level.

As a married woman who has successfully combined motherhood with academic excellence, **Elizabeth Fennema** of the University of Wisconsin in Madison was Gilah's personal role model. Despite being separated by the vast Pacific Ocean, Professor Fennema's writings and research strongly influenced Gilah's work. They shared common concerns about the underrepresentation of women in mathematics-related fields and about the gender differences in achievement that had frequently been reported to favor men—particularly on timed tests and for the most demanding mathematical tasks. On the basis of their research, both have developed models that suggest explanations for these phenomena. They have found that attitudes and beliefs, as well as a range of other factors external to the learner, are strongly implicated in contributing to these gender-differentiated outcomes. In 1990 Leder and Fennema jointly edited and published *Mathematics and Gender*, a leading reference text on the range of issues encompassed by this topic.

During her academic career, Leder has worked with many people who encouraged her. A kindred spirit on the education faculty was educational sociologist Dr. Shirley Sampson. In 1989 they coedited *Educating Girls: Practice and Research*. In the book, a broad range of issues associated with Australian girls' educational disadvantages and needs are discussed and supported with research findings. Leder has also been intrigued by the additional pressures on women who are capable of high achievement. She believes that undue emphasis has been placed on the detrimental effects that a career might have on family life. In her own situation, she feels it has been a positive influence on her children that both parents have worked at jobs they enjoy.

Leder believes there is a strong link between societal and cultural values and mathematics learning. Her research on children who are gifted in mathematics has shed light on the role of societal pressures, values, and expectations. She has found that teachers more often identify boys than girls to be talented mathematics students and that high-achieving girls often underestimate their abilities and potential. She has written of children as young as age 4 who already view mathematics as a gender-dependent field that is more closely associated with men's than with women's occupations, interests, and achievements. Her classroom research has shown that teachers interact more frequently with boys than with girls, particularly when asking more difficult mathematical questions. Boys are also given greater opportunities than girls to answer and demonstrate what they know, because teachers often allow boys more thinking time. More recently, Leder's work has broadened to encompass questions about the influence of culture and ethnicity on mathematics learning and on the nature of mathematics itself.

Leder has published numerous papers in scholarly journals, presented papers and keynote addresses at international conferences, and written several books. Along with two colleagues, Penna and McNamara, she produced a teaching resource video, *Trout Also Multiply*, that received the Australian Society for Educational Technology Merit Award in 1992. She also maintains an active interest in the professional development of teachers. Her own professional contacts are maintained through attendance at international conferences, joint publications, serving on editorial boards, and more recently, over the Internet. She is currently president of the Mathematics Education Research Group of Australasia and is an executive member of the International Congress on Mathematics Instruction Board and its Australian subcommittee.

Leder believes that a sound understanding of mathematics is needed to live with dignity in today's society; she always enjoys working with students who want to improve their mathematics teaching and reflect on what they are doing. She has become increasingly aware of the extent to which her personal experiences have influenced the direction of her professional life. Her career opportunities have been a source of deep satisfaction. She has served as an exemplary role model to her students and to teachers of mathematics. The mathematics education of young women and the opportunities now available to them owe much to her research endeavors.

Note

The information included in this biography is based in part on an interview conducted by the author.

Selected Works by Gilah Leder

(1989). *Educating Girls: Practice and Research* (with S. Sampson). Sydney: Allen and Unwin.

(1990). *Mathematics and Gender* (with E. Fennema). New York: Teachers College Press. (Also published in 1997 by the University of Queensland Press with a special introductory chapter.)

(1992). *Quantitative Methods in Education Research: A Case Study* (with R. Gunstone). Geelong: Deakin University Press.

(1995). Guest Editor, *Educational Studies in Mathematics*, 28(3). Special Issue on Mathematics and Gender.

(1995). Mathematics and Gender: Changing Perspectives. In D. A. Grouws, Ed., *Handbook of Research in Mathematics Teaching and Learning* (pp. 597–622). New York: MacMillan.

(1996). Research and Intervention Programs: A Gendered Issue (with H. Forgasz and C. Solar). In A. Bishop, Ed., *International Handbook of Mathematics Education*. Dordrecht, The Netherlands: Kluwer.

(1996). *Student Pathways: A Review and Overview of National Databases on Gender Equity* (with L. Yates). Canberra, Australia: Department of Education and Training, and Children's Youth and Family Bureau.

Selected Work about Gilah Leder

Butler, A. (1984). *Girls and Mathematics: A Review of Gilah Leder's Work 1974–1984.* Melbourne: Equal Opportunity Unit of Victoria.

HELEN J. FORGASZ

EMMA TROTSKAYA LEHMER
(1906–   )
Birthplace: Samara, Russia

Throughout her life, Emma Lehmer worked in the area of mathematics known as number theory. She and her husband, Derrick Henry Lehmer, became known as a famous number theory team. At age 90 she has finished her work, written up her husband's unfinished work, and overseen the publication of these materials.

Emma was born in a Russian town with the lovely-sounding name of

Emma Lehmer. Photo courtesy of Laura Gould.

Samara on the great Volga River on November 6, 1906. In her journal she wrote that she had always hoped to visit it someday, till they changed its name to the horrific-sounding Kuybyshev, and she lost all interest in it. In 1910 Emma's family traveled by rail from Russia to Harbin, Manchuria. Her father, Motvey Trotsky, had been transferred to Manchuria to be the Far East representative of a large Russian sugar company. Emma's mother, Nadejda, had been a dentist before her marriage.

Not until 1920, when a new community high school opened in Harbin, was Emma allowed to attend school. Before that she had been tutored at home. She recalls a wonderful mathematics teacher in high school: a displaced engineer from Moscow who now taught algebra, geometry, and trigonometry in all the classes and still somehow had time to run a mathematics club after hours—which Emma never missed. She believes he ignited a spark that still keeps her going.

Having abandoned early dreams of continuing her higher education in Russia, which was now in the throes of revolution and general chaos, Emma spent a year working at odd jobs (babysitting, translating, coaching, and giving piano lessons to youngsters) and saving her money to go to college in the United States. She was admitted to Berkeley and finally got there via Japan and Canada, where she was delayed for many weeks before obtaining a student visa.

Arriving a week late for classes, Emma launched right in. She signed up for mathematics, physics, chemistry, and English and had her hands full. After trying an engineering course, where she soon found out that she was not very good with her hands, she decided to change her major to mathematics, which she could do easily and which was much more enjoyable. Emma didn't mind being the only woman in her classes, as she was very independent. Although Berkeley was home to several Russian-speaking students from Harbin, she preferred not to spend time with them because she was eager to improve her English.

Emma was extremely resourceful in supporting herself. After waitressing, which she learned on the job, she did odd jobs such as serving at university banquets, babysitting, and housecleaning. As her English improved she did more translating, which she found easy and which paid well. Soon she got a job with her future father-in-law, Derrick Norman Lehmer, a mathematics professor at Berkeley. Emma remembers him as a fine gentleman and her favorite teacher. She took as many of his courses as she could. It was while working on a research project for him that she met Derrick Henry Lehmer, known as Dick, the man who was to become her husband.

In the mid-1920s Emma was involved in research to find numbers known as pseudosquares. A pseudosquare is a number that is defined relative to a given set of primes called moduli. It is a non-square with the property that it becomes a square when some multiple of each prime modulus is added to it. The number 3, for example, is a pseudosquare relative to the prime 2, because 3 is not a square, but $3 + (3 \times 2) = 9$ is a square. The number 31 is a pseudosquare relative to the moduli 2, 3, and 5 because 31 is not a square, but the three numbers $31 + (9 \times 2) = 49$, $31 + (6 \times 3) = 49$, and $31 + (1 \times 5) = 36$ are squares. Emma worked on finding the smallest pseudosquare relative to the moduli 2, 3, 5, . . . , 97 (all the primes less than 100). Only much later, in 1970, did she and her husband find that the answer to this difficult question is 2,805,544,681.

The Lehmers were married in 1928 in the break between the end of classes and finals. After a luncheon celebration and a weekend honeymoon, Emma spent the next week taking all her finals while Dick prepared for their trip. They began by touring the redwood forest, then went on to Japan and, finally, Mukden (now Shenyang) to introduce Emma's family to their new son-in-law. After a difficult return trip by sea and a few weeks in Berkeley, the couple drove across the country to Brown University in Providence, Rhode Island, where Dick had been offered a teaching assistantship.

While her husband was earning his Ph.D. at Brown, Lehmer was enrolled in the master's degree program. The only other female graduate student in mathematics was Gertrude Stith. She and Emma became friends at once. Emma remembers the time at Brown as a happy one: Dick worked on his thesis; Emma typed it; both took courses, with Emma reading papers and doing a bit of coaching as well. After getting their respective degrees, the young couple returned to California to work for a semester at Cal Tech in Pasadena and then at Stanford for a little more than a year.

Laura, their first child, was born in 1932 in the midst of the Great Depression. Dick was having problems obtaining a proper faculty position because at that time universities were unable to afford new faculty. Then he got a summer job at the Chicago World's Fair, exhibiting an early computing machine he had invented and constructed from large metal gears. This was one of a series of "numerical sieves" that the Lehmers were to work on together, machines that scanned numbers in sequence searching for those that satisfied certain properties.

After the Chicago Fair came a year at Princeton University, where Dick had an Institute fellowship and Emma did some translating. An offer to teach summer school at Stanford in 1934 sent them back across the country. Then came five years at Lehigh University in Pennsylvania, where their second child, son Donald, was born at the end of 1934. Emma writes about "grinding the Monroe [an early, heavy, noisy desk calculator] that we were buying on the installment plan for a project. We could not use it in the evening as it blinked the lights not only in our house but also in the house next door."

The Lehigh years were followed by a Guggenheim fellowship spent at Cambridge University in England, where several prestigious number theorists were working. The Lehmers ran out of money and had to return to the States a few weeks earlier than originally planned. Had they not done so, they might have had to remain indefinitely in England, because the ship they were originally scheduled to sail on never left owing to the outbreak of war in Europe.

After another year at Lehigh, Dick finally got the offer he had been hoping for: a professorship at the University of California. Emma writes about the rich life they enjoyed on their return to Berkeley: They attended colloquia, had lunch and dinner parties for visiting professionals, went to big parties at the homes of colleagues, joined the drama and music sections, gave talks and wrote papers, and went to concerts and plays. "I am exhausted just thinking about it, but we had a lot of energy in those days." The Lehmers also invited graduate students to go hiking with them in the Berkeley hills on Saturdays.

During some of this time, Emma worked at the statistics lab at the university. When the lab work turned into war work, Dick started teaching night classes and was a block warden. Finally succumbing to peer pressure to do their part for the war effort, the Lehmers spent the last year of the war at the Ballistic Research Laboratory of the Aberdeen Proving Grounds in Maryland. Dick's job was to assist in the completion of the ENIAC, an early digital computer, and to participate in its testing. It was to be used primarily for computing ballistic trajectories; but the Lehmers had permission on some weekends to reset the ENIAC, using it as a numerical sieve for their number theory problems. When they could arrange child care, they often stayed at the lab all night long while the ENIAC processed one of their problems. They would return home at the break of dawn. They were pleased to find that the sieve worked in successfully solving problems.

Emma Lehmer considers that she is quite fortunate in the way her career turned out. She would have liked to teach more (she taught some during the World War II under special wartime exceptions to the university nepotism rules that usually prevented more than one member of a family from holding a faculty position). She considered that not having to teach freed her to do research. Nepotism rules didn't seem unfair during the Depression years, when so many people were unemployed. Not being a particularly competitive person, Emma did not miss the prestige of holding a faculty position. As a faculty wife she was a member of the university community, had library privileges, and never felt excluded from the mathematics community. She was able to attend department seminars whenever she wished. She was free to travel with her husband to attend mathematics conferences around the world. Together they shared friends within the mathematics community and were especially close to Raphael and **Julia Robinson**.

Emma Lehmer's long, rich life has been filled with challenges, pleasures, opportunities, and intellectual rewards. She now enjoys a wonderful view of the San Francisco Bay from her living room and plays the piano. When we took a walk and came upon a dense stand of pampas grass blocking her favorite view, I noticed a narrow path through the grass and asked if she was "up to" walking through. "Sure!" said the 90-year-old Lehmer, "I always like to try new things."

Note

The information included in this biography is based in part on an interview conducted in Berkeley, California, in 1996 by the author.

Selected Works by Emma Lehmer

(1935). On a Resultant Connected with Fermat's Last Theorem. *Bulletin of the American Mathematical Society* 41, pp. 864–67.

(1941). (with D. H. Lehmer). On the First Case of Fermat's Last Theorem, *Bulletin of the American Mathematical Society* 47, pp. 139–42.

(1962). (with D. H. Lehmer). Heuristics, Anyone? In G. Szego et al. (Eds), *Studies in Mathematical Analysis and Related Topics*: Essays in Honor of George Polya. (Stanford: Stanford University Press), pp. 202–10.

(1967). On the Quadratic Character of the Fibonacci Root. *Fibonacci Quarterly* 5, pp. 135–38.

(1974). An Outcropping of Combinatorics in Number Theory. *Proceedings of the Fifth Southeastern Conference on Combinatorics, Graph Theory, and Computing*, Boca Raton, pp. 75–92.

(1978). Rational Reciprocity Laws. *American Mathematical Monthly* 85, pp. 467–72.

(1985). On Special Primes. *Pacific Journal of Mathematics*. 118, pp. 471–78.

(1985). (with D. H. Lehmer). On Square-Separable Primes, *American Mathematical Monthly* 92, pp. 719–20.

(1988). Connection between Gaussian Periods and Cyclic Units. *Mathematics and Computation* 50, pp. 535–41.

(1989). An Indeterminate in Number Theory. *Journal of the Australian Mathematical Society* 46, Ser. A, pp. 469–72.

(1993). (with D. H. Lehmer). The Lehmer Project, *Mathematics and Computation* 61, pp. 313–17.

TERI PERL

ADA AUGUSTA BYRON LOVELACE
(1815–1852)
Birthplace: London, England

It was during the London season of 1833 that Ada Augusta Byron Lovelace, who later became a pioneer in the development of computers, entered the grown-up world. She was thrilled with the splendor of the Court of Saint James and of the Palace itself as she was introduced to King William IV and Queen Adelaide. Ada had attended few parties in the past, but in the winter of her "coming out" season she went to many balls and dinners where—for the first time in her life—she met numerous important and famous people. Ada yearned to be part of their group, many of whom were not only famous but intelligent, accomplished, and witty as well.

In fact, this young woman, sired but not raised by the notorious and talented English poet Lord George Byron, was looking for others to share

Ada Lovelace. Photo courtesy of Stock Montage, Inc.

her great love of mathematics, music, riding, and anything else that was interesting and new. In particular she wished to meet the famous **Mary Somerville**, now living in London, who had just published *The Mechanism of the Heavens*, a book on mathematical astronomy. This best-seller was being read with great fascination by the educated people of the day. Ada dreamed of becoming a famous mathematician like Mrs. Somerville.

Another bright star of the London scene was Charles Babbage, an inventor who had studied at Cambridge University. Babbage traveled widely and involved himself in many scientific projects. He also loved to be seen at the best parties and balls. Ada was delighted to be introduced to him at one of these parties, and Babbage invited both her and her mother to see his pet project, an early computer. When the 17-year-old Ada saw Babbage's invention, the Difference Engine, she was enthralled. The next evening Ada went to the Queen's Ball and again conversed with Babbage, thus beginning a professional tie and friendship that was to last throughout her life.

In order to work with Babbage, Ada began studying differential equations so that, as she wrote to him, "at some future time . . . my head may be made by you subservient to some of your purposes and plans."[1] This pursuit was an extension of an already-established pattern of mathematical interest on Ada's part. When she was 17 years old and studying algebra and astronomy (which she had mostly taught herself), Ada wrote playfully to a friend, "So this you see is commencement of 'A Sentimental Mathematical Correspondence between two Young Ladies of Rank' to be hereinafter published no doubt for the edification of womankind. . . . Ever Yours Mathematically."[2]

An interesting glimpse into nineteenth-century attitudes toward women and mathematics is contained in a note from the well-known mathematician Augustus DeMorgan, Ada's occasional mathematics tutor, to Ada's mother Lady Byron: "I feel bound to tell you that . . . [Ada's] power of thinking on these matters . . . has been something so utterly out of the common way for any beginner, man or woman, (that) . . . had any young beginner, about to go to Cambridge, shown the same power, I should have prophesied [that he would become] . . . an original mathematical investigator, perhaps of first-rate eminence."[3]

It was through her subsequent acquaintance with Mary Somerville and Mrs. Somerville's son by her first marriage, Woronzow Greig, that Ada Lovelace met her future husband, Lord William King. Three years after their marriage, and after the birth of two of their three children, Lord King inherited another title and became Earl of Lovelace; Ada became the Countess of Lovelace. Although this title brought no money, Lord Lovelace was given a place in the House of Lords in Parliament.

By this time Charles Babbage was working on plans for a far more complex machine, which he called the Analytical Engine. Indeed, the large-scale electronic digital computers of the twentieth century copy the logical structure of Babbage's Analytical Engine, for which he drew plans in the 1830s. Ada's enthusiasm for this early computer matched Babbage's. Another admirer of Babbage, L. F. Menabrea, wrote an article in French describing the Analytical Engine and its principles of operation. Because Babbage had not written about his machine, this work filled a real need. Ada translated Menabrea's article into English and, in the process, expanded the contents in important ways. Her notes, three times the length of the original article, set down in concrete terms the powers and limitations of the machine.

The work was published, and Babbage, tremendously impressed with Ada's paper, distributed copies to the leading scientists of the time. When Babbage asked why she had not written a separate original article on the subject, she replied that the thought had not occurred to her. To do such a thing seemed out of the question. In fact, even signing her own work brought her great anxiety. Although her paper was clearly the work of an expert, it was highly unusual for any woman—especially a woman of rank—to publish a scientific article. It was even more unusual when the area in question was such an "unfeminine" one as mathematical computation. After much indecision, Ada signed her paper "A. A. L.," using her initials only. It was many years before the actual identity of the author was commonly known.

Ada's paper, in fact, provided the public with an excellent account of the Analytical Engine, an account that Babbage realized was far clearer than any he himself could possibly have written. Babbage had proposed using punched cards for putting data into the Analytical Engine. This process was similar to the ingenious method invented by J. M. Jacquard, who used punched cards to control the sequence of threads in a loom in order to weave fabulous fabric designs. Here Lovelace saw an interesting and lovely analogy between the workings and products of the Analytical Engine and the Jacquard loom. Ada wrote: "We may see most aptly that the Analytical Engine weaves algebraical patterns just as the Jacquard loom weaves flowers and leaves." In her paper, Ada might be said to have predicted computer music a whole century before it was actually produced! She suggested that the computer might be used to compose music, "if the fundamental relations of pitched sounds in the science of harmony and musical composition were susceptible of sufficiently precise formulation."[4]

As it turned out, this paper was the summit of Ada's career. It was never clear why she did not go on, but poor health made it difficult for her to focus on intellectual matters. She wrote to Woronzow Greig: "I am not dropping the thread of Science, Mathematics, & this may probably still be my ultimate vocation. Although it is likely perhaps to have a formidable rival to its being other than just my pastime should I take it seriously with undivided mind to musical composition."[5]

By her thirty-sixth year Ada was diagnosed with cancer of the uterus, one of the most lethal forms of cancer. Lord Lovelace wrote in his journal eleven months before her death at age 37 that Babbage was a constant intellectual companion in whom she found a match for her powerful understanding, and their constant philosophical discussions produced an increased esteem and mutual affection.

By her own wish, she was carried to the old Newstead country, and laid by the father whom she had never known.

In the brief time she lived, Ada Lovelace distinguished herself as an important participant in the early history of modern computers. Many people consider her to be the first to articulate the methodology of computer programming. She used her gifts against tremendous obstacles and showed a spirit that would not be crushed. As to Babbage and the influence of his Analytical Engine, it was never built, though Charles Babbage lived nearly two decades longer. The Menabrea/Lovelace paper remains the sole witness of the power and scope of the ideas of Babbage's Analytical Engine, ideas which lay essentially dormant for another century.

In a similar way, the Lovelace paper remains the sole witness to the power and scope of Ada Lovelace's special genius. Now, a century later, her early contributions to the history of the machines of our own day are gratefully acknowledged. In fact, in the 1980s the computer programming language known as Ada was named in her honor.

Notes

1. Ada Lovelace letter to Charles Babbage. January 12, 1841. British Museum Library, Manuscript 37191, Folder 543.
2. Lovelace Papers 168. 10 November 1845. Bodleian Library, Oxford University.
3. Lovelace Papers 67, Folder 127. 10 January 1844. Bodleian Library, Oxford University.
4. B. V. Bowden. (1953) *Faster Than Thought*. London: Pitman & Sons, p. 369.
5. Somerville Papers 367. Friday, 16 December 1842. Bodleian Library, Oxford University.

Selected Work by Ada Augusta Lovelace

(1961). Sketch of the Analytical Engine invented by Charles Babbage, Esq., by L. F. Menabrea of Turin, officer of the Military Engineers. Translation with extensive notes. Reprinted in Philip Morrison and Emily Morrison, eds., *Charles Babbage and His Calculating Engines* (pp. 225–97). New York: Dover.

Selected Works about Ada Augusta Lovelace

Angluin, Dana. (1976). Lady Lovelace and the Analytical Engine. *Association for Women in Mathematics Newsletter* 5(1), p. 10, and 6(2), pp. 6–8.
Baum, Joan. (1986). *The Calculating Passion of Ada Byron*. Hamden, CT: Archon Books/Shoe String Press.
Bowden, B. V., Ed. (1953). *Faster Than Thought*. London: Pitman and Sons.
Huskey, Velma R., and Huskey, Harry D. (1980). Lady Lovelace and Charles Babbage. *Annals of the History of Computing* 2(4), pp. 299–329.
Kean, David W. (1973). The Countess and the Computer. *Datamation* 19, pp. 60–63.
Moore, Doris L. (1977). *Ada, Countess of Lovelace: Byron's Legitimate Daughter*. New York: Harper & Row.
Moseley, Maboth. (1964). *Irascible Genius: A Life of Charles Babbage, Inventor*. London: Hutchinson.
Neumann, B. H. (1973). Byron's Daughter. *Mathematical Gazette* 57(400), pp. 94–97.
Perl, Teri. (1978). Ada Byron Lovelace. In *Math Equals* (pp. 100–125). Menlo Park, CA: Addison-Wesley.
———. (1993). Ada Lovelace. In *Women and Numbers* (pp. 15–29). San Carlos, CA: Wide World Publishing/Tetra.

Rappaport, Karen. (1987). Augusta Ada Lovelace. In Louise S. Grinstein and Paul
    J. Campbell, Eds., *Women of Mathematics* (pp. 135–39). Westport, CT:
    Greenwood Press.
Stein, Dorothy. (1985). *Ada: A Life and a Legacy*. Cambridge, MA: MIT Press.
Tee, G. J. (1981). The Pioneering Woman Mathematicians. *Mathematical Chronicle*
    10(1–2), pp. 31–56.

TERI PERL

VIVIENNE MALONE-MAYES
(1932–1995)
Birthplace: Texas

Working to make things better for those who followed was a prevalent
theme throughout the life of Vivienne Malone-Mayes. Even though as a
black woman she was denied the opportunity to enroll in classes at Baylor University in 1961, she led the way for others by earning her Ph.D.
in 1966 from the University of Texas and becoming the first black faculty
member at Baylor, man or woman.

Malone-Mayes was one of many black women who were victimized
educationally by segregated schools. She was born on February 10, 1932,
in Waco, Texas; her precollege education took place there in strictly separate and strictly unequal schools. As was common among schools in
the 1930s and 1940s, the "separate" part of the law was rigidly enforced
but the "equal" provision was conveniently ignored. Fortunately Vivienne did receive support to achieve academically and encouragement
to pursue a college education.

At 16 years of age she entered Fisk University, a prestigious black
college in Nashville, Tennessee. As a junior she was undecided about
majoring in mathematics or chemistry, but when she sought a job as a
grader in the mathematics department Dr. Lee Lorch offered her the job
of grading for a freshman-level class in elementary analysis. It was during this time that she developed confidence in her ability to do and
understand mathematics. Her teachers remember her as personable and
outspoken. After earning her B.A., she completed her masters' degree at
Fisk.

Malone-Mayes's philosophy of teaching and love of mathematics was
influenced by significant people throughout her life. As a student at Fisk
University she was personally influenced by **Evelyn Boyd Granville**, one
of the first two black women Ph.D.s in the United States. Granville's
presence and professionalism inspired Malone-Mayes to pursue ad-

Vivienne Malone-Mayes.

vanced degrees in mathematics. Malone-Mayes also credits Lee Lorch's superior teaching skills as important to her successful pursuit of a Ph.D. Lorch was ahead of his time in promoting the rights of all people and in encouraging black women such as Malone-Mayes to pursue a career in mathematics. The idea of promoting blacks, and especially women, to prepare for academic careers was unheard of because there were few teaching appointments in the small number of black colleges. Malone-Mayes said, "In those days, we were counseled to prepare for health professions, the ministry, or public school teaching, the few careers which offered an opportunity for livelihood" (Mayes, 1976, p. 709). Other black women affected her life as well. She pointed out, "In every Black school I've attended there's always been at least one Black woman teacher or professor with whom I could identify as a model I'd like to emulate" (Mayes, 1975, p. 5).

Returning to her hometown, Waco, she chaired the mathematics departments at Paul Quinn College for seven years and at Bishop College for one year before deciding to take graduate mathematics courses to "refresh herself." At these black colleges, as at Fisk, women were the majority in her math classes. This may have been because black women believed that through education they could escape the extremely low-paying jobs designated for black women. Malone-Mayes had the opportunity to be a role model to these black students in the same way that Evelyn Boyd Granville and others had inspired her.

After eight years of teaching she applied to Baylor for graduate courses but was rejected because of the university's segregation policy. She then decided to take summer courses at the University of Texas. Having been educated exclusively at black schools and colleges, Malone-Mayes experienced culture shock at the predominantly white school where she was the only black and only one of two women in her classes. She felt like she was attending school in a vacuum, as she was ignored by the white men in her classes. "At times I felt that I might as well have been taking a correspondence course" (Mayes, 1988, p. 9). She, as well as other black women, wondered if her experiences were primarily due to being black, being a woman, or both.

Even though the social atmosphere was challenging during her first summer at the University of Texas, Malone-Mayes experienced success as a graduate student and believed that she could pursue doctoral studies. After teaching for another year at Bishop College, she decided to become a full-time graduate student. She was denied a teaching assistantship despite her experience and excellence as a teacher. In fact, many opportunities and privileges granted to other graduate students were withheld from Malone-Mayes because she was black. When her adviser and other classmates discussed mathematics over coffee at Hilsberg's café, she was not able to join them because the café would not serve blacks. She pointed out, however, that even after Hilsberg's was required by law to serve blacks, women were seldom included in informal problem-solving sessions. She felt that the lack of interchange with fellow students was a profound hindrance to academic achievement. Although much discrimination was indirect, one instance of direct racism and sexism occurred when a professor prohibited her from enrolling in his class because he refused to teach blacks and, furthermore, believed that the education of women was a waste of taxpayers' money.

Malone-Mayes had an abundance of mathematical talent, but it was her enormous courage and determination that enabled her to become a mathematician. She became the first black woman, and only the second black person, to earn a Ph.D. in mathematics from the University of Texas. She was the fifth black woman in the United States to receive a Ph.D. in mathematics. As she said herself, "It took a faith in scholarship almost beyond measure to endure the stress of earning a Ph.D. degree as a Black, female graduate student" (Mayes, 1988, p. 9).

Malone-Mayes's work in mathematics was in the area of functional analysis, specifically on the properties of functions. In addition, her interests in working with students resulted in papers and presentations involving audio-tutorial approaches to teaching precalculus. While teaching at Baylor in the early 1970s using a self-paced audio-tutorial precalculus program that provided for differences in abilities, backgrounds, and career goals, Malone-Mayes made efforts to identify students who were dissatisfied with the course as early as possible in the semester in order to provide them with the attention they required. The student congress elected her Outstanding Faculty Member of the Year in 1971. Vivienne's professional career in mathematics and the teaching of mathematics was primarily spent at Baylor University, from which she retired in 1994 owing to illness. She died in 1995, leaving a lasting influence.

An active involvement in mathematical organizations was another component of Malone-Mayes's professional work. She was a member of the Board of Directors of the National Association of Mathematics and was the first black person elected to the Executive Committee of the Association of Women in Mathematics. She was elected director-at-large for the Texas section of the Mathematical Association of America, and served as director of the High School Lecture Program for the Texas section.

Her commitment to helping others was also apparent in her community work. She was a member of the Board of Directors for Goodwill Industries, the Board of Directors for Family Counseling and Children, the Texas State Advisory Council for Construction of Community Mental Health Centers, and the Board of Directors of Cerebral Palsy. In addition, she was director of the youth choir and organist at New Hope Baptist Church. At one time she was married to a dentist; they had one daughter, Patsyanne Mayes.

Certainly the civil rights movement and the national emphasis on science education came at the right time for Vivienne Malone-Mayes. She had a positive outlook on life and was willing to take on challenges, saying "I always feel like so many of the things that you think are bad when they're happening can turn into things that are good. It was a blessing, really. If they'd accepted me at Baylor, I would have just taken a few courses and not pursued a doctorate" (Cantwell, 1986, p. 9). Vivienne strongly believed that women should participate in decisions that shape their destiny. As best stated by her colleagues and friends, **Etta Falconer** and Lee Lorch, "With skill, integrity, steadfastness, and love she fought racism and sexism her entire life, never yielding to the pressures or problems which beset her path" (Falconer and Lorch, 1995, p. 9).

Selected Works by Vivienne Malone-Mayes

(1969). Some Steady State Properties of (the integral from 0 to x) f(t)dt/f(x). *Proceedings of the American Mathematical Society* 22, pp. 672–77.
(1975). Black and Female. *Association of Women in Mathematics Newsletter* 5(6), pp. 4–6.
(1976). Lee Lorch at Fisk: A Tribute. *American Mathematical Monthly* 83, pp. 708–11.

(1977). Student Attitudes toward an Audio-Visual Presentation of Pre-Calculus (with L. Brigham and S. Virginia). *Mathematics Teacher* 70, pp. 229–31.
(1988). Untitled. *Association of Women in Mathematics Newsletter* 18(6), pp. 8–10.

Selected Works about Vivienne Malone-Mayes

Cantwell, C. (1986). BU Math Professor's Life Filled with Firsts. *Waco Times-Herald*, February 26; reprinted in *Association of Women in Mathematics Newsletter* 16(4), pp. 8–9.
Falconer, E. Z., and Lorch, L. (1995). Vivienne Malone-Mayes: In Memoriam. *Association of Women in Mathematics Newsletter* 25(6), pp. 8–10.
Kenschaft, P. (1981). Black Women in Mathematics in the United States. *American Mathematics Monthly* 88, pp. 592–604.

JUDITH OLSON and KAY A. WOHLHUTER

DUSA WADDINGTON MCDUFF
(1945–)
Birthplace: Edinburgh, Scotland

Margaret Duse (nicknamed Dusa) Waddington, professor of mathematics at Stony Brook University in New York, is an internationally known geometer. Her appreciation for mathematics began early. When she was only 4 years old, growing up in Edinburgh, Scotland, she remembers her grandfather taking her on his knee and showing her the beauty of the multiplication tables. It wasn't just that he taught her about the magic of the sequence of the nine times table—how the tens place increases as the units decrease—and the pattern of the perfect squares; but somehow he also conveyed the magic and beauty of it all. Little Dusa, nicknamed for her grandmother, decided it must be wonderful to be a mathematician who discovers such beauty.

Her grandfather, Rivers Blanco-White, was on vacation from his own home in England and left an indelible impression on his granddaughter. He was a lawyer who, in typical British fashion, had had an undergraduate major in mathematics. Indeed, he had achieved one of the highest grades in mathematics when he took the final undergraduate examination at Cambridge University. He was a "second Wrangler," which meant that his grade was the second highest in the entire university.

Both of Dusa's parents were successful professionals. Her father was a professor of genetics, and her mother was an architect. It was unusual for any woman to have a career at that time and place, and Dusa's

Dusa Waddington McDuff. Photo courtesy of Dusa Waddington McDuff.

mother didn't tell her two daughters how difficult it was. In fact, Dusa cannot remember any conversations about getting along in a society dominated by men or about how a woman might combine career and personal life.

Dusa was exceedingly well prepared for the entrance examination to St. George's School for Girls, which she attended from age 7 to 16. She remembers being asked to multiply 3 times 4 and answering that she would rather multiply 1534 times 2876. A great fuss was made over the precocious 6-year-old. She remembers liking both the fuss and the intrinsic pleasure of doing the problems. Miss Cobban, the high school "maths" teacher, was one of the most inspiring teachers at St. George's. She was very good at doing and explaining mathematics, but she also saw and conveyed its beauty. In particular Dr. McDuff remembers the moments when her teacher presented and proved how to find the derivative of x^2. She let her star student guess the solution first. Then she made sure the rest of the class was following as she showed the formal proof to the entire group.

Young Dusa was a hardworking, extremely gifted, "goodie-good" girl until her mid-teens. Then, like many teenagers, she wanted more variety in her life. Some of it was provided by David McDuff, who was later to become her husband. Indeed, when she graduated from St. George's she decided not to follow her older sister to Cambridge University, England, on the scholarship she had won because she wanted to remain near David. However, after she received her bachelor's degree from the University of Edinburgh in 1967, she went on to Cambridge as a graduate student. David followed and they were subsequently married.

When students enter Cambridge University as graduate students, they are assigned advisers. George Reid was Dusa's, and he suggested she do research in von Neumann algebras. Her research results were published in the *Annals of Mathematics*, one of the leading mathematics journals in the world. Dusa McDuff was now established as one of the world's most promising young mathematicians. However, she still didn't know how to identify interesting new problems in order to continue functioning as a creative mathematician. Nor was she confident that she could ever do so.

The next few years were a time of uncertainty and isolation, a perfect time to accompany her husband to Moscow so he could study Russian poets. In response to a question on her entry visa asking her to justify her own travel to the Soviet Union, McDuff wrote that she would be working with I. M. Gelfand, the only mathematician—in fact, the only individual—she had heard of in Moscow. This turned out to be fortuitous, since studying under Gelfand was to change the entire way she perceived mathematics.

Gelfand amazed her by combining mathematics and poetry. For example, he said he "saw" hedgehogs in the "bottom row" of a certain mathematical structure called a spectral sequence, meaning that there were many complex novelties there. (Hedgehogs are European animals smaller than rabbits that have spikey spines somewhat like these of porcupines.) Using hedgehogs as a metaphor for mathematical structures tickled the young mathematician's imagination.

After only six months in Moscow, McDuff returned again to a mathematically lonely landscape in England, as she pondered how to stimulate her own mathematical creativity. This state of mind continued during a postdoctoral position at Cambridge University. Here McDuff attended lectures on topology, read books in algebraic topology that Gelfand had suggested, and gave birth to her daughter, Anna. Even at Cambridge, however, she experienced no inspiring mathematical conversations such as those with Gelfand. She continued to feel creatively lost and uncertain.

When she took a job at York University in 1972 she felt desperately busy with pursuing a career, keeping house, and being responsible for a toddler; altogether no time to breathe. She was willing to be the primary breadwinner, since poets make little money, but David was not a dedicated househusband.

During this time McDuff essentially wrote another Ph.D. thesis with Graeme Segal that established the direction of her future research. She subsequently was appointed to a special position at the Massachusetts Institute of Technology that had been created to help increase the number of women faculty there; her husband followed her to the United States. Here she was encouraged to closely reexamine both her mathematics and her life. Her marriage ended when she returned to England.

Subsequent years saw her career see-sawing back and forth between two continents. She worked for two separate semesters at the Institute for Advanced Study in Princeton, New Jersey; returned to a tenured position at the University of Warwick in England; and finally came to the State University of New York at Stony Brook in Long Island, where she is now a full professor. She had come into her own as an independent mathematician, pursuing her own ideas but in continual conversation with other colleagues. In 1988 she gave an Invited Address to the American Mathematical Society; this gave her the visibility that doubtless set the stage for the international honor she was to be awarded in Japan in 1990. Giving an Invited Address at an International Congress of Mathematicians is one of the highest honors a mathematician can receive. Dusa McDuff was thus honored at the Congress that met in Kyoto, Japan, in 1990.

In 1991 Dusa McDuff won the first Ruth Lyttle Satter prize from the American Mathematical Society "for her outstanding work . . . on symplectic geometry." Her interest in this area grew out of her conversations with Gelfand during her visit to Moscow. First working with transformations (changes) that preserve volumes, she decided to continue to look at transformations that preserve symplectic structures, a less well known measure than volume. This led to some truly innovative questions and her ground-breaking answers.

The idea of a symplectic structure arose in the nineteenth century as a way of describing the laws of motion of systems such as the planets circling the sun, a pendulum, or a vibrating string. It is the mathematical structure that underlies the set of equations that describes the movement. Throughout history, research in mathematics and research in physics have tended to stimulate each other. This interaction continues between physics and symplectic geometry, an area of mathematics in which McDuff is a leader. In particular, important equations that describe physical situations (called the Seiberg-Witten equations, after the physicists who developed them in 1994) have had a dramatic effect on symplectic geometry.

Symplectic geometry describes what happens when certain geometric figures are deformed or changed. Indeed, much of mathematics describes how shapes—or the algebraic equations that describe them—change when they are transformed by some motion or process applied to the algebraic equation. For example, we could wonder what happens to a given circle or line if the x-y plane is rotated or stretched in certain ways.

From a symplectic geometer's point of view, a circle is the same as an ellipse of the same area, and a square is the same as a rectangle or even a parallelogram of the same area. Thus in a symplectic transformation or change, these measurements remain the same before and after the transformation.

Mathematicians still do not have a good intuitive feel for what a symplectic structure really is. Of course, there are equations; but by themselves equations do not generate much real human understanding. It is particularly difficult to imagine them in four-dimensional space, where many interesting symplectic structures are studied, but that is what McDuff has been doing. One of her recent papers (written in collaboration with a Canadian mathematician, François Lalonde, and published in the *Annals of Mathematics*) investigates in detail the ways in which a four-dimensional ball can move in four-dimensional symplectic space. McDuff has spent many hours twisting this ball around in her mind until she could move it the way she wanted to.

While investigating these esoteric subjects, McDuff met John Milnor, another outstanding mathematician. He had a permanent post at the Institute for Advanced Study in Princeton, so for years theirs was a weekend relationship—and eventually a weekend marriage. After Thomas was born in 1984, however, Dr. Milnor decided to move to Stony Brook so that the family could live together in the same house. As this biography is written, Dusa's daughter, Anna McDuff, is an undergraduate studying psychology at the University of London.

Dusa McDuff enjoys sharing ideas with other mathematicians and visiting mathematics institutes in many countries. She has given talks not only in Japan but also in the United States, Britain, Switzerland, Germany, France, and Turkey. In 1994 she was elected a fellow of the Royal Society of London, an institution founded in the 1650s. She was the only woman among the forty new fellows to receive that distinction in 1994 and only the second woman mathematician ever to do so, following Dame Mary Cartwright. Joining the Royal Society included using a special pen to sign the parchment pages of the same book signed by Isaac Newton and other British luminaries. In 1995 McDuff was elected a fellow of the American Academy of Arts and Sciences as well.

Mathematical research is generally a highly collaborative activity, often across international borders. Mathematicians have frequently visited each other in faraway places. Now, in the era of electronic mail (e-mail) these long-distance collaborations can take place more easily and frequently. For example, McDuff collaborates closely via e-mail with Lalonde, her colleague in Montreal, Canada. Besides spanning long distances cheaply, electronic communication has other advantages as well. In this case it supports different lifestyles: Lalonde, a nocturnal individual, sometimes works all night and e-mails his results to McDuff, an early riser, for her to download and continue their work.

McDuff considers herself very fortunate to be a thriving mathematician, with over fifty journal articles and two books published. She credits the feminist movement with helping her both emotionally and practically. She believes that opportunities for women are better now; there is more institutional recognition and support for women's needs. Further, the increasing number of women mathematicians suggests that newcomers need not be as isolated as before. However, she recognizes that many problems remain.

Note

The information included in this biography is based in part on an interview conducted by the author.

Selected Works by Dusa Waddington McDuff

(1969). A Countable Infinity of II(sub)1 Factors. *Annals of Mathematics* 90, pp. 361–71.

(1969). Uncountably Many II(sub)1 Factors. *Annals of Mathematics* 90, pp. 372–77.

(1976). Homology Fibrations and the "Group-Completion" Theorem (with G. Segal). *Inventiones Mathematicae* 31, pp. 279–81.

(1987). Examples of Symplectic Structures. *Inventiones Mathematicae* 89, pp. 13–36.

(1995). The Geometry of Symplectic Energy (with F. Lalonde). *Annals of Mathematics* 141(2), pp. 349–71.

Selected Work about Dusa Waddington McDuff

1991 Ruth Lyttle Satter Prize in Mathematics Awarded in San Francisco. *Notices of the American Mathematical Society* 38(3), pp. 185–87.

PATRICIA CLARK KENSCHAFT

MARIE-LOUISE MICHELSOHN
(1941–   )
Birthplace: New York

Marie-Louise Michelsohn is a professor of mathematics and internationally known mathematics scholar; however, early in life she was more

Marie-Louise Michelsohn. Photo courtesy of Marie-Louise Michelsohn.

interested in physics. When she was about 10 years old she saw a movie starring a nuclear physicist. She then began telling everyone who asked that she wanted to be a nuclear physicist when she grew up. This fact has always puzzled Marie-Louise, since she is convinced that she had absolutely no idea what physicists did.

Marie-Louise was born in 1941 in New York City. Until the age of 13 she attended public school on Long Island, New York. Although she was good in arithmetic at school, she was not at all precocious. For example, at the end of the second grade Marie-Louise's father wanted her to learn the multiplication tables, but Marie-Louise resisted, feeling it was just fine to learn them when everyone else did—in the third grade. Her determination to be a physicist lasted for several years. By the eighth grade Marie-Louise had found two books that intrigued her: One was *The Sourcebook on Atomic Energy*, and the other was a book about nuclear physics written for nonscientists by the famous physicist Heisenberg.

When she was in the eighth grade Marie-Louise was selected by competitive examination to attend a special school in the New York City

Public School System, the Bronx High School of Science. Bronx Science draws bright students from all over the city. She recalls working in the mathematics office, to which students who were in the honors math class gravitated. Although the work wasn't particularly interesting, Marie-Louise liked "hanging out" there. Perhaps this was because the other students there had similar interests; or perhaps it was just that she liked her teacher, who was department chair.

Marie-Louise began to believe that she was not learning very much in high school, so she decided to apply to college a year early. She chose the University of Chicago because some members of her family had told her that it had a very strong mathematics department; it also had a reputation as a very interesting place to be a student. These recommendations turned out to be accurate.

Marie-Louise remembers a Modern Algebra class that she took from Saunders Mac Lane, a well-known mathematician, in her very first year at the University of Chicago. Mac Lane's enthusiasm and his vibrancy about what he was teaching was infectious; clearly everything he was talking about was real and alive for him. In all her college mathematics classes, Marie-Louise was very much involved. She asked many questions, answered questions put to the class, and never felt ignored. Her professors encouraged her to be inquisitive and interactive. In fact, she recalls that she got positive feedback from her professors all the time. Subsequently, because of her interest and talent in mathematics, she was encouraged to attend graduate school at the University of Chicago.

One professor, Antoni Zygmund, another well-known mathematician, was particularly inspirational during her undergraduate years and during the beginning of graduate school. He went out of his way to encourage her. For example, a weekly seminar for faculty and graduate students usually dealt with current work in which Professor Zygmund was involved. One week he announced that the following seminar would be about the works of Nina Bari. This was unusual, since Bari's work had been done some decades earlier. Another faculty member told Marie-Louise he had no idea that Bari was a woman; all her work had been signed "N. Bari." He was sure that Zygmund had arranged this lecture just to provide encouragement for Marie-Louise by featuring a suitable role model. She recalls that Zygmund was extraordinary in his sensitivity to such issues long before others thought about them at all.

Indeed, it was Professor Zygmund who pointed out that graduate students learn a great deal from one another and that female students are handicapped by generally being isolated, often being the only woman in a program. Marie-Louise remembers that throughout her school years she always studied by herself, and now she realizes the enormous benefits of studying with others. She encourages her own students to form study groups, because students often learn best by teaching one another and by learning to feel comfortable asking questions about things they don't understand.

At age 21, Michelsohn took on the enormous task of helping the man she loved raise his four young children from a previous marriage. Along with this new and demanding role, Marie-Louise continued with her mathematics. She studied hard and organized her time as well as she could in order to pass her master's examinations. These exams were very difficult—usually about half the students failed. Passing them two months after the children had moved into her apartment gave Marie-Louise a tremendous sense of achievement. She thinks the added pressure of child care made her study harder and learn to be more efficient with her time. However, it took her two years instead of the usual one year to prepare for the next set of examinations: oral Ph.D. qualifying exams. She had to pass these to begin working on her Ph.D. thesis.

Michelsohn's orals were on two topics: analysis and algebraic topology. While preparing for her exams she became very excited about topology and, as a result, changed her specialty to topology, although her original intent had been to specialize in analysis. Topology is the study of shapes and their properties—in particular those properties that remain unchanged even if the shape is stretched and distorted, as long as it is not torn or punctured. To a topologist, a doughnut and a coffee cup are the same.

As time went on Michelsohn began to feel added pressure to spend time with her family rather than at school. She gave birth to her first child in 1968. Unfortunately, the Hong Kong influenza epidemic was at its height, and her baby girl, Didi, was diagnosed with encephalitis (an inflammation of the brain), most likely as a complication of influenza. This caused Didi's brain to be severely stunted as she grew, requiring constant nursing care. Michelsohn gave birth to a second daughter in 1969. There were now eight members in the family. Caring for a family this size was a full-time job, and Michelsohn found herself diverted from her career for the time being.

In the fall of 1971, Professor Mark Mahowald suggested that she get back to work on her Ph.D. as his student. This simplified matters because Michelsohn was living close to Northwestern University, where Mahowald was a professor. Working with him eliminated the problem of traveling to the University of Chicago, where she was technically enrolled. In the following year she made the difficult decision to place her daughter, Didi, in a nursing care facility. It was hard to accept the need to do this and hard to adjust to doing it. For the past three years Michelsohn's whole life had revolved around the care of Didi. However, she finally realized that this sacrifice was not just her own; she had been shortchanging her infant daughter, Michelle, as well.

During the summer Michelsohn made a renewed effort to learn more about homotopy theory, the part of algebraic topology that was Professor Mahowald's area of expertise. In the following fall she made the decision to leave her husband after years of trying to make the marriage work. By January she had moved out on her own with their 3-year-old daughter, Michelle. Michelsohn now began to work on her Ph.D. in earnest and by 1974 had completed her degree.

She recalls walking onto campus one early morning at the University of California at San Diego, where she had taken a position as a visiting assistant professor of mathematics. "Am I really going to be a faculty member here?" She recalls the strange feeling of having leapt from being a graduate student to faculty member. The following year she joined the faculty at the University of California at Berkeley. Two years later she spent a year working at a research institute outside of Paris, l'Institut des Hautes Études Scientifiques. Upon her return she became a member of the faculty at the State University of New York at Stony Brook, where she is now a professor and director of the graduate program.

Professor Michelsohn's achievements include research in complex geometry, characterization of balanced manifolds, Clifford and spinor cohomology, the geometry of spin manifolds and the Dirac operator, Riemannian manifolds of positive scalar curvature, and the theory of algebraic cycles. She has contributed research articles to the *American Journal of Mathematics, Acta Mathematica, Inventiones Mathematicae*, and the *Journal of Differential Geometry*. She has authored a book, *Spin Geometry*.

Over the years Michelsohn has been a visitor at several mathematics research institutes in different parts of the world. She has spent several short periods of time at the Instituto de Matematica Pura e Aplicada in Rio de Janeiro, Brazil; the Research Institute in Mathematical Sciences in Kyoto, Japan; and the Tata Institute in Bombay, India. She has revisited l'Institut des Hautes Études Scientifiques several times.

Michelsohn has also attended international conferences. These are wonderful opportunities to find out what other mathematicians are doing, to learn about new results in mathematics, and to share and get valuable feedback on her own work. Places she has visited—both giving and attending lectures—include Italy, Germany, China, Israel, Canada, and Denmark. All this travel has brought Marie-Louise friends from all parts of the world. It has added a special richness to her life, as she has to the world of mathematics.

Note

The information included in this biography is based on an interview by the author.

Selected Works by Marie-Louise Michelsohn

(1996). Algebraic Cycles and Equivariant Cohomology Theories (with H. B. Lawson Jr. and P. Lima-Filho). *Proceedings of the London Mathematical Society* 73(3), pp. 679–720.

(1993). Algebraic Cycles and Infinite Loop Spaces (with C. P. Boyer, H. B. Lawson Jr., P. Lima-Filho, and B. M. Mann). *Inventiones Mathematicae* 113(2), pp. 373–88.

(1991). Algebraic Cycles and Group Actions (with H. B. Lawson Jr.). *Differential Geometry* (pp. 261–77). *Pitman Monographs Surveys on Pure and Applied Mathematics* 52, Longman, New York.

(1989). *Spin Geometry* (with H. B. Lawson Jr.). Princeton Mathematical Series, Vol. 38. Princeton, NJ: Princeton University Press.

(1984). Choosing a Nice Metric for a Complex Manifold. In *Proceedings of the 1981 Shanghai Symposium on Differential Geometry and Differential Equations* (pp. 227–32). Beijing: Science Press.

(1984). Approximation by Positive Mean Curvature Immersions: Frizzing. (with H. B. Lawson Jr.). *Inventiones Mathematicae* 77(3), pp. 421–26.

DYANNE M. TRACY

CATHLEEN SYNGE MORAWETZ
(1923–)
Birthplace: Toronto, Canada

> My father was a mathematician, so as a very small child, if I was asked what I wanted to be, I would say I wanted to be a mathematician, but I had no idea what that was.
> —Cathleen Morawetz

Cathleen Morawetz, a highly respected mathematician, was born in Canada in 1923 of Irish parents. She was the second of three daughters. Her father, John L. Synge, was a prominent mathematician; her mother, Elizabeth Allen, had studied mathematics as an undergraduate but switched to history on the advice of her brother, who said there was no future in mathematics. Allen had quit college in order to support her husband until he finished school. She never received her own degree, which Cathleen believes she regretted.

Cathleen thinks of her mother as a strong influence. Although she doesn't think her mother was a suffragette, she believes her mother was very interested in women's independence. The attitude of Cathleen's fa-

Cathleen Morawetz. Photo courtesy of Cathleen Morawetz.

ther, however, was that of Mr. Higgins in *Pygmalion*: A woman could do anything a man could do if she would just give up certain things. One could say that the literary tradition is stronger in the family than mathematics; her father's uncle is the notable Irish playwright J. M. Synge.

Cathleen grew up in Toronto, a city in the Canadian province of Ontario. She was diverted from her initial interest in history when a high school teacher, who recognized her mathematical talent, coached her to win a scholarship to the University of Toronto. Here she found herself majoring in mathematics merely because she was good at it. In graduate school she returned again to mathematics after trying electrical engineering and finding she didn't have the talent for it. It has always been her feeling that mathematics was what she fell back on, rather than something she elected to do.

The program at the University of Toronto was very good but highly specialized. Cathleen was required to take almost no courses other than math and physics. Later, when she went on to receive a master's degree at the Massachusetts Institute of Technology (MIT), she remembers being told that she had received an inadequate cultural background in her undergraduate courses, and might be asked to leave.

In 1945, halfway through MIT, Cathleen married Herbert Morawetz, a chemist whom she had met while still in school in Toronto. At the time they were married Herbert was working at a company in New Jersey. Getting his first job had been extremely difficult: Although he was the best student in his class, everywhere Morawetz went he was told, "We don't hire Jews." The job he finally got was through a family friend.

After earning her first graduate degree at MIT, Cathleen joined her husband in New Jersey. At about that time her father mentioned her situation to a colleague at a professional meeting. Richard Courant, a professor at New York University, replied that his own daughter had also just gotten married and interrupted her career. "You can't help *my* daughter—she's in biology—but I *can* help yours." Thus Morawetz set off to the Courant Institute at New York University (NYU). She was initially hired to solder connections on a machine being developed to solve linear equations; later she continued her graduate work in mathematics there.

Cathleen fondly recalls the comfortable atmosphere at the Courant Institute when she interviewed there for the first time. The Institute was a relatively small place that had developed around war work. She was immediately charmed. All the graduate courses there were taught in the evening, and the twenty or so students who were supported on war-related grants and contracts created a lively intellectual atmosphere.

The problems being solved at the Institute during the war had been very concrete—such as studying the effect of a shell hitting a wall. With the end of the war there was a resurgence of interest in more theoretical problems. In many places, as soon as the war was over, grants were discontinued. Professor Courant, however, realized that the future of his group depended on government funding; and he was able to generate new support from the Office of Naval Research. Thus the late 1940s and early 1950s saw a growing group at the Courant Institute. In the stimulating, congenial environment there was a great deal of interaction between faculty and students as well as the many engineers who were taking mathematics classes in the evening. "This was the only place around where you could get good mathematics taught in a way that engineers could start learning and using it. I really felt happy and at home in that group," Cathleen recalls. As a student of Kurt Friedrichs at the Institute, Morawetz became much more ambitious about her own mathematics.

Cathleen and Herbert Morawetz had been married for two years when their first daughter was born; their son was born two years after that.

This was a difficult time for the young couple living in a small apartment, struggling with two children and two dissertation theses. Despite the difficulties, however, both managed to get their doctoral degrees by 1951.

After receiving their Ph.D.s, both Morawetzes returned to Cambridge. Herbert went to the Harvard Medical School as a postdoctoral student; Cathleen returned to MIT, where she worked with C. C. Lin. An excellent mentor, Lin never let her sit around stewing about a problem. If she became stuck on a particular problem, Lin would take it away from her and give her another one. Her first two papers came out of her work at MIT.

Soon thereafter, Courant, visiting Cambridge for an International Mathematics Congress, told her that if she wanted to return to the Institute they would be glad to find her a position there. When her husband was also offered a job in the New York area, the couple happily returned to the city. (Herbert Morawetz has recently retired from his chemistry professorship at Polytechnic University in Brooklyn.)

Cathleen Morawetz works in applications of partial differential equations. One of her main areas concerns applications involving the so-called mixed equations that describe patterns, like the airflow around an airplane just before it becomes supersonic. In the 1950s many aspects of the mathematics of such problems were unknown, and there was controversy about what really happened owing to contradictions with wind tunnel experiments, theory, and so on. Morawetz's later work has involved scattering theory, which has to do with the reflection of linear waves such as electromagnetic or light or sound waves. Her work here has addressed questions about patterns generated by reflection on different objects.

It would be most surprising if Cathleen Morawetz—who now has four children and five grandchildren and who has interacted with students as learners throughout most of her professional life—were not to have opinions about education and current educational issues. Morawetz has long believed in the importance of public schooling. Although she herself initially attended a private school for girls, her parents decided to send the children to public schools in Canada. As a result, Morawetz grew up with a strong sense that this was the right thing to do. However, she is well aware of the problems associated with public education today, including classes that are much too large. She believes that the autonomy of local school boards inhibits the development of uniform standards. After spending several years on the Mayor's Commission for Science and Technology, Morawetz concluded that spending education dollars on teachers' salaries is a more productive approach than spending funds directly on curriculum. Those with just a bachelor's degree in mathematics can do far better in work other than teaching, she believes. Low salaries for teachers make it difficult for those with more extensive mathematics training to remain in teaching. In addition, Morawetz worries that the motivation to go to college is reduced now that college graduates are no longer assured of good jobs when they graduate.

Also the population of mathematics applicants to American graduate schools has changed significantly. Morawetz believes it is difficult to select Americans over Europeans for admission to graduate schools in mathematics when Europeans' credentials are so much better. This disparity may partly be due to the fact that high school lasts longer in some European countries, such as France and Germany. However, even accounting for that factor, Morawetz sees the difference in prior training as striking.

Morawetz has spent her entire professional career, from associate to full professor in 1965, at NYU. In 1978 she became associate director of the Courant Institute; she rose to full directorship in 1984, the first woman to head such a prestigious institute in the United States. Now that she is retired, Morawetz rarely teaches or serves on committees. As immediate past president of the American Mathematical Society, an outstanding honor that placed her at the top of her profession, she travels widely and today remains closely involved with the entire world of mathematics.

Note

The information included in this biography is based in part on an interview conducted in New York City in 1996.

Selected Works by Cathleen Morawetz

(1981). A Formulation for Higher-Dimensional Inverse Problems for the Wave Equation. *Computers and Mathematics with Applications* 7, pp. 319–31.

(1981). *Lectures on Nonlinear Waves and Shocks*. Bombay: Tata Institute of Fundamental Research.

(1982). The Mathematical Approach to the Sonic Barrier. *Bulletin of the American Mathematical Society* 6, pp. 127–45.

(1983). (with G. A. Kriegsmann). The Calculations of an Inverse Potential Problem, *SIAM Journal of Applied Mathematics* 43, pp. 844–54.

(1983). (with A. Bayliss and G. A. Kriegsmann). The Nonlinear Interaction of a Laser Beam with a Plasma Pellet. *Communications on Pure and Applied Mathematics* 36, pp. 399–414.

Selected Works about Cathleen Morawetz

Albers, Don, and Reid, Constance, Interviewers. (1990). Cathleen S. Morawetz. In Donald J. Albers, Gerald L. Alexanderson, and Constance Reid, Eds., *More Mathematical People* (pp. 220–38). Boston: Harcourt Brace Jovanovich.

Cathleen Morawetz, First Woman to Head a Mathematics Institute. (1984). *SIAM News* 17(4), p. 5. Reprinted in *Association for Women in Mathematics Newsletter* 15(1) (January–February 1985), pp. 7–8.

Kolata, Gina Bari. (1979). Cathleen Morawetz: The Mathematics of Waves. *Science* 206, pp. 206–7.

Patterson, James D. (1987). Cathleen Synge Morawetz (1923–   ). In Louise S. Grinstein and Paul J. Campbell, Eds., *Women of Mathematics* (pp. 152–55). Westport, CT: Greenwood Press.

TERI PERL

Emmy Noether
(1882–1935)
Birthplace: Erlangen, Germany

Mathematicians like to honor the great people who have preceded them and who have created structures of power and beauty, as did Emmy Noether. Her work in algebra was groundbreaking; it provided significant new directions for mathematicians. As we honor those greats, we often recall their personal characteristics. A widely circulated wall chart of great mathematicians (ironically entitled "Men of Mathematics") says of Emmy Noether: "rough, and loud . . . all who knew her loved her."

Imagine this woman, Amalie Emmy Noether, in 1931, 49 years old, at the height of her career and working in the Mathematische Institut in Göttingen, Germany. Emmy's students often came to her apartment to share food, conversation, and mathematics. They would take long walks in the beautiful surrounding countryside, talking mathematics and stopping for a picnic or at a café for a bite to eat. Famous mathematicians came for extended stays at the Mathematische Institut, which was considered by many to be the best center for mathematics in the world at that time. Emmy (as she was known by all) spent long hours working out and communicating mathematical theory. The mathematicians around her were the most active and productive at the Institut. She had a stimulating and contented life.

How did she develop an interest in mathematics and become a mathematician? The story begins in Germany at the end of the nineteenth century. Emmy's school education was, by all accounts, rather ordinary. She prepared to be a schoolteacher of the "foreign" languages English and French. However, when she finished her studies for certification the climate for women in mathematics was beginning to improve, and Emmy saw a chance to do what she loved. She immersed herself in

Emmy Noether. Photo courtesy of Stock Montage, Inc.

mathematics and prepared for university work. This was not an easy matter for a woman at the beginning of the twentieth century. At German universities, women could not take classes for official credit. They could only audit classes, and they could audit only by permission of the lecturer—which was not always given. And because teachers usually had low expectations of their female students, even where they were allowed to audit, women often were not ready for the university courses because of the inferior education they had received earlier. Emmy's own academic preparation was probably not quite adequate for the rigors of university-level courses.

Emmy's father, who was a mathematician at Erlangen, supported her interest in mathematics. She began to attend mathematics lectures at the University at Erlangen as an auditor, because women were not allowed to be regular students. Simultaneously she studied for the examination that she would have to pass in order to enter a university. With two more years of study, she passed the required examination and was admitted to the university at Göttingen, but still only as an auditor. In the winter of 1904, at the age of 21, she was able to attend lectures given by the great mathematicians at Göttingen. Finally, when German law was changed to allow women to be regular students in universities, she entered the University at Erlangen with the same rights as male students. Emmy appears to have accepted the constraints of the times. When becoming a language teacher was considered a suitable pursuit, she planned to do that. When it became possible for women to audit courses at Göttingen, she went to Göttingen; and when in 1904 she was able to become a regular student at Erlangen, she went to Erlangen, where her father taught and was engaged in research.

Now, as a regular student, she studied mathematics—her true love—virtually all the time. Her fellow students were nearly all men, doubtless unaccustomed to having a young woman studying alongside them. It would be interesting to know what Emmy experienced in those classes, but she did not record any of her thoughts of that time. With the chance to study mathematics full-time and a few years' hard work she wrote her thesis and was awarded a Ph.D. in mathematics with the highest honors, *summa cum laude*. The year was 1907. Her doctoral thesis, which involved a considerable amount of computation, recorded over 300 of what are called invariants of ternary biquadratic forms.

To get a sense of what her thesis involved, think about a quadratic (degree 2) expression such as $2x^2 + 3xy - 5y^2$. The points (x, y) for which this expression is constant form a two-dimensional curve. Emmy's thesis involved looking at similar expressions that have three variables, instead of just two, and that have degree 4 instead of degree 2. She studied the coefficients of such expressions when the corresponding points were shifted or rotated. Her work was related to theoretical physics in that it became part of the research effort related to developing Einsteinian differential invariants. She later referred to her thesis as "a jungle of formulas."[1]

After she completed her degree, the times hadn't changed all that much for women; Emmy was unable to obtain a paying position. She was only able to assist her father in his teaching and research duties while pursuing her own research interests. These interests still involved a tremendous amount of computation. In fact, her creative mathematical work continued to involve such computations for some time. Although her work was solid and prolific, it was not considered groundbreaking. Gradually, however, she moved to a more abstract approach—indeed, she made the process of abstraction a guiding principle. In doing so, her work became influential. By 1918 she was recognized for the "extreme generality and abstractness of approach that would eventually be seen as her most distinguishing characteristic."[2]

Emmy was invited to Göttingen in 1915 as what is called a *Privatdozent*, with the right to teach but not to be paid! Although petitions were made on her behalf for the university to pay her, those petitions were rejected.

After many years her colleagues recommended that she be made a full professor, but this recommendation was rejected by the faculty as a whole, for many members of the faculty outside mathematics still felt that university teaching and research were inappropriate for a woman.

Emmy was most productive as a mathematician during the tumultuous and eventually catastrophic times in Germany of the 1920s and early 1930s. With massive unemployment, and runaway inflation decreasing the purchasing power of money every day, she considered herself lucky to have a job at all. Her job title and financial position, however, were not in keeping with the respect that those who knew her work accorded her. "[I]n the view of Weyl, Hilbert, and the others [the full mathematics professors at Göttingen], she was right on the level of any of the full professors. Her work was much admired and her influence widespread."[3]

The eminent mathematician Saunders Mac Lane writes about how Noether taught "enthusiastic but obscure courses on group representations and on algebras."[4] Her enthusiasm was so great that she would sometimes hold class, outside the classroom, when there were state holidays! She had a style of lecturing in which she did not make a polished presentation but worked out the details as she lectured. Some students found this exhilarating and stimulating to their own ability to "work mathematics out" (and thereby become productive mathematicians); others were frustrated by the lack of polish. Such courses may have been obscure; but Noether's ideas, novel at the time, became central to mathematical thinking throughout the latter half of the twentieth century.

Noether's name lives on with all graduate students of mathematics who study a mathematical structure called Noetherian rings, named in her honor. (A ring is a mathematical structure, in a branch of mathematics known as abstract algebra, that consists of a set and two operations, all related according to some specific rules. An example of a ring is the collection of integers with the operations of ordinary addition and multiplication.) Israel Kleiner, reviewing the genesis of the abstract ring concept, remarked that Noether (along with Emil Artin) was a master algebraist who transformed the study of structures—such as rings of polynomials and hypercomplex numbers—into powerful, abstract theories.[5]

Emmy Noether's satisfying and mathematically productive career was interrupted by the dramatic rise to power of Hitler: By the simple fact of her being Jewish, she could no longer teach in Germany. In April 1933 her permission to teach was withdrawn by the Prussian Ministry of Science, Art, and Public Education. However, with the help of leaders of the international mathematics community, by October 1933 she was safely in America as a visiting professor at Bryn Mawr College. Along with this position, she often lectured in Princeton at the Flexner Institute (now the Institute for Advanced Study). More important, she was able to talk about mathematics with many of America's leading mathematicians. It seemed that she could now get back to her incredible work, which was highly regarded throughout the United States.

Unfortunately, Noether's active research life was not to continue for long. In 1935, suffering from deteriorating health diagnosed as resulting from a tumor, she underwent seemingly successful surgery; a few hours later she was dead from sudden and mysterious complications. The mathematical world had lost a great leader.

Many gathered following her unexpected death to pay tribute. In a letter to the *New York Times* dated May 5, 1935, Albert Einstein wrote:

> Within the past few days a distinguished mathematician, Professor Emmy Noether . . . died. . . . In the judgment of the most competent living mathematicians, Fraeulein Noether was the most significant creative mathematical genius thus far produced since the higher education of women began. In the realm of algebra . . . she discovered methods which have proved of enormous importance. Her unselfish, significant work . . . was rewarded . . . with a dismissal [by German authorities]. . . . she found in America . . . grateful pupils whose enthusiasm made her last years the happiest and perhaps the most fruitful of her entire career.[6]

Professor Noether is considered to be the preeminent female representative of the community of mathematicians that developed in Europe during the eighteenth and nineteenth centuries. This community consists of people in universities throughout the world who devote their lives to developing new mathematics. They communicate extensively with one another, ask each other questions, try to convince each other of mathematical facts, and encourage others to study ideas that they themselves find interesting. Gradually more and more women are joining this community, inspired by the genius, perseverance, and vitality of the woman who is known to all mathematicians as "Emmy."

Notes

1. Clark Kimberling, "Emmy Noether and Her Influence," in James W. Brewer and Martha K. Smith, eds., *Emmy Noether: A Tribute to Her Life and Work* (New York: Marcel Dekker, 1981), p. 11.

2. Ibid., p. 13.

3. Saunders Mac Lane, "Mathematics at the University of Göttingen, 1931–1933," in James W. Brewer and Martha K. Smith, eds., *Emmy Noether: A Tribute to Her Life and Work* (New York: Marcel Dekker, 1981), p. 70.

4. Saunders Mac Lane, "Mathematics at Göttingen under the Nazis," *Notices of the American Mathematical Society*, October 1995.

5. Israel Kleiner, "The Genesis of the Abstract Ring Concept," *Mathematical Monthly* 103, no. 5 (May 1996): 423.

6. Quoted in Auguste Dick (translated by Heidi Blocher), *Emmy Noether, 1882–1935* (Boston: Birkhäuser-Boston, 1981), pp. 93–94.

Selected Works by Emmy Noether

(1926). Abstrakter aufbau der idealtheorie in algebraischen zahl-und funkthion-skörpern (Abstract structures of ideal theory in algebraic number and function fields). *Mathematische Annalen* 96, pp. 26–61.

(1933). Nichtkommutative algebren (Non-commutative algebras). *Mathematische Zeitschrift* 37, pp. 514–41.

Selected Works about Emmy Noether

Dick, Auguste (translated by Heidi Blocher). (1981). *Emmy Noether, 1882–1935.* Boston: Birkhäuser-Boston.

Kimberling, Clark. (1981). Emmy Noether and Her Influence. In James W. Brewer and Martha K. Smith, Eds., *Emmy Noether: A Tribute to Her Life and Work* (pp. 3–61). New York: Marcel Dekker.

Kleiner, Israel. (1996, May). The Genesis of the Abstract Ring Concept. *Mathematical Monthly* 103(5), p. 423.

Mac Lane, Saunders. (1981). Mathematics at the University of Göttingen 1931–1933. In James W. Brewer and Martha K. Smith, Eds., *Emmy Noether: A Tribute to Her Life and Work* (pp. 65–78). New York: Marcel Dekker.

———. (1995, October). Mathematics at Göttingen under the Nazis. *Notices of the American Mathematical Society.*

JAMES MORROW

KAREN PARSHALL
(1955–   )
Birthplace: Virginia

Karen Parshall, Ph.D., holds a joint appointment in the mathematics and history departments at the University of Virginia. Her pathway to this career began in a graduate French Literature course at the University of Virginia in 1976 during her senior year. The professor who taught the course was visiting from France and was, in fact, a historian of science rather than a literary scholar. In his class, Parshall became aware of an entire field she had never heard of before: the history of science.

Karen Parshall. Photo courtesy of Karen Parshall.

Parshall, born Karen Virginia Hunger in Virginia in 1955, was a talented student who liked to study and now thinks that she was probably viewed as a "total nerd." Her mother was an elementary school teacher in Virginia Beach, and her father worked for the government. Her only sister, trained as a nurse, now works in a family business.

Karen was interested in French from an early age. She was influenced by her adventurous grandmother who had come to the United States from France as a young woman, making her way as a translator, first in London and finally arriving in Virginia Beach. Her grandmother stimulated Karen's enthusiam for the French language. Attending Colonial High School in Virginia Beach was a wonderful experience for Karen. She enjoyed all her classes and especially appreciated her English teacher, who taught her how to write. She kept to herself and spent a great deal of time in the library. She was strongly interested in science as well.

Karen considered various colleges, initially being most interested in studying genetics. She choose the University of Virginia (which had begun admitting women only a few years earlier) because it seemed to offer the best choices. There she pursued her interest in science by taking astronomy, physics, and mathematics classes. She majored in French and mathematics, was elected to Phi Beta Kappa, and graduated in 1977 with highest distinction. While taking the previously mentioned French literature course during her senior year, she began to shape her career goals around a combined interest in both history and mathematics by pursuing a higher-level degree in the history of science. She discussed her interest with the visiting professor and was urged to study the history of science in graduate school.

Awarded a Governor's Fellowship for graduate school at the University of Virginia, Karen took the first step toward her career goal by earning a master's degree in mathematics in 1978. Finding a graduate school for her doctoral degree meant looking for a school with both a mathematics and a history of science department. The University of Chicago had both, as well as a sympathetic and friendly science historian, Allen G. Debus, who became her adviser. Karen Parshall felt Professor Debus was vital to her work, although his area of expertise is the sixteenth century and her own interest lies in nineteenth-century American mathematics. A Noyes Fellow at the university in 1979–1980, Karen was also fortunate to have as a mathematics adviser the late I. N. Herstein. She received her Ph.D. in history in 1982; her dissertation was entitled *The Contributions of J.H.M. Wedderburn to the Theory of Algebras*.

Parshall's research in the history of mathematics concentrates on Lie groups and algebraic groups, which is also the field of study pursued by her husband, Brian. She feels fortunate to be able to talk in depth about mathematics, which they do "all the time," since they share a common field. Both Karen and Brian are faculty members at the University of Virginia; Brian holds a chair in mathematics and Karen holds a joint appointment in the history and mathematics departments. They travel often to professional meetings, giving talks abroad more than once a year. As they travel, they enjoy good food and sample local wines. They delight in their interactions with foreign hosts, who make sure that they sample food and culture they would never be able to find on their own. Parshall was able to connect with her family roots when she taught in Paris for a semester in 1985, holding the position of Foreign Director of Studies in the History of Science at l'École des Hautes Études en Sciences Sociales.

Parshall's work, both her talks and published work, has received wide acclaim. She has published two books and numerous scholarly articles, and has been invited to give several major addresses. In August 1994 she was an invited speaker on the history of mathematics at the International Congress of Mathematics in Zurich, where she gave a talk entitled "Mathematics in National Contexts (1875–1900)." She has enjoyed work with her own doctoral students, Della Dumbaugh and Patti Wilger, with whom she has coauthored papers. She is happy to be advising students in the next generation of researchers in the history of science.

Note

The information included in this biography is based in part on an interview.

Selected Works by Karen Parshall

(1982). Varieties as Independent Species: Darwin's Numerical Analysis. *Journal of the History of Biology* 15 (Summer), pp. 191–214.

(1983). In Search of the Finite Division Algebra Theorem and Beyond: Joseph H. M. Wedderburn, Leonard E. Dickson, and Oswald Veblen. *Archives Internationales d'Histoires des Sciences* 35 (December), pp. 274–99.

(1984). E. H. Moore and the Founding of a Mathematical Community in America: 1892–1902. *Annals of Science* 41, pp. 313–33.

(1985). Joseph H. M. Wedderburn and the Structure Theory of Algebras. *Archive for History of Exact Sciences* 32, pp. 223–349.

(1988). The Art of Algebra from Al-Khwarizmi to Viäte: A Study of Natural Selection of Ideas. *History of Science* 26, pp. 129–64.

(1989). (with David E. Rowe). American Mathematics Comes of Age: 1875–1900. In Peter Duren et al., Eds., *A Century of Mathematics in America, Part III* (pp. 1–24). Providence, RI: American Mathematical Society.

(1990). A Century-Old Snapshot of American Mathematics. *Mathematical Intelligencer* 12(3), pp. 7–11.

(1991). A Study in Group Theory: Leonard Eugene Dickson's Linear Groups. *Mathematical Intelligencer* 13(1), pp. 7–11.

(1993). (with David E. Rowe). Embedded in the Culture: Mathematics at the World's Columbian Exposition. *Mathematical Intelligencer* 15(2), pp. 40–45.

(1994). (with David E. Rowe). *The Emergence of the American Mathematical Research Community (1876–1900): James Joseph Sylvester, Felix Klein, Eliakim Hastings Moore.* Providence: American Mathematical Society; London: London Mathematical Society.

(1994). (with Della Dumbaugh Fenster). Women in the American Mathematical Research Community: 1891–1906. In Eberhard Knobloch and David E. Rowe, Eds., *The History of Modern Mathematics* (Vol. 3, pp. 229–61). Boston: Academic Press.

(1995). Mathematics in National Contexts (1875–1900): An International Overview. In *Proceedings of the International Congress of Mathematics* (pp. 1581–91). Zurich/Basel/Boston/Berlin: Birkhäuser Verlag.

(1996). (with Paul Theerman, Eds.). *Experiencing Nature: Proceedings of a Conference in Honor of Allen G. Debus.* Boston/Dordrecht: Kluwer.

(1996). How We Got Where We Are: An International Overview of Mathematics in National Contexts 1875–1900. *Notices of the American Mathematical Society* 43 (March), pp. 287–96.

FLORENCE FASANELLI

BERNADETTE PERRIN-RIOU
(1955–   )
Birthplace: Ardèche, France

From her office Bernadette Perrin-Riou, professor of mathematics, looks out onto a restful scene of trees, bushes, and birds, which pleases her as a nature lover and hiker. Her office is located at one of the campuses of the University of Paris-Sud (South) in a small suburb of Paris called Orsay. The uphill walk to the campus from the train station passes through lovely grounds, perhaps conducive to the contemplation in which research mathematicians like to engage.

Perrin-Riou was born in 1955 in Ardèche, France, the same town in which her parents had been born. The family subsequently moved to Neuilly-sur-Seine, where she was raised along with her two sisters. Her mother is a professor of physics and her father is a chemist; this professional orientation apparently has had a profound influence on their three daughters—both of Perrin-Riou's sisters are physicists. Although Perrin-Riou was a serious and talented student in all areas throughout school, it was not until she had a young, enthusiastic mathematics teacher in *lycée* (secondary school) that she began to have more than a passing interest in the subject.

She entered l'École Normale Supériure de Jeunes Filles (a women's college) in 1974. Her class was very small, consisting of only twenty other women with whom she took all her classes. The small-scale, personal atmosphere was well suited to Perrin-Riou, and she found that she liked to delve deeply into subjects. The spark of interest in mathematics she had experienced in *lycée* was ignited, and she began to specialize in it. She completed her undergraduate work in 1977, and the next year obtained a research assistantship at the Pierre and Marie Curie University in Paris.

While there, she began work on advanced mathematics research with Georges Poitou, for which she received an advanced degree from the University of Paris-Sud in 1979. As she completed more work in the area of theoretical mathematics, she became increasingly aware of both her talent and her deep interest in mathematical research. She was encouraged to complete a doctoral degree in mathematics at the Pierre and Marie Curie University and did so, studying with John Coates. Perrin-Riou obtained her doctorate in 1983 and became an assistant professor there during the summer. In the fall of 1983 she was invited to spend a

Bernadette Perrin-Riou. Photo courtesy of Charlene Morrow.

year as a visiting professor at Harvard University. She had never been to the United States and was quite excited about the opportunity to exchange ideas with a new community of mathematicians.

Although she enjoyed the intellectual interchange at Harvard, she found that splitting her time between work and family was difficult. Her husband, also a mathematician, and her 18-month-old son accompanied her on this trip, and the demands of family life left little time to socialize. The constant need to speak and work in English caused further stress. At the end of the year she was happy to return to France, continuing her research at Pierre and Marie Curie University. In 1987 she had another opportunity to work in the United States for a month at the Mathematical and Sciences Research Institute (MSRI) in Berkeley, California.

In 1987 Perrin-Riou began teaching at the University of Paris, Paris 6, a post that she held until 1994 while continuing her mathematical research. She moved from the rank of assistant professor to professor. Also during this time she and her husband had two more sons, born in 1985 and 1989. (Her husband teaches mathematics at a different branch of the university, Paris 7.) Although her work occupies a great deal of her time, family and other interests are also very important to her. For instance, each year she spends a month hiking with her husband and sons in the Alps. She also enjoys weaving and theater.

Although Perrin-Riou enjoyed her teaching experience, it was very time consuming and made it difficult to continue her mathematical research, which she did remarkably well nonetheless. In 1994 she obtained her present position at the University of Paris-Sud in Orsay. This position is almost exclusively a research position. Although she still teaches an occasional course and likes the contact with students, she is freed from the constant time demands of teaching. Research posts in mathematics are rare, and her ability to obtain such a post speaks to her accomplishments. She occasionally collaborates with colleagues, but mainly she likes to do research alone. She does enjoy the collegiality and exchange of ideas at meetings. She is known internationally for her work and is regularly invited to speak at mathematics conferences.

Perrin-Riou's research is in the area of number theory. She does not like to use what she calls "big theorems," but instead prefers the quest for a simple, elegant proof. Her emphasis is on understanding—she likes to discover how and why things work in a certain way. Another aspect of her work that is particularly meaningful to her is discovering how different things in mathematics are linked: for example, finding connections between the complex numbers and algebra, or between the areas of algebra and geometry.

Perrin-Riou's specialty is "p-adic functions," which, she says with an apologetic smile, is *very* abstract. The study of p-adic functions involves the sophisticated and complex use of functions of special numbers that are constructed using the prime numbers in order to gain insight into the way functions operate in other number systems. The "p" in the word "p-adic" stands for any prime number, so that, for example, there are 2-adic, 3-adic, and 5-adic functions. These functions are different from the functions commonly studied in school. Instead of having the real numbers as input and output, they take special p-adic numbers as input and output. One reason for studying these functions is to put together all the information from each prime number and from the real numbers to say something about the rational numbers. The study of p-adic functions is a newly emerging approach for understanding some old, unsolved problems and thinking about number systems in new ways. The tools of Perrin-Riou's trade are paper and pencil or chalk. She says she only uses the computer for word processing and e-mail.

Perrin-Riou is a soft-spoken and pensive woman, which belies the stature she has attained in her area of research—especially at such a young age. At least professionally, she seems to lead a calm and contemplative existence, working steadily on her quest for mathematical knowledge.

Note

This biography was based on an interview that was conducted in Orsay, France, in March 1995.

Selected Works by Bernadette Perrin-Riou

(1988). *p*-adic *L*-functions Associated to a Modular Form and an Imaginary Quadratic Field. *Journal of the London Mathematical Society* 38, pp. 1–32.

(1989). (with John Coates). On *p*-adic *L*-functions Attached to Motives over **Q**. *Algebraic Number Theory*, pp. 23–54, in *Advanced Studies in Pure Mathematics*, Vol. 17. Boston: Academic Press.

(1989). Variation of the *p*-adic *L*-function under Isogeny. *Algebraic Number Theory*, pp. 347–58, in *Advanced Studies in Pure Mathematics*, Vol. 17. Boston: Academic Press.

(1992). Théorie d'Iwasawa et hauteurs *p*-adiques [Iwasawa theory and *p*-adic heights]. *Inventiones Mathematicae* 109, 137–185.

(1994). Théorie d'Iwasawa des représentations *p*-adiques sur un corps local [Iwasawa theory of *p*-adic representations over a local field]. *Inventiones Mathematicae* 115(1), 81–161.

(1994). La fonction *L p*-adique de Kubota-Leopoldt [The Kubota-Leopoldt *p*-adic *L*-function]. *Arithmetic geometry*, pp. 65–93, *Contemporary Mathematics* 174, American Mathematical Society, Providence, RI.

(1995). *p*-adic *L*-functions. In *Proceedings of the International Congress of Mathematicians* (Vol. 1, no. 2, pp. 400–410). Basel: Birkhäuser.

CHARLENE MORROW

HARRIET POLLATSEK
(1942–   )
Birthplace: Michigan

Harriet Pollatsek, professor of mathematics at Mount Holyoke College, has served as an important role model for young women for the past three decades. She has combined a commitment to mathematical research with a devotion to teaching that has helped many generations of students envision an appealing life in mathematics.

Pollatsek was born Harriet Katcher on May 2, 1942, in Detroit, Michigan, the oldest of three daughters born to first-generation American parents. Her paternal grandparents had come to the United States from Ukraine in the early 1900s as part of the Jewish emigration from Eastern Europe. They originally settled in North Dakota and Saskatchewan as homestead farmers but eventually moved to Detroit, where her maternal

Harriet Pollatsek. Photo courtesy of Elsa Laughlin.

grandparents lived, also having come from Eastern Europe. Harriet attended Oak Park High School in Detroit; although she was an excellent student, she actively disliked arithmetic in grade school. Her attitude began to change when she was assigned to a pre-algebra class with an energetic, female teacher. The novelty of this class was not only in the teacher (a feisty New Yorker) but in the beauty of mathematics that began to emerge through her teaching. Harriet was fortunate to have this same teacher in the tenth through twelfth grades; consequently her outlook on mathematics became increasingly positive throughout high school.

In 1959 Harriet, the first in her family to attend college, was admitted to the Honors Program at the University of Michigan. She had originally planned to major in architecture—after all, she had been the first woman in her high school to take a mechanical drawing class, and she had a strong interest in drawing and painting—but on reflection she realized that mathematics had a much stronger appeal. She registered for honors calculus and had the good fortune of being assigned to Professor Edwin Moise, a well-known topologist who truly cared about teaching this class. In fact, he thought that the forty registered students were too many for one class, so he split the class in half and taught two sections. In this class the seeds of attraction to mathematics that were planted by Harriet's high school teacher began to germinate and grow.

Her sophomore year, however, did not go smoothly. The group of mathematics majors had dwindled to twenty-five, with only two women, and was further diminished as a result of the attitude of a professor who thought that twenty-five majors in one class were too many. By the end of her sophomore year Harriet was the lone woman in a group of fifteen majors. Fortunately there were also very good professors, and she continued to enjoy her mathematics studies—especially algebra, which she chose as her area of emphasis. She earned a B.A. in mathematics in 1963.

After graduation Harriet explored the idea of working in industry, but through job interviews she discovered that she was not at all comfortable in this atmosphere. She decided to stay on at Michigan in the doctoral program in mathematics to study algebra, earning her Ph.D. in 1967. Reflecting on graduate school, she says that she did not experience overt gender discrimination, but she was not pushed or challenged. The only mistreatment was being treated "too nicely." She remembers that she survived the frustrations by being determined not to confirm the stereotypes of women as unable to do advanced mathematics.

One important factor in her decision to stay on at Michigan was that she had met Sandy Pollatsek, her future husband, who was already in a doctoral program at Michigan in mathematical psychology. After graduating in 1967, Harriet taught at Western Michigan University in Kalamazoo and the University of Toledo while waiting for Sandy to finish his degree, which he did in 1969. The Pollatseks moved to Amherst, Massachusetts, in 1969 to take teaching positions at the University of Massachusetts. Harriet had also been offered a three-semester position at Mount Holyoke College to follow her semester of teaching at the University of Massachusetts. By the time she arrived in 1970 for the temporary position at Mount Holyoke, the person she was replacing (Fred Kiokemeister, a well-known calculus textbook author) had died. Consequently she was offered a tenure track position instead of a temporary position; she earned tenure in 1974. She was honored in 1990 by being named the Julia and Sarah Ann Adams Professor of Science at Mount Holyoke College. On three sabbatical leaves she has been a visiting professor at the University of Oregon.

Pollatsek describes herself as a Platonist, that is, someone who delights in abstraction as a method for tying things together. She starts with things that appear to be very different, looks for and defines their qualities, then uses these qualities to explore connections among the original objects. Her particular area of research is in Lie (pronounced "lee") theory, a system developed in the nineteenth century for examining symmetry groups of differential equations. Although Lie theory was initially developed for a very specific mathematical purpose, it has proved useful in making discoveries in many areas. One aspect of her work that particularly appeals to Harriet is the puzzle-playing approach. Her sense of being on a quest for understanding motivates her to delve into solving problems and persist for long periods of time.

Although she had been working in abstract areas of mathematics, her more recent work has moved her closer to real-world applications. In 1990 Pollatsek heard a talk by John Dillon, a mathematician at the National Security Agency, that turned her attention toward difference sets—an area that is closely related to coding theory, in particular error-correcting codes. In developing an error-correcting system, it is essential that the intended "codewords" be as different from each other as possible, so that the presence of errors is less likely to confuse the receiver. Arranging the codewords very symmetrically among the set of all words that can possibly be received accomplishes this goal very efficiently. These codes are particularly essential in computer and satellite systems. Pollatsek's current research has brought her back in contact with a colleague from her graduate school days, Robert Liebler (now at Colorado State University), with whom she finds it very helpful to explore research problems.

Mathematical research is only one important aspect of Pollatsek's busy professional life. She is part of a team of faculty from Mount Holyoke, Smith, Hampshire, and Amherst Colleges that has taken a leadership role in developing new approaches in teaching calculus to college students. Their approach, called Calculus in Context, embeds calculus concepts in specific questions in epidemiology, biology, physics, and environmental science, then moves to more abstract generalizations of the concrete ideas studied. Some of the work is done on computers, thereby enabling students to do more sophisticated analyses earlier in their studies. Her devotion to restructuring a course that has turned so many students away from mathematics comes as no surprise to her colleagues and students, who know her as a dedicated and effective teacher. In addition to her academic-year courses, she has worked on mathematical research with undergraduates during the summer under the auspices of a program funded by the National Science Foundation.

Pollatsek has definite views on teaching. Although she is recognized as a very able mathematician, she works at giving up the role of "classroom oracle," a transition she says is difficult for many teachers. Instead she delights in giving students responsibility for their learning, and in seeing them become successful and empowered. She knows she has succeeded when a student is willing to face a complex problem and show confidence in being able to solve it. She also has definite views of the environment in which she teaches. The impact of being at a small liberal arts college and a women's college, an environment she had not experienced before coming to Mount Holyoke, has become more apparent to Pollatsek as she participates in professional meetings and does other work off campus. She has noticed that in most environments a woman is far less likely than her male colleague to be automatically viewed as a serious scholar. These experiences have led her to become a strong advocate for women's colleges.

In addition to her teaching and research, Pollatsek is well known at Mount Holyoke for her community service. She is often appointed to important committees and turned to for sage advice; she was dean of studies from 1977 to 1980. She is respected for her thoughtful, caring, and insightful contributions to the college and is a major contributor to the mathematics department, which was recently named by the Mathematical Association of America as one of twenty exemplary undergraduate mathematics departments in the United States—one of only three liberal arts colleges represented.

Family is an important part of Pollatsek's life. Harriet and Sandy have two children, now grown. (Their daughter works in New York City as a theater costume designer and their son works for a small computer game company in Minnesota.) Harriet is still an avid reader, having been one course shy of an English major in college. She is active in her community outside of the college, where she has participated in antiwar protests, been a contributor to public education in western Massachusetts, and run for Town Meetings in her hometown of Amherst, Massachusetts. To relax, she likes to paint and draw as well as listen to music.

Note

The information included in this biography is based on an interview conducted at Mount Holyoke College, South Hadley, Massachusetts in 1996.

Selected Works by Harriet Pollatsek

(1974). First Cohomology Groups of Some Orthogonal Groups. *Journal of Algebra*, 28, pp. 477–83.

(1976). Irreducible Groups Generated by Transvections over Finite Fields of Characteristic Two. *Journal of Algebra*, 39 pp. 328–33.

(1990). Case Studies in Quantitative Reasoning (with R. Schwartz). *Sloan New Liberal Arts Program Extended Syllabi Series*. Stony Brook, NY: Research Foundation of SUNY Stony Brook.

(1992). Rates of Change: Modeling Population and Resources (with Eva Paus). *Sloan New Liberal Arts Program Monograph Series*. Stony Brook, NY: SUNY Stony Brook.

(1995). *Calculus in Context* (with J. Callahan, D. Cox, K. Hoffman, D. O'Shea, and L. Senechal). New York: W. H. Freeman.

(1995). Difference Sets in Groups of Order 4p⁴. In *Proceedings of the Ohio State Mathematical Research Institute*. Hawthorne, NY: Walter de Gruyter Verlag.

(1997). *Laboratories in Mathematical Experimentation: A Bridge to Higher Mathematics* (with J. W. Bruce et al.) New York: Springer Verlag.

CHARLENE MORROW

CHERYL PRAEGER

(1948–)

Birthplace: Queensland, Australia

Cheryl Praeger describes herself as someone who goes out and solves other people's problems, and she does so with infectious enthusiasm. She thrives on being in contact with colleagues, both mathematicians and other professionals, and her work has been shaped by the kinds of mathematical problems she has found within the many contexts offered by other people's problems. Therefore it is not surprising that she has developed an international set of colleagues, particularly in Southeast Asia. Her personal journey has taken her from the tiny Humpy Bong State School, just north of Brisbane, where she began her schooling, to becoming only the second woman to be appointed full professor of mathematics in Australia.

Praeger was born on September 7, 1948, in Towoomba, Queensland, about 100 miles from Brisbane, in northern Australia. Her father worked for a commercial bank, and the family (including two younger brothers) moved several times from one small town to another. Although both her parents grew up poor in Brisbane and had to leave school early to work, they placed a high value on schooling. Her mother's dream was that her children would attend the university. When Cheryl was still in grammar school, her father decided to embark on a career change. He went back to school to become trained as a chiropractor. When she was 14 years old, Praeger's family moved to Brisbane so her father could open a chiropractic office. Living in a city was a very different experience, and her schooling experience changed dramatically as well. In the country she had begun high school at a small coeducational school where there were nine girls and eighteen boys in her class and a great deal of pressure not to excel. Her first-semester grades had been 20 percent higher than those of any of the other students, and Praeger had worked hard to conceal

Cheryl Praeger. Photo courtesy of Cheryl
Praeger.

this fact. In fact, her achievement was so socially unacceptable that she
actually made an effort to get lower grades. She was on a path of trying
to fit in and be average. When the family moved to the city, she was
accepted to attend Brisbane Girls Grammar School. Because this was a
special opportunity in that money was in short supply, and because students were expected to achieve, she began to work hard. For the first
time she felt free to do as well as she could.

As she progressed through school Praeger felt attracted to mathematics, but she received no specific encouragement and, furthermore, felt
intimidated by examinations. During high school she received vocational
advice from a government agency that steered her away from mathematics. Results from a vocational test advised her to be a nurse or
teacher. When Praeger told the counselor that she wanted to do mathematics, she was told that women can't pass "maths" (the nickname for
mathematics in many parts of the world). Fortunately her mother was
an able advocate, pushing for her to attend university and seeking out
appropriate advice about courses. At the same time her mother encouraged her to continue her musical training (she was becoming an accom-

plished pianist) so that she would have an option for financial independence. Praeger knew that she did not want to go into engineering because there was not enough math in it, but she had no idea what career paths were open to a person with a degree in mathematics.

Finally, in high school she entered a mathematics contest for all of Queensland and tied for first place. She took this as a sign; she didn't know where she was heading with it, but she knew that she passionately wanted to study mathematics. Following high school graduation she attended the University of Queensland, where she studied both mathematics and physics. She realized that the academic environment would have few women in it when, after the first exam, her college honors class went from eighty students, including ten women, to thirty men and three women. Between her third and fourth years she was awarded a Vacation Scholarship and went to the Australian National University for the summer. Here she studied with Bernard Neumann and finally was able to see what mathematicians really do. During this internship she attended a two-week series of daily lectures on category theory by Saunders Mac Lane. She was electrified by the ideas she heard, which she thought "were going to unify all of math." It was at this point that she chose mathematics over physics. She completed her undergraduate work at Queensland, earning several top honors. In 1970 she received a three-year Commonwealth Scholarship to study at Oxford. Praeger notes that at this point in her life she almost chose to get married, but she is glad that she stayed on the school track instead.

Praeger did travel to England to attend Oxford, where she earned a master's degree in science in 1972 and a doctorate in 1974. She returned home to take up a position as a research fellow in Bernard Neumann's department at the Australian National University. Here she met her husband-to-be, John Henstridge, who is a mathematical statistician. Soon there after she was offered a visiting professorship at the University of Virginia in the United States. She found it both exhilarating to be in a new environment and very difficult to be so far away from home. While she was in Virginia there were terrible floods in northern Australia that affected her parents' home, and she was unable to help.

She married John Henstridge in 1975. In 1976 both she and her husband obtained university positions in Perth in western Australia, and she began teaching at the University of Western Australia. For the first several years she was a lecturer in the mathematics department. (Her husband, in the meantime, left the university to establish a statistical consulting business.) In her quest to expand her work in group theory, she established collaborative working relationships with other mathematicians. Her work has become technically complex, applying deep and powerful theory about finite groups to explain the structure of many mathematical and physical systems. During this time she was also offered visiting professorships in Cambridge, England, and Tel Aviv, Israel. In 1977 she fought for and won permanent job status, rather than continuing to hold temporary replacement positions. She and her husband were also busy raising their two sons, James, born in 1979, and Timothy, born in 1982. Although she loves to spend time with her family, she continued to work full-time during these years.

In 1982 Praeger was promoted to senior lecturer, and in 1983 she was awarded a professor's chair—the second woman in Australia ever to receive such a position in mathematics (the first was Hanna Neumann, who died in 1971). There are now five tenured women professors of mathematics in Australia. Praeger currently serves as dean of postgraduate research studies, as well as continuing on the faculty in the mathematics department.

Praeger has committed her energies not only to mathematical research—with two books and over 150 research papers published—but to improving mathematics education for all students, sharing her expertise with a more general audience, and fostering the inclusion of women in mathematics. She has given talks on a wide variety of topics, including "Why Don't Girls Do Mathematics?," "Research, a Personal Reflection," "Pure and Applied Brain Power," and "The Mathematics Curriculum and Teaching Program." She has served on numerous local and national committees concerned with improving mathematics education and the status of girls and women. Praeger served as president of the Australian Mathematical Society from 1992 to 1994, the only woman thus far to serve in that office. She has supervised many undergraduate and graduate students' work in mathematics, including the direct supervision of nine Ph.D. dissertations. Praeger is currently the director of her husband's consulting business as well.

In her own mathematics work Praeger has focused on group theory, in particular, permutation groups. Group theory is a powerful tool in describing symmetry and classifying systems according to their symmetries. Examples of systems that can have different kinds of symmetries include wallpaper, crystals, and chemical compounds. When a mathematician develops abstract ways to describe symmetry groups, she can notice groups that fit into her system but have not yet been noticed in the "real world." The mathematician can then predict things that might exist but have not yet been discovered. Scientists can look for new things based on the abstract system that has been developed. In this way mathematics and science work together in making new discoveries. Praeger says that she is constantly amazed at the incredible number of different patterns or structures that arise having a relatively small size. In May 1996 she was honored for her work in mathematics by being elected to the Australian Academy of Science, the only woman out of a group of twelve (and only one of two mathematicians).

Finding patterns everywhere that can be described mathematically is a constant joy to Praeger. It is an added bonus when abstract mathematical ideas turn out to have useful applications in the real world. She has developed a workshop for grade school students that uses powerful mathematical ideas to describe traditional weaving patterns, and she has had great fun in leading some of these workshops herself. She is connected to people ouside of mathematics in many other ways as well. Although she never pursued a professional career in music, she has stayed in close touch with those early interests by serving as an organist for her church, where she has also served as a church elder. She also enjoys hiking, cycling, spinning wool, and sailing.

Note

The information included in this biography is based on an interview conducted in Newark, New Jersey in June 1995 by the author.

Selected Works by Cheryl Praeger

(1982). (with P. Schultz, and R. P. Sullivan, Eds.). *Algebraic structures and their applications, Lecture notes in Pure and Applied Mathematics*, Vol. 74, Marcel Dekker.

(1987). Mathematics and weaving: I. Fabrics and how they hang together. *Function* 9, Part 4, 7–10. (Reprinted in *Matimyas Mat.* 11, (1987) No. 2, 5–9.

(1987). Mathematics and weaving: II. Setting up the loom and factorizing matrices. *Function* 9, Part 5, 12–17.

(1994). (with A. A. Miller). Non-Cayley, vertex transitive graphs of order twice the product of two distinct odd primes, *Journal of Algebraic Combinatorics* 3, 77–111.

(1994). (with Wujie Shi). A characterisation of certain finite alternating and symmetric groups. *Communications in Algebra* 22(5), 1507–1530.

(1994). (with A. Gardiner). Transitive permutation groups with bounded movement. *Journal of Algebra* 168, 798–803.

(1995). (with C. Nilrat). Balanced Directed Cycle Designs Based on Cyclic Groups. *Journal of the Australian Mathematical Society* A (58), pp. 1–9.

(1995). (with A. Zalesskii). Orbit Lengths of Permutation Groups, and Group Rings of Locally-Finite Simple Groups of Alternating Type. *Proceedings of the London Mathematical Society* 3(70), pp. 313–35.

(1997). (with L. H. Soicher). Low Rank Representations and Graphs for Sporadic Groups. In *Australian Mathematical Society Lecture Note Series* (Vol. 8). Cambridge: Cambridge University Press.

CHARLENE MORROW

MINA SPIEGEL REES
(1902–)
Birthplace: New York

One of the outstanding achievements of Mina Spiegel Rees is that she created an environment in which great things could be accomplished, both by herself and by others. Referring to her work as an administrator of programs supporting mathematical research, a colleague said in 1962, "Through her personal imagination, initiative, and judgment, as well as her indefatigable leadership in rousing this country's mathematical community . . . she has contributed perhaps more than any other single person to the scope and wealth of present day mathematical research activity in the United States."[1]

Mina's family moved to the Bronx section of New York City when she was 2 years old. Her family did not have a great deal of money, perhaps due in part to her father's generosity toward friends and relatives who asked for loans and gifts. Nonetheless, Mina's family appreciated her success in school. Her father even had her straight-A report cards framed. Children in the Rees household were free to do what mattered most to them. In the eighth grade, Mina's mathematics teacher recognized her abilities and recommended that she take the examination for admission to Hunter High School, a school for gifted girls associated with Hunter College. She was admitted to Hunter High and began a lifelong association with public higher education in the city. She also began a lifelong association with mathematics.

At Hunter High all the girls studied math, but Mina studied it simply because she wanted to. Mina's high marks continued: She graduated from Hunter High as valedictorian of her class; going on to Hunter College, she graduated with highest honors and a Phi Beta Kappa key in 1923. Perhaps anticipating her later work as an organizer and leader, she was elected student body president and was editor of the yearbook. Her mathematical success began early in college. After her first year, the mathematics department asked her to teach the trigonometry laboratory in surveying. After suitable training at Columbia University summer school, she taught for the next three years and earned a significant salary for the work. She says, "When I went to Hunter College, I found that the mathematics department was where I wanted to be. It wasn't because of its practical uses at all; it was because it was such fun!"[2] And Mina wasn't alone; mathematics was one of the most popular courses of study

Mina Rees. Photo courtesy of the Hunter College Archives.

at the college.

In an interview published in 1988, Mina spoke about the appropriateness of young women studying mathematics:

> I want [young women] to be mathematicians if they like mathematics! That's the thing that troubles me. I don't care whether or not there are a lot of women mathematicians, but if other girls have the same motivations I had—and I'm sure they do because there were so many of us at that time—I wish they wouldn't have irrelevant things interfering with their desires. It may well be that in our society a woman must sacrifice too much if she wants a career that's offbeat. It didn't seem like a sacrifice to me because I had plenty of men friends, and I wasn't prepared to get married; that wasn't what I wanted to do.[3]

The Hunter College mathematics department invited Mina to join its faculty after her graduation. She wanted further training, however, and joined the Hunter High faculty instead, while enrolling in the graduate program at Columbia University. In 1926, the year after she earned a master's degree, Mina was ready to teach college students and became a member of the Hunter College faculty.

She still wanted to learn more. Had Columbia University been willing, she would have gone on for her doctoral degree there. However, without officially saying so, Columbia's mathematics department let her understand that because she was a woman she would not be allowed to continue. This was the first time that her gender hindered her progress in mathematics. Since her hometown university would not have her, Rees went to the University of Chicago to study with L. E. Dickson. Professor Dickson had been the author of her college algebra textbook and was at the time distinguished professor of mathematics at Chicago. His work and the quality of his students helped make Chicago one of the three leading mathematics departments in the country at the time. (Harvard and Princeton were the other two.) Mina's doctoral thesis was published in 1932 under the title *Division Algebras Associated with an Equation Whose Group Has Four Generators*. Degree in hand, she rejoined the Hunter College faculty.

Before the United States became directly involved in World War II following the Japanese attack on Pearl Harbor on December 7, 1941, the federal government had established the Office of Scientific Research and Development (OSRD) to focus the country's scientific and technological resources on new weapons research and new ways of fighting. Mathematician and administrator Warren Weaver was brought in to join the work of OSRD. He established an Applied Mathematics Panel, and in 1943 he recruited Mina Rees to serve as technical aide and administrative assistant. In his memoirs Weaver referred to her contribution to the Mathematics Panel's work as "incomparably fine." Her work was fine enough, in fact, to earn her the President's Certificate of Merit from the U.S. government and the King's Medal for Service in the Cause of Freedom from Great Britain after the war.

Rees's career put her in many situations where other women were few and far between. At one meeting during World War II when a mathematician and an Air Force colleague were explaining their logistics system to Navy brass and government officials, Mina was the only woman in the room. She said later that the only expression of discrimination she ever encountered came from a civilian.

Not long after peace was restored, the government decided to continue its wartime practice of support for scientific research and development in the uneasy peace that followed the war. The U.S. Navy was particularly keen to do this, and Congress created the Office of Naval Research (ONR) to make and administer grants of support to academic scientists and engineers. Rees was called to join the ONR as head of its Mathematics Branch. In the course of the next seven years, as the cold war intensified and the Korean War began, she rose to be director of ONR's Mathematical Sciences Division and deputy science director of the agency. She was able to maintain a delicate balance between the mission-specific mathematics research that the Navy wanted and the more creative and open-ended investigation that the mathematicians wanted. As the Mathematical Association of America said later when awarding her its first Award for Distinguished Service to Mathematics in 1962, "During these years in Washington, Mina Rees firmly built into the permanent structure and policies of the ONR the principle that the full scope of mathematics should form part of the total scientific effort properly supported by government sponsored research programs."[4]

When Rees went to Washington in 1946 to join the ONR, it was difficult to obtain housing. There was a nationwide housing shortage, and in the capital there were especially few places to stay. She eventually located a downtown hotel that would rent her a room for two weeks at a time—all the others would allow only a five-day stay. Having to vacate her room regularly, she made a virtue of necessity and used the occasion to travel to one or another of the nation's leading mathematics departments to consult with colleagues about research needs and opportunities. As with Columbia's refusal to let her study for a Ph.D., she turned the adversity into an advantage and built a program of support for mathematical research that became a model for other military agencies and for the National Science Foundation when it was authorized by Congress several years later.

Working for the Applied Mathematics Panel and the ONR, Rees contributed to the development of modern computers. Technological warfare, such as that waged during World War II, demanded an enormous amount of arithmetic. Specific values were needed from innumerable equations for such tasks as controlling artillery, planning bombing raids, planning production, and especially for designing and building atomic weapons. By the end of the war the first digital computers were being built. After the war the federal government supported their continued improvement. Mathematicians, engineers, physicists, and others in that period used funds administered by Rees and her agency to explore the digital frontier.

Support of research enterprises in the midst of the hot and cold wars of the mid-twentieth century represented a major and meaningful demonstration of Rees's ability to balance the theoretical and practical aspects of science. The effort linking mathematics with the natural and social sciences was unprecedented and produced many new findings. "When I was in Washington, I felt that the most important thing I did was to see to it that mathematics got its share of support, chiefly by repeatedly demonstrating its achievements. I got the support only by being on hand all the time and being watchful. It doesn't come automatically."[5]

Rees left Washington in 1953 and returned to Hunter College. Now, she was not only professor of mathematics but also dean of the faculty. Eight years later when the public colleges in New York City were brought together as the City University of New York, she was appointed its first dean of graduate studies. She worked to establish an independent graduate school within the university. Rees became provost in 1968 and then president of the Graduate School and University Center from 1969 to 1972. In 1985 the City University dedicated its new graduate library in her name.

Although she was now based in the academy, Rees continued to contribute to science and mathematics at a national level. From 1954 to 1961 she served on advisory committees and panels for the National Bureau of Standards, the National Science Foundation, the Defense Department, the Navy, the Conference Board of the Mathematical Sciences, and the National Research Council. Between 1967 and 1971 she belonged to the Council of Graduate Schools of the United States, serving as chair for a period. She served on the National Science Board from 1964 to 1970 and held various posts in the American Association for the Advancement of Science (AAAS), culminating with election as president for 1971. "There was a considerable brouhaha in the press when a woman became president of the AAAS."[6]

Notwithstanding the practical nature of much of her work as a scientific and academic administrator, Rees had a love and appreciation for the beauty and elegance of mathematics. Speaking with interviewers when she was in her eighties, she said, "I get so mad at people who talk about mathematicians as practical people!"[7] Speaking to a conference of teachers of mathematics in 1962, she discussed the creative tension between logical rigor and creative intuition that has always characterized mathematics. Perhaps drawing on her administrative experiences as well, she said, "mathematical concepts and techniques, derived solely because of their interest and quite independently of possible use, have repeatedly proved their usefulness."[8] She concluded her talk by offering a series of major positions about mathematics, the "queen of the sciences."

Mathematics is not the only place where Mina Rees has found beauty. She is a an accomplished painter who has taken instruction in the United States and in Mexico and has spent many vacation days on the coast of Maine making full use of her easel and paintbox. In 1955 she married Leopold Brahdy, a physician and her friend for many years. He died in 1977.

Mina Rees achieved great professional success. Her mathematical and personal talents were recognized early and often during her educational years. She earned a doctoral degree from one of the finest mathematics departments in the United States. She took on war work that was complex and demanding. Because she was good at it, the federal government brought her back to lead a postwar program of military support for science and mathematics. Her work served as a model for later programs and agencies. On the strength of her skills and experiences, she was put in charge of the establishment of one of the country's major graduate research and teaching centers. She succeeded because she expected to succeed and demanded no less from herself and those around her.

Notes

1. "Award for Distinguished Service to Mathematics," *American Mathematical Monthly* 69 (1962): 185–186.
2. Quoted in Rosamond Dana and P. J. Hamilton, "Mina Rees," in W. P. Berlinghoff and K. R. Grant, eds., *Mathematical People*, 2nd ed. (New York: Ardsley House, 1988), p. 258.
3. Ibid., p. 261.
4. "Award for Distinguished Service to Mathematics," p. 185.
5. Quoted in Dana and Hamilton, in Berlinghoff and Grant, *Mathematical People*, p. 260.
6. Phyllis Fox, "Mina Rees (1902–   )," in L. S. Grinstein and P. J. Campbell, eds., *Women of Mathematics* (Westport, CT: Greenwood Press, 1987), p. 177.
7. Quoted in Dana and Hamilton, in Berlinghoff and Grant, *Mathematical People*, p. 266.
8. Mina Rees, "The Nature of Mathematics," *Science* 138 (1962) p. 12.

Selected Works by Mina Rees

(1952). Digital Computers—Their Nature and Use. *American Scientist* 40, pp. 328–35.
(1952). (with R. Courant and E. Isaacson). On the Solution of Non-Linear Hyperbolic Differential Equations by Finite Differences. *Communications on Pure and Applied Mathematics* 5, pp. 243–55.
(1958). The Impact of the Computer. *Mathematics Teacher* 51, pp. 162–68.
(1958). Mathematics in the Market Place. *American Mathematical Monthly* 65, pp. 332–43.
(1962). The Nature of Mathematics. *Science* 138, pp. 9–12.
(1982). The Computing Program of the Office of Naval Research, 1946–1953. *Annals of the History of Computing* 4, pp. 102–20.

Selected Works about Mina Rees

Award for Distinguished Service to Mathematics. (1962). *American Mathematical Monthly* 69, pp. 185–87.
Dana, Rosamond, and Hamilton, P. J. (1988). Mina Rees. In W. P. Berlinghoff and K. R. Grant, Eds., *Mathematical People*, 2nd ed. New York: Ardsley House.

Fox, Phyllis. (1987). Mina Rees (1902–   ). In L. S. Grinstein and P. J. Campbell, Eds., *Women of Mathematics* (pp. 121–28). Westport, CT: Greenwood Press.
                                                                HOMER STAVELY

IDA RHODES
(1900–1986)
Birthplace: Ukraine, Russia

Ida Rhodes was a pioneer in the development of the modern electronic digital computer and its use for numerical calculations. While working at the National Bureau of Standards (NBS) until her retirement, she was an outstanding and internationally recognized computer programmer who was in great demand for advice and consulting by other mathematicians, engineers, government agencies, and private firms. Ida Rhodes was also a true humanist; she gave constantly of herself for bettering the human condition around her.

Ida Rhodes was born as Hadassah Itzkowitz on May 15, 1900, in a small Jewish village between Nemirow and Tulcin in Ukraine, about 150 miles southwest of Kiev. Although it was the beginning of a new century, her country was experiencing troubled times. From her early childhood she recalls listening with dread to the sounds of the approaching pogroms (campaigns of violence directed against Jews). However, all was not grim for the young girl. She managed to escape the destitute lives that many of her countryfolk were experiencing, due in large part to her fortuitous friendship with a Russian countess who owned ninety-nine communities. The countess introduced her to the wonders of nature and opened her eyes to various possibilities. Ida Rhodes recalls:

She [the countess] was a great naturalist and set up a school for the poor of the area. She was very kind and wanted to adopt me. I said that was impossible; that I already had a family. Nevertheless, she often had me as a house guest and arranged for the finest of kosher food for me. She took me riding and showed me plants and explained what I could expect of the plants' development by the next time we visited. There was an island we visited in one of her parks where the swans nested. The lady was careful to instruct me never to touch the swan eggs or the mother would disown them. (Weiss, 1992)

Ida Rhodes. Photo courtesy of National Institute of Standards and Technology.

Rhodes was 13 years old in 1913 when her parents, David and Bessie Sinkler Itzkowitz, brought her to the United States (her name was changed upon entering the U.S.) Shortly thereafter, at the time of the Bolshevik revolution, the countess's communities sent a delegation to the local Soviet (the local unit of government) pleading for good treatment of the countess and asking that her life be spared. For a while she was allowed to live, but eventually she suffered the same fate as many of the wealthy in Russia at that time.

In the United States, Rhodes blossomed into a promising student. She was awarded a New York State Cash Scholarship and a Cornell University Tuition Scholarship, enabling her to attend Cornell University, where she studied mathematics. While at Cornell (1919–1923) she was considered somewhat of a prodigy, and professors often changed their schedules so she could take their courses. This was not an easy task, since Rhodes was also very involved in nursing. She worked at Ithaca City Hospital as a nurse's aide, where she performed all delivery room duties not assigned exclusively to nurses and all tasks related to post-natal care of mothers and their infants (NBS, 1959a). She typically left school at 1:00 P.M. and worked for twelve hours at the hospital; this precluded her taking any afternoon classes. In fact, she chose to major in mathematics rather than a science because physics or chemistry, for example, required laboratories, which she couldn't manage along with her nursing commitments.

At Cornell, Rhodes excelled in mathematics. She was elected to the honorary organizations Phi Beta Kappa (1922) and Phi Kappa Phi (1923). She earned a B.A. in mathematics with honors in February 1923, and a M.A. in mathematics in the fall of 1923. Rhodes liked to retell a story of her first encounter with Albert Einstein while at Cornell. In 1922 she met Einstein but was so overwhelmed by his reputation that she said practically nothing. More than ten years later, in 1936, she joined a group of mathematicians who piled into their cars each weekend to race to Princeton to spend weekends in informal seminars with Albert Einstein. When she entered the room with others, Einstein looked at her for a moment and said, "It must have been in 1922 that we first met at Cornell. Have you learned to talk since then?" Indeed she had, and she was an integral part of the community of well-known mathematicians of her day.

After college, Rhodes continued as a nurse's aide until 1926, then had a series of mathematics related jobs, including teaching high school mathematics in Houston, Texas; performing statistical tasks connected with merchandise control at R. H. Macy and Co.; and, finally, performing accounting tasks as secretary of the corporation and co-owner of her father's store, David Itzkowitz Sportswear. While working at the store, she attended graduate school at Columbia for one year in 1931 and studied mathematics. In 1938 Rhodes moved on to other jobs as registrar at the Alpha Business School and statistical clerk at the New York State Labor Department. Finally, in 1940, she joined the Math Tables Project (MTP) in New York City, which launched her illustrious career with the U.S. NBS.

The first program of computing within the NBS, the MTP was started in response to a Works Progress Administration conference on aid for unemployed mathematicians (Blanch and Rhodes, 1974; Aspray and Gunderloy, 1989). The project opened in New York City with a staff of 7 mathematicians and 120 high school graduates; its goal was to prepare basic tables of exponential and circular functions and to solve scientific numerical problems for government and industry. With limited resources, the MTP managed to become known worldwide for its excellence and its production of error-free and accurate volumes of tables.

Rhodes was part of an initial group of young mathematicians (of whom three were women) that were hired in 1940. This group was highly educated in theoretical mathematics but not in numerical analysis;

thus one of their first tasks was to acquire the necessary skills in numerical analysis and approximate numbers. Rhodes did this with her usual vigor and aptitude. Gertrude Blanch of the MTP helped to train this talented group with the cooperation of some members of the British Association of the Advancement of Science, a world-renowned table-making institution. One of the MTP's goals was to publish tables that were as accurate as those of the British school, a goal it did eventually achieve.

Producing high-quality, error-free tables was not the only accomplishment of the MTP. There was also a human factor, where Rhodes played a key role. The majority of the workers on the project were not mathematicians by training. Most of them had a high school education and were chosen from the welfare rolls during the Depression; many of the workers were physically handicapped. At a time when human spirits and self-esteem were extremely low, the MTP provided steady work and a sense of camaraderie that were hard to find in those difficult times. The working staff were made to feel the importance of their contributions and a pride in producing scientifically important work (Gürer, 1996).

In addition to her mathematical prowess, Rhodes's nursing skills were called on during the day, since many of the MTP workers had epilepsy, arrested tuberculosis, or polio disabilities and needed special care. It was during the evening hours that Rhodes and Blanch were able to perform the bulk of their work. Hundreds of worksheets had to be tested for consistency; it was crucial that everything be consistent. In addition, new worksheets had to be developed and prepared.

The MTP mathematicians surmounted all the difficulties they faced with undertrained workers and a low budget. During World War II the MTP was taken over by the National Defense Research Council and started to perform mostly defense-related calculations. However, a great technological change was about to occur: the advent of the electronic computing machine, which allowed computations that had taken minutes, hours, and even days to do with hand calculators, to be performed in a matter of seconds. Rhodes was not left out of this new technological revolution. In 1947 her supervisor, Dr. Arnold Lowan, asked her to go to Washington, D.C., and help out with the new electronic digital computational machine (today known as a computer) the NBS was building, the UNIVAC I.

At first Rhodes felt she was not the appropriate person for the job because she did not have any formal training in electronics. However, the Washington staff was impressed by her capabilities and requested she work there permanently. She accepted and moved to Washington, D.C., to become a part of the original nucleus of the Computation Laboratory at the NBS, where she became one of the foremost experts in the world in the functional design and application of electronic digital computing equipment. For a short time she worked with **Grace Hopper**, another famous woman mathematician and pioneering computer scientist. While at the NBS until her retirement, Rhodes contributed greatly to the development of the UNIVAC I and SEAC machines and took part in the newly developing field of numerical analysis performed on electronic computational digital machines.

Part of her work involved the analysis of systems of programming. She was one of the first programmers to use the C-10 language in the early 1950s for the Census Bureau's UNIVAC I, and she designed the original computer program used by the Social Security Administration. She was also a pioneer in the application of computers to the translation of her native tongue, Russian, to English. She was one of the first to recognize the importance of parsing sentences and separating the roots of words from their prefixes and suffixes as initial steps in developing a natural language process for computers, which is still an active area in the field of artificial intelligence.

Ida Rhodes was continually in demand as a consultant by mathematicians and engineers who were engaged in using and designing electronic digital computers. She gave many orientation lectures about computers to government agencies and private firms in which she explained how computers could enable them to do computations more easily and efficiently. She was also concerned about handicapped users and taught computer coding techniques to the physically handicapped (e.g., deaf mutes and individuals who were totally blind). Rhodes became one of the most called upon scientists to lecture about computers and their applications in many locations of the world. In fact, one of her main interests was Israel. A friend of hers, Golda Meir, who later became prime minister of Israel, encouraged her to go to Israel and work there. She was tempted, but her dedication in caring for her parents outweighed her desire to work in Israel.

Ida Rhodes formally retired from the NBS in 1964 but continued to act as a consultant for its Applied Mathematics Division until 1971. She passed away at age 85 on February 1, 1986. In addition to her substantial technical contributions, she left a legacy in areas outside her technical competence. She had a long-standing interest in the Hebrew calendar that culminated in a paper on computations of the Hebrew New Year and Passover (Rhodes, 1977). She was also quite generous and gave many gifts to Hebrew charities and a much-appreciated gift to the NBS in 1977 for azaleas and rhododendrons to be planted near the Administration Building in honor of the three directors under whom she served (Lyman J. Briggs, Edward U. Condon, and Allen V. Astin).

Rhodes was highly respected and admired by her colleagues. In 1959 the U.S. Department of Commerce awarded her an Exceptional Service Award (Gold Medal) for "significant pioneering leadership and outstanding contribution to the scientific programs of the Nation in the functional design and the application of electronic digital computing equipment" (NBS, 1958; NBS, 1959b). In 1976, the Department of Commerce honored her again with a Certificate of Appreciation "on the occasion of the 25th anniversary of UNIVAC I in recognition of your services to the Information Revolution," and at the 1981 Computer Conference in Chicago she was cited as a "UNIVAC I Pioneer."

Selected Works by Ida Rhodes

(with G. Blanch). (1974). Table-Making at the National Bureau of Standards," In B. K. P. Scaife, Ed., *Studies in Numerical Analysis: Papers in Honor of Cornelius Lanczos* (pp. 1–6). London: Academic Press.
(1977). Computation of the Hebrew New Year and Passover. *Computers and Mathematics with Applications* 3, pp. 193–90.

Selected Works about Ida Rhodes

Aspray, W., and Gunderloy, M. (1989). Early Computing and Numerical Analysis at the National Bureau of Standards. *Annals of the History of Computing* 11(1), pp. 3–12.
Gürer, D. (1996). Women's Contributions to Early Computing at the National Bureau of Standards. *IEEE Annals of the History of Computing* 18(3), pp. 29–35.
National Bureau of Standards. (1958). Nomination for Honor Award Exceptional Service Award National Bureau of Standards Nomination.
———. (1959a). National Bureau of Standards Biographical Data on Ida Rhodes. NBS-28, February 19.
———. (1959b). Mrs. Ida Rhodes Receives Exceptional Service Award from U.S. Department of Commerce. *National Bureau of Standards Announcement*, TRP 8610, August.
Slutz, R. J. (1980). Memories of the Bureau of Standards' SEAC. In N. Metropolis, J. Howlett, and G. C. Rota, Eds., *A History of Computing in the Twentieth Century: A Collection of Essays* (pp. 471–77). New York: Academic Press.
Weiss, E. (1992). Biography of Ida Rhodes. *IEEE Annals of the History of Computing* 14(2).

DENISE GÜRER

JULIA BOWMAN ROBINSON
(1919–1985)
Birthplace: Missouri

Julia Robinson hesitated as she prepared to blow out the candles on her birthday cake. As she did so, she made a wish that either she or someone

Julia Robinson. Photo courtesy of Constance Reid.

else would solve the tenth problem posed by the great mathematician David Hilbert around the turn of the century. She had been working on this problem since receiving her Ph.D. some two decades earlier, and she had been making this birthday wish year after year. She felt that she could not bear to die without knowing the answer. Although she could not have guessed it at the time, her wish was about to be granted.

During her early years, Julia, born on December 8, 1919, gave little outward indication of the mathematical ability she would eventually show. She had been slow to begin speaking as a child, missed more than two years of school as a result of scarlet and rheumatic fever, and scored in the low-average range on an IQ test taken in junior high school. One of her earliest memories, however, was of arranging pebbles on a sunny day in the small desert community in Arizona where she spent her early childhood. She felt this was an indication of her innate interest in the natural numbers, an interest that would eventually lead her to number theory, the branch of mathematics in which she was to make her greatest contribution. Number theory deals with the properties and relationships of integers. What is proved about numbers will be true in any universe, she believed. That was what made number theory so special for her.

The family moved to San Diego, where she attended high school and won awards in advanced mathematics and physics even though she was the only girl in these classes. In high school she was also a great baseball fan, keeping box scores at games and spending her allowance on the *Sporting News*. Robinson recalls that although she was very shy, being the only girl in a roomful of boys did not bother her. Mostly they paid little attention to her unless they needed help with homework.

She completed her undergraduate education at San Diego State College in 1940 and went on to graduate school at the University of California at Berkeley to study mathematics. There she met her future husband, Raphael, a mathematics professor. In this respect Robinson's situation was fairly typical of other women mathematicians—many had also married mathematicians. At that time the professional status of a woman's husband was a major determinant of the doors that would open for her in the mathematics community, especially because most universities had nepotism rules explicitly prohibiting the hiring of both members of a married couple.

While at Berkeley, Robinson worked toward her Ph.D. under the guidance of Alfred Tarski, who was regarded as one of the top international scholars in mathematical logic. In 1948 Robinson earned her Ph.D. degree and took a research position with the Rand Corporation. She also began work on the problem in number theory to which she was to make important contributions over the next twenty years. From 1960 to 1975 she worked intermittently as a lecturer at Berkeley. In 1976 Robinson accepted a professorship in mathematics at Berkeley. This happened, however, only after she was elected to the National Academy of Sciences, the first woman mathematician to achieve this high honor.

The branch of mathematics known as number theory (the field in which Robinson did her most distinguished work) dates back to Diophantes, who lived in the latter part of the third century. Diophantes was in many ways ahead of his time. He wrote the *Arithmetica*, a collection of 150 problems, introducing symbols into the solution process and finding clever ways to solve the problems he had posed by using only one variable wherever possible. For example, to find two numbers whose sum was 20 and the sum of whose squares was 208, Diophantes called the numbers $(10 + x)$ and $(10 - x)$ rather than x and y (here we are using modern algebraic symbolism rather than Diophantes's original symbols). Hence $(10 + x) + (10 - x) = 20$ and $(10 + x)^2 + (10 - x)^2 = 208$, from which it follows that x is 2, and the two numbers are 12 and 8. In this way Diophantes solved his problems without having to resort to methods of solution for simultaneous equations.

Typically Diophantes specified that the solution to a problem had to be in integers or in rational numbers only. Even today, equations on which these conditions are imposed are known as Diophantine equations, and many remained unsolved. In the seventeenth century a Greek and Latin edition of the *Arithmetica* was published, and it was then that aspects of Diophantes's work piqued the curiosity of the French mathematician Pierre Fermat. Fermat, who is now regarded as having established a more modern theory of numbers, was fascinated by such Diophantine topics as magic squares, Pythagorean triples, and perfect and prime numbers. He worked on some of Diophantes's problems, proving, for example, that there is no cube that can be expressed as the sum of two cubes, a problem that reflects the classical connection between number theory and geometry. Fermat generalized this Diophantine result, however, stating that for $n > 2$ there are no positive integers x, y, and z such that $x^n + y^n = z^n$, and writing in his copy of the *Arithmetica* that the margin was too narrow to contain his proof.

Many mathematicians have since attempted the proof of this proposition, now called Fermat's Last Theorem, thinking they had succeeded only to have an error in the proof detected by someone else. E. T. Bell, the author of the celebrated classic *Men of Mathematics*, related how he had spent three weeks trying to find the flaw in one such proof, only to have it discovered within half an hour by a girl who was a student in his trigonometry class. Fermat's Last Theorem is now, finally, thought to be solved.

Julia Robinson read Bell's *Men of Mathematics* in college. It proved to be a very important book for her because prior to reading it, she had had no idea about the kind of work a mathematician does. Later she highly recommended the book to young people interested in mathematics research.

As it developed, Diophantine equations were to play a significant role in Robinson's mathematical work. In 1949 she published a proof in number theory that has been called elegant. Important results in mathematical logic have followed from this work. The problem that most stimulated Robinson's curiosity when she completed her doctorate was one posed by Hilbert as the tenth on a list of important unsolved problems. The tenth problem had to do with whether or not a general method existed for determining if a given Diophantine equation had an integral solution. Robinson published several papers on this problem.

In 1970 Robinson received word that the problem had been solved by a 22-year-old Russian, Yuri Matijasevic, using the Fibonacci numbers to meet the requirements for the solution that she herself had sketched. Robinson was overjoyed that the problem had finally been solved and could not help observing that it was Fibonacci numbers (a mathematical topic known since the thirteenth century) that had led to the solution. In the following year she and her husband went to Russia to meet with Matijasevic, with whom she subsequently collaborated. Robinson, Matijasevic, and Martin Davis, who also worked on the problem, had all made important contributions and were credited with its solution.

In 1976, when Julia Robinson became the first woman elected to membership in the National Academy of Sciences, the university press office called the mathematics department to find out who Julia Robinson was. "Why, that's Professor Robinson's wife," replied someone in the mathematics department. "Well," replied the caller, "Professor Robinson's wife has just been elected to the National Academy of Sciences!" (Albers et al., 1990, p. 279). Only then did the university offer her a professorship.

In 1982 she was elected president of the American Mathematical Society. Although she realized that she had been chosen in part because she was a woman and in part because she had been elected to the National Academy, she decided that as a woman and a mathematician she had no alternative but to accept. "I have always tried to do everything I could to encourage talented women to become research mathematicians" (Albers et al., 1990, p. 280). Robinson received a coveted "genius" grant from the MacArthur Foundation in 1983 and has been listed by the *Ladies Home Journal* as one of 100 outstanding women in America. She has been honored in many other ways, including the Julia Robinson Celebration of Women in Mathematics Conference held in July 1996 at the Mathematical Sciences Research Institute in Berkeley.

When she was not doing mathematics, Robinson enjoyed bicycling. Following open heart surgery in 1961 to correct the damage caused by rheumatic fever in her childhood, she was able to indulge this interest by participating in a number of cycling trips in both America and Holland. She enjoyed many of these activities not only with her husband but with her sister, Constance Reid, with whom she was very close. Reid, although following a literary path, has remained very close to mathematics. She has become a prize-winning writer on mathematics and a leading biographer of several well-known mathematicians, including a new book about the life of her sister, Julia (Reid, 1996).

Julia Robinson died on July 30, 1985, after an unsuccessful struggle with leukemia. She was only 65 years old. She was a mathematician of impressive credentials. This was important to her. Rather than being remembered as the first woman to accomplish a particular thing, she preferred to be remembered simply by the theorems she had proved and the problems she had solved.

Selected Works by Julia Robinson

(1951). An Iterative Method of Solving a Game. *Annals of Mathematics* 54(2), pp. 296–301.

(1962). The Undecidability of Exponential Diophantine Equations. In *Logic, Methodology, and Philosophy* (pp. 12–13). Stanford, CA: Stanford University Press.

(1969). Finitely Generated Classes of Sets of Natural Numbers. *Proceedings of the American Mathematical Society* 21, pp. 608–14.

(1969). Unsolvable Diophantine Problems. *Proceedings of the American Mathematical Society* 22, pp. 534–38.

(1971). Hilbert's Tenth Problem. 1969 Number Theory Institute, American Mathematical Society, Providence, Rhode Island, pp. 191–194.

(1973). Solving Diophantine Equations. In *Logic, methodology, and philosophy of science* (Vol. 4, pp. 63–67). Amsterdam: North-Holland.

(1976). (with M. Davis, Y. Matijasevic, and J. Robinson). Hilbert's Tenth Problem: Diophantine Equations: Positive Aspects of a Negative Solution. In *Mathematical Developments Arising from Hilbert Problems* (pp. 323–78). Providence, RI: American Mathematical Society.

Selected Works about Julia Robinson

Albers, D., Alexanderson, G., and Reid, C., Eds. (1990). Julia Robinson. In *More Mathematical People* (pp. 263–80). Boston: Harcourt, Brace, Jovanovich.

Feferman, S. (1997). *The Collected Works of Julia Robinson*, Vol. 6. Providence, RI: American Mathematical Society.

Reid, C. (1986). The Autobiography of Julia Robinson. *College Mathematics Journal* 17(1), pp. 3–21.

———. (1996). *Julia: A Life in Mathematics*. Washington, DC: Mathematical Association of America.

JEAN SCHMITTAU

JUDITH ROITMAN
(1945–   )
Birthplace: New York

As a child growing up in New York City, Judith Roitman never imagined herself as a mathematician. This, however, is exactly what she is; a mathematics professor and researcher at the University of Kansas. She excelled in reading and writing, and has written poetry seriously since the age of 8. Roitman was also a minor prodigy in music but decided against a career as a classical musician and concert pianist because she didn't want to spend all her time at a piano bench, practicing. She was encouraged to pursue music, literature, and writing; but at the time girls and women were discouraged from careers in areas such as mathematics

Judith Roitman. Photo courtesy of
Judith Roitman.

and physics. Roitman remembers feeling that no matter how well she
did in mathematics she could never achieve real understanding, because
real understanding was, by definition, something only boys could have.

In junior high school Judith remembers reading George Gamow's book
1-2-3 Infinity and being struck by Cantor's proof that the real numbers
are uncountable. The idea that there was more than one kind of infinity,
and that one could explore infinity by using the mind alone, absolutely
stunned her. Judith also remembers spending a sleepless night as a 12-
year-old when she first learned about imaginary numbers. She was very
excited and began to think about how to graph them. She visualized two
real axes and one imaginary axis, and was very excited because she had
invented this in her mind. (In hindsight she realizes that she was actually
graphing functions from the real numbers to the complex plane, but she
didn't have the vocabulary to understand this at the time.) When she
explained this way of representing complex numbers to her teacher, he
dismissively told her that it could be done much more simply with only
two axes. Discouraged, she felt that mathematics allowed no room for
creativity and insight. It was very unlike her experiences writing poetry
or performing Bach on the piano, where things were always new, different, wonderful. At school, mathematics was mainly arithmetic, a sub-

ject that Roitman found incredibly boring. Nevertheless she loved reading; and still intrigued by mathematical and scientific phenomena, she read whatever was available in math and science for people her age.

Although reading *1–2–3 Infinity* had a profound influence on her, it had no effect on her future career plans for a long time. She says this was because she was a girl, and because the mathematics she encountered in the book was nothing like any other mathematics she'd ever seen. Many years later, after finally finding her way into mathematics, Roitman continues to have a fascination with infinity.

Having graduated from high school in 1962, Roitman went on to Oberlin College and planned to become a high school English teacher. After a year at Oberlin she transferred to Sarah Lawrence College, and there was convinced to plan a career teaching college literature. In 1966 she graduated from Sarah Lawrence and applied for a graduate school fellowship in English literature. Realizing that what she really wanted was to write literature, not *study* it, her career plans changed again and she began searching for something that better fit her interests.

Except for a "Math for Poets" course, Roitman hadn't taken any mathematics in college. Attending a women's college (Sarah Lawrence), however, had radically changed her notions of what she could and could not do. As a poet interested in language—and particularly the connection between language, mind, and reality—Roitman decided to enter the mathematical linguistics program at the Massachusetts Institute of Technology (MIT). To do that, however, she needed to take calculus. That requirement sent her out to Berkeley, California, to take a summer course in calculus. (It was now the late 1960s, and like many in her generation Roitman lived in the San Francisco Bay area as a "kind of" hippie, working days as a secretary.) After taking first- and second-year mathematics courses part-time to prepare for a career in mathematical linguistics, Roitman quit her job and spent a year at Berkeley taking a combination of philosophy and mathematics courses.

Roitman subsequently applied to the linguistics program at the University of Pennsylvania and was offered a full fellowship. When she inquired about mathematics she was told that although she could take an abstract algebra course, there wasn't room for much mathematics in the linguistics program. That caused her to turn down the University of Pennsylvania fellowship. In 1969 Roitman instead entered the logic and methodology of science program at Berkeley. A short while later she switched to mathematics because she realized that she liked mathematics better than philosophy. The fact that mathematicians were constantly inventing new ways of thinking appealed to her.

Roitman encountered a great deal of sexism during her formative years in graduate school. The climate was not supportive of women in mathematics. Recognizing the importance of having a peer group and maintaining connections with other women mathematicians, Roitman met regularly with a group of women graduate students and postdoctoral instructors. She found their support very important. Roitman was also fortunate to be close friends with **Lenore Blum**, a highly regarded young postdoctoral instructor. Blum helped Roitman bolster her self-confidence and belief in herself, and maintain a vision of herself as a professional mathematician.

When Roitman was starting to consider a thesis topic, Ken Kunen was at Berkeley as a visiting professor from University of Wisconsin at Madison. He interested Roitman and a fellow graduate student, Bill Fleissner, in applying set theory to general topology (see discussion below). Since none of the Berkeley faculty were interested in this topic, both she and Fleissner went to Madison to work with Kunen and **Mary Ellen Rudin**. A well-known mathematician who throughout her career has cared greatly about the next generation of mathematicians, Rudin was extremely supportive. For Roitman, Mary Ellen Rudin was an "existence proof" demonstrating that a woman could have a salaried professional life as a research mathematician. At the time, two other distinguished women mathematicians, **Julia Robinson** and **Emma Lehmer**, were working at Berkeley as adjunct faculty, mainly because they were faculty wives and could not obtain formal faculty positions.

After receiving her Ph.D. from Berkeley in 1974, Roitman's first teaching job in mathematics was at Wellesley College, where she was an assistant professor from 1974 to 1977. Roitman has been teaching at the University of Kansas since 1977, with the exception of a leave during the fall of 1997 to study at the Institute for Advanced Study in Princeton, New Jersey. In addition to her research work in mathematics, Roitman has been active in mathematics education reform and issues related to women in mathematics. In the mid-1970s she was president of the Association for Women in Mathematics. Her interest in mathematics education and teaching stem from her early graduate school experiences as a Community Teaching Fellow, when she taught in elementary mathematics classrooms.

Roitman's research is in the area of set theoretic topology and infinitary Boolean algebra, subjects in which she studies infinite sets and their properties. Her mathematical interests focus on infinity and models of set theory. Using different models of set theory, she focuses on results of modern mathematics outside set theory that cannot be solved without modern set theoretic techniques. Historically, set theory belongs to a quasi-philosophical branch of mathematics known as foundations, which most mathematicians felt they could safely ignore. Roitman's article "The Uses of Set Theory" (1992) describes, for a general mathematical audience, some recent mathematical results that clearly demonstrate that set theory cannot be safely ignored.

Why is this so? To paraphrase her article, set theory is based on three truths and two beliefs. The first truth, attributed to Georg Cantor, was discovered in the nineteenth century and is the root of set theory. *Truth #1*: Not all infinite sets look alike. Cantor's great nineteenth-century discovery was that infinite sets can differ in size; in fact, this is the simplest way that infinite sets can differ. For example, the integers and the reals are both infinite sets, but they differ in size. Most of what set theorists work on involves seeing and describing all the ways in which infinite sets can differ.

The two other truths are as follows. *Truth #2*: Not all formulas look alike. There are different ways to define sets, ways that don't look alike; but if one knows the simplest way of defining a set, then one already knows quite a bit about the set. *Truth #3*: Not all approximations to the mathematical universe look alike. Set theorists develop models of set theory that attempt to model the mathematical universe. A model, or an approximation to the mathematical universe, begins with a fairly small, easily described set of axioms or assumptions about this universe. Unfortunately, there are no ways of knowing which approximations to the mathematical universe are better than others. And sometimes the models don't agree on what's true.

None of this would matter to most mathematicians except for two beliefs that are widely held in the mathematical community: (1) that set theory is a consistent theory, that is, it makes sense to work within it; and (2) that mathematics can be embedded in set theory.

In her own work, Roitman considers the differences between infinite numbers and sets as well as the relationships among them. She builds or uses alternative models to see how the differences between infinite numbers play out in the structures of topology and Boolean algebra. What she finds interesting is that she can prove that many of the questions she studies can't be answered absolutely; you get one answer if you use one model, and another answer using another model. Much of her work is in constructing counterexamples—examples that show a reasonable conjecture is not true.

Roitman finds working in mathematics both satisfying and frustrating; in many ways the satisfaction comes from overcoming the frustrations. She feels it is important for students and teachers to know that doing mathematics is difficult; it is important to keep that perspective in mind and not give up easily. For her, mathematics is a comfortable world in which to move around and think. She almost always finds it soothing to return to mathematics after doing something else. She is still fascinated by using mathematics to explore the human mind and see how far it can be taken in a given direction.

Roitman lives in Lawrence, Kansas, with her husband, Stan Lombardo, a classics professor, and their teenage son. She continues to write and publish poetry. In addition to her research work in mathematics, Roitman has recently been deeply involved in mathematics education reform and works extensively with elementary mathematics teachers. She has served on a number of panels and boards—including the Mathematical Sciences Education Board Panel on College and University Programs, the American Mathematical Society Committee on Education, and the Mathematicians for Educational Reform Advisory Board—and has served as the Association for Women in Mathematics president in 1979–1981. For her outstanding work, she received the Louise Hay Award for Contributions to Mathematics Education from the Association for Women in Mathematics in 1990.

Note

The information included in this biography is based in part on an interview by the author.

Selected Works by Judith Roitman

(1990). *Introduction to Modern Set Theory*. New York: John Wiley.
(1992). The Uses of Set Theory. *Mathematical Intelligencer* 14(1).
(1993). Autohomeomorphisms of Thin-Tall Locally Compact Scattered Spaces in ZFC. *Annals of the New York Academy of Sciences* 704.
(1994). A Space Homeomorphic to Each Uncountable Closed Subspace under CH. *Topology and Its Applications* 55.
(1995). What Will Be the Effect of a Standards-Based Education on College Students? *Mathematical Association of America Focus* v. 15, No. 2, pp. 9–10.
(1996). Association of Women in Mathematics Hay Award for Contributions to Mathematics Education. *Notices of the American Mathematical Society* 43(4), pp. 432–35.

JUNE MARK

MARY ELLEN RUDIN
(1924–   )
Birthplace: Texas

I grew up in very primitive, simple surroundings where I had lots of time just to think. But there was never any question about the fact that I would go to the university and that I would do something with my education. My mother had been a teacher before she had married. She expected that I should earn my living, and that what I did should be an interesting thing to do.[1]

Mary Ellen Rudin. Photo courtesy of Mary Ellen
Rudin.

A look at the life of Mary Ellen (Estill) Rudin will show that she fulfilled
the high expectations that her family held for her. She is a professor
emerita of mathematics at the University of Wisconsin and an internationally respected mathematical researcher. Mary Ellen was born on December 7, 1924, in a small town in Texas. Her father worked for the Texas
Highway Department as a civil engineer, and her mother was a high
school English teacher. She went to a very small school, with only five
students in her graduating class. She liked school and was a serious
student, but did not feel a special affinity for one subject over another.

Mary Ellen entered the University of Texas on the advice of her father,
who had been a student there and considered it an excellent school. On
arrival, she had a conversation with Professor R. L. Moore at the mathematics registration table. She was completely unaware at that time of
his reputation as a mathematician and his unorthodox way of selecting,

teaching, and mentoring very talented mathematics students. As a result of that meeting, he enrolled her in his trigonometry course. She had not been planning to focus on mathematics when she arrived at the university, since she had enjoyed all subjects equally well in high school. As it turned out, she took a mathematics course from Moore each semester for the rest of her time at the University of Texas. Rudin earned a B.A. degree in mathematics in 1944 and stayed on for graduate school, earning her Ph.D. in mathematics in 1949. An interview conducted in 1986[2] gives a fascinating account of her development as a mathematician while a student at Texas.

After earning her Ph.D. she taught at Duke University. It was there that she met Walter Rudin, who was a student at Duke and subsequently earned his Ph.D. in mathematics. They were married in 1953 and moved to Rochester, where Walter had obtained a position. Rudin and everyone else assumed that when she married, her career as a professional mathematician would be over. That didn't mean that she would stop doing research. She continued to teach but did not hold a position as a professor in the standard line for promotion to tenure. A tenure track position is the usual pathway to permanent employment in the university, allowing the enjoyment of the benefits of academic life. Rudin was, instead, more or less dependent on her husband for money and all the things that made it easy for her to be a mathematician at that time—primarily his position at a university.

Rudin did indeed carry on with her mathematical research and teaching, always in temporary or informally arranged positions. During their time at Rochester their first two children were born, and they had two more children after moving to Madison, Wiconsin, in 1959 when Walter was offered a mathematics position at the university. Her mentors and colleagues seemed to realize from the beginning what an important contribution she would make in mathematics and were always on the lookout for positions for her. In some ways, the lack of a formal and permanent position relieved her of some of the "busy work" of a university professorship, and she could better concentrate on her research and devote time to her children.

In 1971, when the nepotism rules preventing spouses from holding jobs at the same university were eliminated, Rudin was made a professor of mathematics at the University of Wisconsin in recognition of her highly respected mathematical research. In 1981 she was awarded the **Grace Chisholm Young** professorship, an honor that Rudin was the first to receive. Mary Ellen and Walter are now both retired. In addition to publishing more than seventy papers, she has been invited to give honorary lectures at mathematics meetings.

Rudin never saw any conflict between having a career as being a research mathematician and being a woman or being the mother of four children. She says that mathematics requires imagination and persistence and a joy of words, much more than of number—things that are traditional qualities for women. Being a professional mathematician allows one to work at home, and therefore it fits well with having a family. One can work on mathematics while there are small children around; in fact, it may actually be harder to clean the house with them there because they want to get involved. Rudin's experiences have shown her that mathematical ideas can come to you at odd times.

Rudin has published many papers in the area of mathematics known as set theoretic topology, a branch of topology in which methodology from set theory is applied to solve problems. She is most noted for the counterexamples she has found to well-known conjectures. (Conjectures are mathematical statements that are either true or false; there is no middle ground.) Part of the work of a research mathematician is to find a way to prove the conjecture true or to find an example that shows the conjecture is false. This kind of example is called a counterexample— literally an example that is "counter" to the conjecture. For example, consider the following statement from high school geometry: The diagonals of a quadrilateral bisect each other. There are many examples of quadrilaterals for which this statement is true (e.g., squares, rectangles, rhombuses, and isosceles trapezoids). It is important to note that all these examples are not enough to prove the statement is always true. In fact, the statement is false because one can also find many counterexamples, that is, examples for which the statement is not true (e.g., the kite shape, which has one diagonal that is bisected and one that is not). A single counterexample is enough to show that the statement is false. Rudin has achieved a great deal by believing that if a problem has been worked on for a long time and hasn't been proved, there is probably a counterexample.

In her work, Rudin investigates whether there exist sets that have a particular kind of intersection, a particular kind of union, or a particular kind of pattern over a large set. Her research is often at the very foundation of mathematics. In fact, she describes her mathematical research as being more like doing philosophy. As a research mathematician, Rudin is constantly working on problems. She works on something for a little while, thinking about it in various kinds of ways, perhaps drawing pictures. She says, "You develop your own ways of thinking about it in your head, and sometimes you work at it very intensely for a little while, but you can't work at it very intensely for many hours at a time. You need to have some time for it to mature; your mind does some work on its own that you are unaware of."

Now that both Rudins are retired, they are free to do extensive traveling. Their trips usually include visiting with colleagues around the world, attending conferences, giving lectures, and collaborating with other mathematicians. Recently Rudin has traveled to the Netherlands, Japan, Spain, the Canary Islands, and Switzerland. When asked if she is still doing mathematics now that she is retired, her answer was quick and certain, "Oh, yes. Absolutely!" And does she ever run out of problems? "Oh never, ever. Every time you do something, you make [new] problems. If you solve something, you ask the question 'What happens if I do this now?' You can think of a half dozen things. If you have a counterexample of some known conjecture, then you want to know what sort of conditions you might add to make the theorem be true.... You don't kill the problem; you just open it up."

What does a retired mathematician do for recreation? "Math is my principal recreation. I enjoy walking. I enjoy the beautiful outdoors. I love to swim. We went to Hawaii for a month this winter and we rented a little tiny shack on the beach. We both love to swim and this was wonderful. We sat under a tree and did math and swam and went for walks. I love to read ... murder mysteries ... anything ... I like to read almost anything. I enjoy plays and music." Fundamentally, however, mathematics is where she has always spent her extra time.

Notes

The information included in this biography is based in part on an interview by the author.

1. Mary Ellen Rudin, quoted in D. J. Albers, G. L. Alexanderson, and C. Reid, *More Mathematical People: Contemporary Conversations* (Orlando, FL: Harcourt Brace Jovanovich, 1990), p. 286.

2. Ibid., pp. 283–291.

Selected Works by Mary Ellen Rudin

(1957). A Note on Certain Function Spaces (with V. L. Klee). *Achivum Mathematicum* 7, pp. 469–70.

(1957). A Subset of the Countable Ordinals. *American Mathematical Monthly* 64, p. 351.

(1965). A Technique for Constructing Examples. *Proceedings of the American Mathematical Society* 16, pp. 1320–23.

(1972). The Box Product of Countably Many Compact Metric Spaces. *General Topology and its Applications* 2, pp. 293–98.

(1975). *Lectures on Set Theoretic Topology*. Providence, RI: American Mathematical Society.

(1977). Some Examples of Normal Moore Spaces (with M. Starbird). *Canadian Journal of Mathematics* 29, p. 84.

(1981). Directed Sets Which Converge. In L. F. McAuley and M. M. Rao, Eds., *General Topology and Modern Analysis* (pp. 295–305). New York: Academic Press.

(1990). Two Nonmetrizable Manifolds. *Topology and its Applications* 35, pp. 137–52.

(1992). Monotone Normality (with A. Balogh). *Topology and its Applications* 47, pp. 115–27.

Selected Works about Mary Ellen Rudin

Albers, D. J., Alexanderson, G. L., and Reid, C. (1990). *More Mathematical People: Contemporary Conversations* (pp. 283–303). Orlando, FL: Harcourt Brace Jovanovich.

Karr, R. M., Rezaie, J., and Wilson, J. E. (1987). Mary Ellen Rudin. In L. Grinstein and P. Campbell, Eds., *Women of Mathematics* (pp. 190–92). Westport, CT: Greenwood Press.

Tall, F. D., Ed. (1993). *The Work of Mary Ellen Rudin.* New York: New York Academy of Sciences.

MARGARET R. MEYER

MARY BETH RUSKAI
(1944–)
Birthplace: Ohio

There is a vast difference between the mathematics learned in elementary and secondary school and the actual practice of research mathematics. If we taught music the way we teach science and math, we'd teach the students to tune the instruments precisely, just so, but we'd never allow them to play. And then they'd say they hate music.
—Mary Beth Ruskai

Mary Beth Ruskai, a professor of mathematics at the University of Massachusetts in Lowell, always liked mathematics and knew that she wanted to be "some kind of scientist." She finds mathematics satisfying because it rewards understanding rather than memorization.

Ruskai's parents, first-generation college graduates, provided encouragement for academic achievement during her early years in Cleveland, Ohio. Her father, an engineer, and her mother, a professional dietician, while perhaps not appreciating their daughter's "tomboy" activities, did support Ruskai's love of science and mathematics.

Sputnik I was launched in 1957, the year that Ruskai was in the eighth grade. This unmanned satellite, the first of a series launched by the Soviet Union, sparked a drive to build a science program in the United States in order to compete with the Soviet achievement. Even though women

Mary Beth Ruskai. Photo courtesy of Lilian Kemp.

scientists were not the norm at this time, there was a feeling that the country needed scientists so badly that even women should go into scientific fields. This atmosphere had a great impact on the aspiring scientist/mathematician. Ruskai concluded that if she became a scientist she would be successful and appreciated.

Ruskai graduated from Notre Dame College in Cleveland, Ohio, in 1965 with a B.S. in chemistry and enough credits for a second major in mathematics. Realizing how much she enjoyed the mathematical part of her undergraduate education, she continued to study mathematics as well as physics and chemistry in graduate school. She simultaneously received her M.A in mathematics and Ph.D. in physical chemistry from the University of Wisconsin in 1969. Upon graduation she was offered a Battelle postdoctoral fellowship in mathematical physics at the Institut de Physique Théorique in Geneva, Switzerland, from 1969 to 1971. Ruskai found this to be one of the first of many satisfying professional experiences. Subsequently she has held positions at the Courant Institute of Mathematical Sciences in New York, the Bunting Institute at Radcliffe College, and MIT, the latter two in Cambridge, Massachusetts. Currently she is a professor in the Department of Mathematics at the University of Massachusetts in Lowell, Massachusetts.

Ruskai's research focuses on mathematical problems that arise in the study of quantum mechanics, particularly those that relate to atoms and molecules with many electrons. In 1972, while holding a postdoctoral position at MIT, she and her adviser, Elliot Lieb, proved the strong subadditivity of quantum mechanical entropy. The quest for this proof had been going on for five years and was considered quite important to the professional community.

In 1981 Ruskai developed the first proof that an atom could have only finite numbers of electrons bound to it. The negative electrons are attracted to the positive nucleus but repel one another, with the number of repulsions growing in the form of $N^2/2$, where N is the number of electrons. If the nuclear charge is $+z$, the total attraction is in the form of Nz, so that, as one tries to add more and more electrons, it seems as if the quadratic repulsion must eventually "win," limiting the number of electrons that can be bound. However, the sizes of the attractive and repulsive terms vary with the location of the electrons. This leads to difficult mathematical problems in both classical and quantum physics. Ruskai also studied the related problem of how many electrons could be removed from a stable molecule before the repulsion of the positive nuclei would cause the molecule to split apart in what is called a Coulomb explosion.

Ruskai became interested in wavelet theory in the late 1980s, recognizing it as potentially very powerful. Wavelet theory can be described as a mathematical tool for multiscale analysis. Wavelets are sets of functions that are useful for transmitting pictures with different amounts of detail. Wavelets allow efficient algorithms to be built that use scale adjustment, like a zoom lens, to analyze fine detail. One wavelet-based algorithm has been adopted by the FBI for fingerprint compression. This algorithm allows the FBI to store, on computer disks, the 200 million fingerprint files that otherwise would take up over an acre of office space. Using this algorithm 95 percent of the data can be selectively discarded, yet the fingerprints may still be reconstructed with sufficient accuracy to make reliable identifications. In 1990 Ruskai organized the first U.S conference on wavelet theory, the NSF/CBMS Regional Conference in the Mathematical Sciences on Wavelets in Lowell, Massachusetts.

In conjunction with her research, Ruskai has published and edited over thirty articles and books. She has become an advocate for women in mathematics and science and has written and published papers on issues of gender and science. She has been an invited speaker at international conferences such as the Conference on Women and Science at Barnard

College, and the International Commission on Mathematical Instruction Study on Gender Issues in Mathematics Education in Hoor, Sweden. In addition, from 1992 to 1995 she chaired the Joint Committee on Women in Mathematical Sciences. This committee includes representatives from seven national organizations in the mathematical sciences. She is involved, as well, in the Association for Women in Mathematics.

Ruskai emphasizes that mathematics is not so much about following rules as it is about inventing new rules and examining their consequences. She believes it is important for women to understand that much of what they enjoy has a mathematical aspect. Many girls like to work puzzles, but most people don't realize that working puzzles involves mathematical thinking. Ruskai has shared the frustration of fellow female mathematicians and scientists who are rarely able to share their joy with other women, many of whom retain the negative attitudes they developed toward mathematics in school. Ruskai further questions the belief that women are only interested in practical applications and not in the theoretical aspects of science. Perhaps the greatest loss to our culture is not in the lack of career opportunities, but in the lack of opportunities for women to find pleasure within science. Societal perceptions of science as eccentric and nonconformist present a challenge to both sexes.

Ruskai's work has given her the opportunity to travel throughout Europe and North America, visiting and working with colleagues in many different countries. During her postdoctoral work in Geneva she developed a love of mountain climbing, skiing, and backpacking, activities that she continues to pursue. As a backcountry hiker she is among those who pioneered a route on the ridge above Tourist Creek recorded in the *Field Book of the Wind River Range*, a backcountry guide to Wyoming by Orrin H. and Lorraine G. Bonney. She is also an avid squash player. For entertainment Ruskai loves reading a good mystery; she also enjoys live theater, particularly serious drama.

Mary Beth Ruskai continues to influence the world of mathematical physics, not only in her professional work but also in her support of the advancement of women in mathematics and science. She hopes that women will study and be successful in mathematics because they like the field, because they feel comfortable and accepted in it, and because they are as excited about it as she is. She believes in the old adage, "Do what you love first and success will follow."

Note

The information included in this biography is based in part on an interview by the author.

Selected Works by Mary Beth Ruskai

(1973). Proof of the Strong Subadditivity of Quantum Mechanical Entropy, *Journal of Mathematical Physics* 14, 1938 1941 (with E. Lieb).

(1988). Location of Essential Spectrum of Intermediate Hamiltonians Restricted To Symmetry Subspaces, *Journal of Mathematical Physics*, 29, 2236–2240 (with C. Beattie).

(1991). Absence of Bound States in Extremely Asymmetric Positive Diatomic Molecules, *Communications in Mathematical Physics* 137, 553–566.

(1992). Editor-in-Chief, *Wavelets and Their Applications* (Boston: Jones & Bartlett Publishers) with an introduction by M. B. Ruskai (co-edited with G. Beylkin, R. Coifman, I. Daubechies, S. Mallat, Y. Meyer, and L. Raphael).

(1992). Relative Entropy under Mappings by Stochastic Matrices, (with J. E. Cohen, Y. Isawa, G. Rautu, E. Seneta, and G. Zbaganu). *Linear Algebra and its Applications* 179, pp. 211–35.

(1994). Beyond Strong Subadditivity? Improved Bounds on the Contraction of Relative Entropy. *Reviews in Mathematical Physics* 6, pp. 1147–61. Reprinted in M. Aizenman and H. Araki, Eds., *The State of Matter* (River Edge, NJ: World Scientific, 1994).

(1994). Equivalence of Certain Entropy Contraction Coefficients (with M. D. Choi and E. Seneta). *Linear Algebra and its Applications* 208/209, pp. 29–36.

SUSAN ZACHARKIW

CORA SADOSKY

(1940–   )

Birthplace: Buenos Aires, Argentina

Cora Sadosky, professor of mathematics at Howard University in Washington, D.C., was born in Buenos Aires, Argentina. In the course of her education and mathematical work she has lived in South America, North America, and Europe. Cora's mother, Cora Ratto de Sadosky, an Argentinean mathematician, was both a professor at the University of Buenos Aires and an organizer in the fight for human rights. Her father, Manuel Sadosky, was founding director of the Computer Science Center at the University of Buenos Aires. Cora Sadosky has earned a reputation as a respected researcher and has been an active leader in the continued quest for equal rights. Her aspiration is that, "In the next century everybody will have the right to mathematics."

As a child, Sadosky accompanied her parents to Europe when they traveled to pursue postdoctoral studies. She started elementary school in Paris and ended her secondary schooling by studying at home in Buenos Aires, attending a total of eleven different schools in three dif-

Cora Sadosky. Photo courtesy of Cora
Sadosky and the Association of Women
in Mathematics.

ferent countries along the way. Perhaps it was this combination of factors
that caused her to start college at age 15. During her high school education she was tutored in physics by Mario Bunge, a physicist and close
family friend who later became a world-renowned philosopher of science. Under his tutelage Cora became fascinated with the workings of
the universe and thus entered the School of Sciences of the University
of Buenos Aires with the intention of majoring in physics.

However, Cora was soon captivated by the beauty of structures in
modern algebra. By the end of her first semester she had switched her
major to mathematics. During her junior year the eminent Polish mathematician Antoni Zygmund visited Argentina and lectured at the University of Buenos Aires. Zygmund had emigrated to the United States
at the beginning of World War II and had created an important school
of analysis at the University of Chicago. His teaching, and that of his
collaborators who later visited Buenos Aires, had a marked influence on
Cora's future as a mathematician. In 1960, upon earning the degree of
Licenciada (comparable to the M.S. degree in the United States), she was
offered a research assistantship by Zygmund to work on her doctorate
in mathematics at the University of Chicago.

Sadosky arrived in Chicago in the winter of 1961; in spite of the rough weather, she felt intensely happy to attend such a fine university and meet such brilliant mathematicians. She was, however, quite surprised to be the only woman in the Ph.D. program (in all the sciences, not only in mathematics), but she wrote it off as "American savagery." She certainly did not think that being a woman was at all detrimental to her studies. "It just never crossed my mind. I always felt equal to the boys."

While working on her doctorate Sadosky met Daniel Goldstein, a recently graduated Argentinean physician interested in molecular biology, who was then at Yale University. Cora earned her doctorate in early 1965 and returned to Argentina to marry Daniel. She was appointed assistant professor of mathematics at the University of Buenos Aires, where she stayed until July 1966. Then, following a brutal police assault on the School of Sciences, Sadosky, with 400 other faculty members (including her mother), resigned her position in protest. Sadosky taught for a semester at the Uruguay National University and then joined her husband, who was doing postdoctoral work at Johns Hopkins University. She was appointed assistant professor at Johns Hopkins, and there she realized for the first time a striking fact about being a woman in mathematics: Her salary was two-thirds that of her male counterparts.

Sadosky and her husband returned to Buenos Aires in 1968, but she was unable to gain an academic position in Argentina, which was still ruled by the military. That meant much more than not having a job: She did not have access to a mathematics library, seminars, or any other accouterments of academic life. Finally, isolation forced a long hiatus in her mathematical work. To make a living she worked as a technical translator, editor, and proofreader. Fortunately, in 1973 the leading Argentinean mathematician Mischa Cotlar returned to the country; he and Sadosky started a productive collaboration that continues today.

In 1971, during the period of mathematical isolation, one of the happiest events of her life took place: Cora and Daniel had a daughter, Cora Sol Goldstein. It worked out well to have flexible hours and no outside work demands. Still, Sadosky's mother convinced her of the need to remain connected to her academic work, and she helped by paying for daycare to ensure daily study time for the new mother at a public library.

In 1974 the campaign of terror unleashed by the military and its paramilitary groups—against intellectuals, human right activists, and many others—forced Sadosky and her family to flee Argentina. Thanks to her collaboration with Cotlar, who had relocated to Caracas, she was invited to join the faculty of the School of Sciences at the Central University of Venezuela, where Cotlar and Sadosky continued their joint research work. Sadosky began to publish again and prepared the manuscript for a graduate textbook. This work was based on her graduate student notes from Chicago and her teaching notes from Uruguay, Argentina, and Venezuela. The book was published in 1979 in the United States. For the academic year 1978–1979, Sadosky was a member-in-residence at the Institute for Advanced Study (IAS) in Princeton, New Jersey. This was a critical year for her return to mathematics. In 1980 her career resumed fully with her appointment as associate professor of mathematics at Howard University. She was promoted to full professor in 1985 and is frequently sought out as an inspiring lecturer.

Sadosky's mathematics career has been centered in the United States since her return in 1980, although her international ties remain strong. In 1985, after the ignominious departure from power of the last Argentinean military junta, Sadosky and her family returned to Buenos Aires for a year of work "back home." It was wonderful to find bright and enthusiastic students there, but the academic situation in mathematics was not hospitable to her permanent return. She has made an increasing number of working trips abroad to Spain, France, Italy, Germany, Sweden, Scotland, England, Canada, Argentina, Venezuela, and Mexico. These trips are facilitated by her fluency in Spanish, French, Italian, and English. Many awards have been bestowed on Sadosky during her research career. In 1983–1984 she was awarded a visiting professorship for women (VPW) in science and technology from the National Science Foundation (NSF) and returned to Princeton as a member of the IAS. In 1987–1988 Sadosky received a Career Advancement Award from the NSF, which allowed her to spend a year as a member of the Classical Analysis Program at the Mathematical Sciences Research Institute (MSRI) in Berkeley, California. She later returned to MSRI as a research professor and co-organizer of the Holomorphic Spaces Program. In 1995 a second VPW from the NSF enabled Sadosky to accept an invitation as visiting professor at the University of California at Berkeley.

Sadosky's mathematical work is in analysis, a branch of mathematics that, although theoretical, has applications to probability and control theories. This work is increasingly significant in engineering. Her research over the last twenty years has centered on developing, in collaboration with Mischa Cotlar, an abstract extension theory for operators that commute with evolutions in scattering structures. Such operators model many transformations occurring in several engineering fields. Their extension properties provide a wide array of applications to signal processing and to the theory of feedback control of automatic devices, such as the control system of the space shuttle. Sadosky has published more than forty articles on her research in harmonic analysis and operator theory.

About her work Sadosky says, "Teaching lets me feel like I'm doing something right. I can finish a class and say to myself that it was successful. When one is doing research, it is more difficult to be equally satisfied. Most of the time the problem is not being solved. Then when you solve the problem you are working on, you feel fantastic. But that moment of euphoria is quite short. In no time you're frustrated by the next problem." Her research comes from a strong inner drive, yielding the utmost satisfaction; teaching, however, provides much more immediate and positive feedback. Yet she finds that her research provides her the inspiration for teaching mathematics in new and dynamic ways.

As she reached her thirties, Sadosky began to notice that many talented women mathematicians of her generation were no longer working in their fields. The inequality of opportunity and lack of support for women in science became unacceptable to her. In the 1970s the women's movement facilitated the breaking down of barriers that had prevented many women from having equal access to education and careers. Sadosky welcomed the movement with enthusiasm and became active in promoting women in mathematics. Then came a golden opportunity: She was elected president of the Association for Women in Mathematics (AWM), the organization that brought about real changes in the status of women in mathematics, both in the United States and abroad. These changes were achieved through the dedication and hard work of the Association's members, and Sadosky threw herself into AWM work with passion.

Equity is a theme that reaches into every corner of Sadosky's life. In addition to her continuing work through AWM to improve the status of women in mathematics, she is a strong advocate for actions to increase the participation of groups that have been denied equal access to mathematics and the sciences. As a tenured faculty member of a historically black university (Howard University), she has worked toward greater participation of African Americans in mathematics.

As a teacher she strives to return to others some of the wonders she received from her own teachers. As a researcher she expects to continue proving theorems, hoping for good mathematical results. One of her main preoccupations remains undergraduate teaching, where she thinks many people become deeply discouraged and never gain the indispensable mastery of the mathematical basics. "Mathematics," she says, "gives the most incredible intellectual pleasure. It allows you to reach with your fingers and touch the fingers of the gods."

Note

The information included in this biography is based in part on an interview by the authors.

Selected Works by Cora Sadosky

(1979). (Ed.). *Analysis and Partial Differential Equations, Lecture Notes in Pure and Applied Mathematics* 122. New York: Marcel Dekker.
(1990). (Ed.). *Analysis and Partial Differential Equations, Lecture Notes in Pure and Applied Mathematics* 122, New York: Marcel Dekker.

(1994). (with M. Cotlar). The Adamyan-Arov-Krein Theorem in General and Regular Representations of the Plane and the Symplectic Plane. *Operator Theory: Advances and Applications* 71, pp. 54–78.

(1994). (with M. Cotlar). Nehari and Nevanlinna-Pick Problems and Holomorphic Extensions in the Polydisk in Terms of Restricted BMO. *Journal of Functional Analysis* 124, pp. 205–10.

(1996). (with M. Cotlar). Two Distinguished Subspaces of Product BMO and the Nehari-AAK Theory for Hankel Operators on the Torus. *Integral Equations and Operator Theory* 26, pp. 276–304.

(1997). Liftings of Kernels Shift-Invariant in Scattering Systems. In *Holomorphic Spaces*, MSRI Book Series, Vol. 32. London: Cambridge University Press.

CHARLENE MORROW and LYNN BENANDER

ALICE TURNER SCHAFER
(1915–)
Birthplace: Virginia

Alice Schafer, professor emerita at Wellesley College, wrote that "In the past fifteen years, many individuals and many organizations in the United States have worked long and hard to ensure that women have the same opportunities for education, for professional careers, and for advancement in their careers as men."[1] Schafer herself has made her mark as one of these hardworking individuals in the world of mathematics. She is a person with tremendous energy and determination. At a very early point in her life she observed that women and girls were treated unfairly in society, and she has spent her life and energy in trying to provide women with equal opportunities in mathematics.

Alice lost her parents at a very early age and was reared by her two aunts. She lived with one of her aunts in Scottsburg, Virginia. Her other aunt, who was married and lived in Richmond, provided Alice with financial support. She describes herself as having been protesting all her life. She recalls as a child "always being jealous of what the boys were allowed to do and [she] wasn't," from climbing trees to having an Indian outfit like her best friend Johnny. Even at that early age her struggles were not in vain. It took some work, but she finally managed to persuade her aunts to buy her a boy's Indian outfit.

Although Alice's aunts may have had traditional ideas of what girls should play with, they had no preconceived notions of what careers women should hold. Alice was never discouraged from her love of mathematics by her aunts or her uncle. They were always supportive of her

Alice Schafer. Photo courtesy of Ron Agnir.

decision to pursue a career in mathematics. Her family's support was undoubtedly a source of strength for Alice during her school years.

Alice finished high school in 1932. She had developed an interest in mathematics by then and wanted to attend the University of Richmond, but her high school principal believed that "girls don't do mathematics" and would not write a letter of recommendation for her. In spite of this Alice was awarded a full scholarship to the University of Richmond and started school there in the fall of 1932.

Once she got to Richmond her battles continued. At that time the University of Richmond students were segregated by gender. The library and all the laboratories were located on the men's section of the campus. Women students were not allowed in the library. They requested the books they wanted; the books were then delivered to a reading room in the women's section of the campus. After a long and hard battle Schafer was granted entry into the library. The first day she had access to the building she sat in the reading room to read Cyrano de Bergerac, thought it hilariously funny, and was kicked out for laughing aloud. She was told never to darken the doors of the library again. Later that summer the librarian, who thought that mathematics majors could alphabetize well, hired Alice to do cataloguing work for the library. Alice sums up the incident in her own words: "I was good enough to work in the library, but not good enough to sit at the tables to study and think."

Alice did have some women mentors at the University of Richmond. In particular, in the first two years of mathematics courses the women students were taught by a female faculty member. Alice recalls that this woman never finished her doctoral degree because she said it would be futile. She knew she would never be promoted at the University of Richmond or allowed to teach a course beyond analytic geometry.

After the first two years, students of both sexes were in the same classes in mathematics and in the sciences. Alice was an outstanding mathematics student, and the faculty treated her with a mixture of prejudice against her gender and grudging support of her performance as an outstanding student. At one point in her junior year the dean of Westhampton College (the women's college) called Alice to her office. She wanted to warn Alice that the chairman of the mathematics department had been heard to say that he wanted to flunk every woman who took his analysis class because he wanted no women mathematics majors. The dean encouraged Alice to "stand her ground." Alice says that in fact she was so young and naive that it never would have occurred to her not to continue studying mathematics.

At that time there was a Crump Prize for juniors majoring in mathematics. The students were given a set of problems to solve within twenty-four hours. Alice, who was now the sole woman mathematics major, won the prize over all the other students. The mathematics department chairman's only comment to her was: "I never thought you would win." Alice was so angry that it was twenty years before she realized that the men on the mathematics faculty, including the chairman, at least must have graded the papers fairly.

After finishing college Alice decided to pursue a career in mathematics. For several reasons the University of Chicago seemed a good choice for graduate school. The woman who was her mentor in the mathematics department at Richmond had experience with the University of Chicago, as two of her colleagues in the history department had received doctorates there. After teaching high school for three years in Virginia (she needed the money), Alice started graduate school at the University of Chicago in the fall of 1939 on a full scholarship. During the last two years of her graduate work she held a University of Chicago Fellowship. She worked in metric and projective differential geometry, respectively, for her master's and doctoral degrees.

Not surprisingly, Alice's graduate school experience was also riddled with incidents of discrimination. Only four of the approximately sixty graduate students were women. A striking example of inequity among the graduate students occurred during the weekly colloquia. The women students were in charge of ordering cakes, serving tea after the talk, and cleaning up. Alice saw how unfair it was that the men would be able to talk mathematics with the speakers and mathematics faculty while the women served them. She "put up a row." As a result the men, of their own accord, started to help clean up after the colloquia.

When Alice completed her doctoral degree she and Richard Schafer, a fellow graduate student at Chicago, were married. (They now have two sons and three grandchildren.) Alice Schafer held faculty positions at several schools including Douglas College (now a part of Rutgers University), the University of Michigan, and Swarthmore College. While her husband was in the Navy and stationed in San Francisco, she worked for a time writing a history of the Army in World War II. In 1959, while Schafer was teaching at Connecticut College, her husband found a job in Massachusetts. They had a commuting marriage for three years. In 1962 Schafer also moved to Massachusetts and began teaching at Wellesley College. She retired from there in 1980.

Given her limitless energy, it is not surprising that Schafer kept working after she retired. She was a lecturer at Simmons College and at the Radcliffe College Seminars until her husband retired in 1988. They then moved to Virginia, where she is currently a professor at Marymount College. She was chair of the mathematics department at Marymount until the fall of 1995.

Throughout her career Alice Schafer has been involved in many projects and organizations designed to encourage and provide opportunities for women in mathematics. She was one of the founding members of the Association for Women in Mathematics (AWM). During the early 1970s in several parts of the country women in mathematics were organizing informal meetings to discuss discrimination faced by women in the mathematics community. These meetings were being held independently of one another. Schafer organized the meetings in the Boston area. The format of the meetings varied but usually involved mathematical talks by women graduate students as well as some discussion time.

In 1971, at an American Mathematical Society meeting, the women who had been involved in these informal meetings joined to form an organization. This organization is now the Association for Women in Mathematics. The purpose of the AWM is to improve the status of women mathematicians in the mathematics community. **Mary Gray** of American University was the first president of the AWM. In 1972 Schafer was elected the second president. She has, since her presidency, been an active and important contributing member of the AWM.

Schafer has always recognized the importance of encouraging women at the outset of their careers. Her efforts in this direction were honored by the AWM in 1989 when it established the Alice T. Schafer Prize for

Excellence in Mathematics by an undergraduate woman. The Schafer Prize was first awarded in 1990.

One of her outstanding efforts in reaching high school students and encouraging them to pursue careers in mathematics is her involvement in the Sonia Kovalevsky High School Days for women students and their teachers. The Days are an opportunity for young women and their teachers to learn about the pioneering work of **Sofya Kovalevskaia**[2] and to attend workshops where they are exposed to accessible topics in mathematics.[3] In 1985 the AWM sponsored a symposium on the legacy of Sofya Kovalevskaia, celebrating the fifteenth anniversary of the AWM and the twenty-fifth anniversary of the Bunting Institute at Radcliffe College. Pamela Coxson, one of the fellows at the Bunting Institute, suggested that a program for high school women students and their teachers be included as part of the celebration. The day's activities were modeled on earlier work Coxson had done for inner-city students in Los Angeles. That first Sonia Kovalevsky High School Day was a huge success. Simmons College has held a Sonia Kovalevsky High School Day each spring since then. Schafer was among the primary fundraisers and organizers for the event during part of her tenure at Simmons. Other institutions now also hold Days, and they are always tremendously popular.[4]

Schafer has also supported the development and collaboration of women scientists at an international level. She was to lead the first tour of women mathematicians to the People's Republic of China in 1989, sponsored by People to People International. Unfortunately the trip was cancelled because of political violence in China. Instead, Schafer led a tour of eighteen women and two men in 1990. In 1995 she was invited by the Citizen Ambassador Program of People to People to join with a Chinese scientist to lead the Women in Mathematics and Science session of the U.S./China Joint Conference on Women's Issues. The meeting was scheduled to coincide with the fourth United Nations Conference on Women in Beijing.

In comparing the situation for women mathematicians between the beginning of her career and now, Schafer states that even though the situation has improved, discrimination against women in mathematics has not vanished. In her own words, "This has not been an easy task, and much remains to be done; but there has been some progress."[5] What is true beyond a doubt is that Schafer's energy, determination, and work have not only touched and encouraged the individual women she has mentored, but helped provide many more young women with the opportunity to pursue a career in mathematics.

Notes

The information included in this biography is based in part on an interview by the author.

1. Foreword, Louise Grinstein and Paul Campbell, *Women of Mathematics* (Westport, CT: Greenwood Press, 1987).

2. There is confusion about the spelling of Kovalevskaia's name, probably because of different translations from the Russian. "Kovalevskaia" is probably the more accurate spelling because all female Russian patronymics end in the letter 'a'. However, we have kept the alternate spelling when referring to the Sonia Kovalevsky High School Days because that has been the spelling since the beginning of the program.

3. For a description of the Days held at American University in 1994, see *AWM Newsletter* 24, no. 4 (July–August 1994).

4. For information about organizing Sonia Kovalevsky High School Days, contact the AWM, 4114 Computer & Space Sciences Bldg., University of Maryland, College Park, MD 20742–2461.

5. Foreword, Grinstein and Campbell, *Women of Mathematics*.

Selected Works by Alice Schafer

(1944). Two Singularities of Space Curves. *Duke Mathematical Journal* 11, pp. 655–70.

(1948). The Neighborhood of an Undulation Point of a Space Curve. *American Journal of Mathematics* 70, pp. 351–63.

(1965). Some Theorems on Finite Groups. *American Mathematical Monthly* 72.

(1981). (with M. W. Gray). Sex and Mathematics, *Science* 16.

(1981). Women and Mathematics. In L. A. Steen (Ed.), *Mathematics Tomorrow*. New York: Springer-Verlag.

(1991). Mathematics and Women: Perspectives and Progress. *American Mathematical Society Notices* (September). Reprinted in the Mathematical Association of America Notes Series, 1994.

AYSE A. SAHIN

DORIS WOOD SCHATTSCHNEIDER
(1939–)
Birthplace: New York

The work of Doris (Wood) Schattschneider, professor of mathematics at Moravian College, has been instrumental in opening the world of visual geometry not only to mathematicians but to students of mathematics. Doris, born on October 19, 1939, was the second of four children. As a daughter of two professional parents, there was no question that Doris and her siblings would be fully educated. Family expectations were high, and her father was very demanding. Doris's mother, Charlotte Lucile Ingalls Wood, had received a master's degree in classics from Cornell

Doris Schattschneider. Photo courtesy of Doris
Schattschneider.

University and taught Regents Latin in high schools on Staten Island.
She was also coauthor of a widely used Latin textbook. Doris's father,
Robert W. Wood Jr., a graduate of City College of New York, was a
mechanical engineer for the Bureau of Bridges of the City of New York.
Both her sisters are nurses; her brother, formerly a systems analyst for
the Navy, is now an independent contractor.

During Doris's youth, the Wood household revolved around lively
dinner table discussions. Her father always wanted to know what had
happened at school that day. If anyone asked a question about the meaning of a word or topic, the questioner had to leave the table and look
up the answer before dinner could proceed. Thus, Doris and her siblings
were introduced to research skills, at the dinner table, every day.

Doris's first recollection of school is that of enjoying kindergarten in
Lake Placid, New York. She spent her day doing first grade work because she had been reading and printing since the age of 4. The next

year, she remembers reading the Dick and Jane stories and learning to write in cursive. Her family had moved to Lake Placid from Staten Island, New York, when her father was overseas with the Army's 36th Engineers during World War II. She remembers waiting for letters from her father, who was stationed in North Africa and Sicily; these letters were crude photostats of the originals, censored for security purposes. When she returned to Staten Island, Doris, a third-generation Staten Islander, was two years ahead of her classmates.

In school, Doris enjoyed all subjects. She was a voracious reader of popular girls' series such as Nancy Drew and Judy Bolton. For a time she considered becoming a nurse, but blood did not appeal to her. Throughout both elementary and high school, close friendships were very important to Doris. This affinity was nurtured over the years in both church and community organizations; Doris progressed from being a Bluebird to a Camp Fire Girl to a Horizon Girl with the same leader and the same group of friends all the way through twelfth grade. These friendships remained stable throughout college and beyond to post-college reunions.

In high school Doris tutored her peers for the mathematics portion of the Regents examinations, worrying more about her friends' success than her own. Teaching is in her blood; not only was her mother a teacher, but her maternal grandfather, Frank G. Ingalls, had been an elementary school teacher and a principal on Staten Island.

Mathematics came easily to Doris, and she enjoyed its challenges. She was encouraged by her high school mathematics teacher, a woman who tantalized her with the suggestion that some questions not answered by algebra would be answered when she learned calculus in college. In college she enjoyed physics, but that instructor did not encourage her. Studio art and sculpture were also favorite activities. Doris wanted to create work rather than analyze the work of others. She finally decided to study mathematics and, in the process, discovered more about mathematics, found answers to intriguing questions, and shared her learning through her writings and lectures throughout the world.

After receiving an A.B. degree in mathematics from the University of Rochester, Doris went on to Yale University, where she earned her M.A. and Ph.D. degrees, both in mathematics. She is currently professor of mathematics at Moravian College in Bethlehem, Pennsylvania. Prior to this she taught at the University of Illinois in Chicago and at Northwestern University. She has served as department chair at Moravian College for several periods (1971–1974, 1985–1988, and 1989–1992).

Symmetry, the artwork of M. C. Escher, and geometric models have long held a special fascination for Schattschneider. Geometry offers a world of exciting ideas to ponder and explore. Symmetry, one aspect of geometry, appears everywhere in the world around us. In nature we notice that the wings of a butterfly have mirror, or bilateral, symmetry. In kaleidoscopes, mirrors are used to produce beautiful and ever-changing symmetric patterns. Dancers produce rotational symmetry as they hold hands and move in circles. Most traditional symbols and designs are symmetric in one or more ways. Even our own bodies offer numerous examples of symmetry.

Schattschneider's dual interest in geometry and art led naturally to her study of tiling problems and the work of the Dutch artist M. C. Escher. (A tiling is the repetition of one shape, or several shapes, that can be repeated to completely cover the plane.) Over the years she has authored many scholarly articles on tiling the plane and has revealed to the professional world the mathematical investigations of M. C. Escher and of homemaker and amatuer mathematician Marjorie Rice. Schattschneider is coauthor of a book and collection of geometric models, *M. C. Escher Kaleidocycles*, that has been translated into sixteen European languages.

As senior associate of the Visual Geometry Project, a project funded by the National Science Foundation, she collaborated with colleagues (including Eugene Klotz from Swarthmore College) to develop and produce three activity books with hands-on geometric models and computer-animated videotapes. These materials, designed to teach about two- and three-dimensional forms, include a videotape on the computer program The Geometer's Sketchpad to be used in teaching geometry. All materials are published by Key Curriculum Press. The newest video is entitled *Three-Dimensional Symmetry*.

Professor Schattschneider has lectured and given workshops on numerous campuses, and at national and international meetings, on the topics of tiling and polyhedra, dynamic geometry, geometry and art, and visualization in teaching. She is the author of more than thirty articles, and author or coauthor of several books. Research for her books has been supported by the National Endowment for the Humanities and the Fund for the Improvement of Post-Secondary Education (FIPSE), an agency of the U.S. Department of Education. Her article entitled "Tiling the Plane with Congruent Pentagons" earned the MAA Carl B. Allendoerfer award in 1986. In 1996 Schattschneider was the invited keynote speaker for the U.S. Mathematics Olympiad winners' awards banquet.

Presently, Schattschneider is first vice president of the Mathematical Association of America (MAA). Previously she has served the organization as vice chair of the Eastern Pennsylvania and Delaware (EPADEL) section of the MAA, as chair from 1977 to 1979, and as governor from 1986 to 1989. In 1991 she received the MAA's certificate of meritorious service. She has served on the editorial board of *Mathematics Magazine* and was its editor from 1981 to 1985. In 1993 she received the MAA Award for Distinguished Teaching of College or University Mathematics.

In addition to her extensive professional affiliation with the MAA,

Schattschneider is involved with the American Mathematical Society; the Association for Women in Mathematics; the National Council of Teachers of Mathematics; and the Association of Teachers of Mathematics; a British organization. She is a member of Phi Beta Kappa and Pi Mu Epsilon, having served as national councillor from 1990 to the present.

Doris has been married for over thirty years to David Schattschneider, who is a church historian and dean of the Moravian Theological Seminary. Their daughter, Laura, received a master's degree in comparative literature from the University of California, Berkeley; taught in Germany on a Fulbright Fellowship; and is currently completing her studies for a Ph.D. in comparative literature at Berkeley.

In her leisure time Doris enjoys visiting art museums, an interest she has had since childhood. Since ninth grade she has enjoyed designing and making her own clothes including dresses, suits, coats, and even her wedding gown. Her other interests include reading, walking, and extensive travel all over the world.

In thinking back on her life so far, Schattschneider notes that the majority of her work has been done in collaboration with others. The Visual Geometry Project, for example, was a collaboration of a team of people. *A Companion to Calculus* (1995) was produced as a group project. Contrary to some stereotypes, communication skills can be very important to success in mathematics (as in many other fields). Not only has Schattschneider had to communicate with her colleagues and peers, but at times she has had to communicate with nonmathematicians as well. In writing the *Kaleidocycles* book, for example, she worked with a graphic designer who had failed geometry three times. She could not communicate with him in the traditional sense; rather, they communicated intuitively. Schattschneider has become aware of different learning styles and how difficult it is for some people to learn in a traditional way; some people must invent their own ways of understanding.

Doris Schattschneider has never stopped learning about mathematics and geometric relationships. Her own enthusiasm for learning and her desire to help others learn have been the cornerstones of her professional and personal life.

Note

The information included in this biography is based in part on an interview by the author.

Selected Works by Doris Schattschneider

(1977). *M. C. Escher Kaleidocycles* (with Wallace Walker). New York: Ballantine Books. Rev. ed., Corte Madera, CA: Pomegranate Artbooks, 1987. European language ed., Berlin: TACO, 1987.

(1978). Tiling the Plane with Congruent Pentagons. *Mathematics Magazine* 51, pp. 29–44. Reprinted in G. Andrews, Ed., *Percy Alexander MacMahon, Collected Papers*, Vol. 2. Cambridge, MA: MIT Press. (Article won MAA Carl B. Allendoerfer award.)

(1981). In Praise of Amateurs. In D. Klaner, ed., *The Mathematical Gardener* (pp. 140–66). Boston: Prindle, Weber & Schmidt.

(1987). The Polya-Escher Connection. *Mathematics Magazine* 60, pp. 293–298.

(1991, 1996). *The Stella Octangula* (1991), *The Platonic Solids* (1991), and *Symmetry* (1996) (with Cynthia Schmalzreid, Hilary Best, and Annie Fetter). Berkeley, CA: Key Curriculum Press. (Activity books with accompanying videotapes.)

(1992). The Fascination of Tiling. *LEONARDO* 25(3/4), pp. 341–48.

(1992). *Visions of Symmetry: Notebooks, Periodic Drawings, and Related Work of M. C. Escher*. New York: W. H. Freeman.

(1994). Escher's Metaphors: The Prints and Drawings of M. C. Escher Give Expression to Abstract Concepts of Mathematics and Science. *Scientific American* (November), pp. 66–71.

(1995). *A Companion to Calculus* (with Dennis Ebersole, Alicia Sevilla, and Kay Somers). Pacific Grove: CA: Brooks/Cole.

REGINA BARON BRUNNER

CHARLOTTE ANGAS SCOTT
(1858–1931)
Birthplace: England

When Charlotte Scott, a highly respected mathematics researcher and professor, was born in England, there were almost no schools open to girls in that country—and no colleges whatsoever. While she was growing up, the first college for women opened in association with Cambridge University. When she was 18 years old Charlotte was offered a scholarship to join its freshman class, which had only eleven students. It was called Girton College, as if it were one of the "colleges" making up the university. In 1880 she took the undergraduate final exams of Cambridge University. To do this, she had to apply for and obtain special permission, because women were not allowed to be official students or to receive degrees. Many decades later she remembered the bitter cold of the six January days when she sat for a total of fifty hours taking tests. It was worth it. Only seven men in all of Cambridge University scored higher than she did in mathematics! Because she was a woman, she was not allowed to be present at the award ceremony or even have her name read. However, the young men protested such injustice. When the name

Charlotte Angas Scott.

of one of them was read aloud as Eighth Wrangler (eighth best student), they threw their hats into the air and shouted, "Scott of Girton! Scott of Girton!"

The news spread all over England. People responded by circulating petitions asking that all women who attended Cambridge women's colleges (by then there were two) be allowed to take the examinations with Cambridge men. Previously some Girton students who had spent over three years at the college were told they would not be allowed to take the final exams—simply because they were women. The Senate of Cambridge University considered the petitions. The following year it decided that henceforth, duly prepared students from its women's colleges would have the right to take the university's "Tripos" exams that qualified men for Honors, and to have their ratings posted among the men's. Decades later a man remembered that even schoolboys in 1880 talked about Scott's achievement.

To achieve so much without attending any school before college, a girl had to have a very supportive family—as did Charlotte Scott, born on

June 8, 1858. Her father, Caleb Scott, was an extremely gifted, energetic, and innovative man; and her mother, Eliza, was "a source of profound happiness" to him, according to his obituary. Little else is known about her mother. Charlotte's father was a Congregational minister who strongly supported intellectual attainment for all people and joy as a legitimate part of life. At home he played mathematical games with his own children. (For example: "Think of a number. Double it. Add six. Take half of the answer. Subtract the original number. Your answer is three!") When Charlotte was 7 years old he joined the staff of a college that prepared future Congregational minister and was renowned for its fine mathematics department. Four years later he became its president.

Clearly, Caleb Scott was unusually able to recruit tutors for his children. The first two of his seven children were girls, and he apparently made sure they had an excellent mathematics education. His firstborn, Charlotte's companion in childhood, died five months before Charlotte entered Girton College. One can only imagine the effect this had on the surviving sister's determination to use well her privilege of having a full lifetime.

One of the leaders in the 1880 Cambridge Senate fight for women was Arthur Cayley, an outstanding mathematician. He subsequently began to mentor Scott, and he was her close friend until his death fourteen years later. Under his supervision she completed the requirements for a doctorate in mathematics in 1885. Because women could not receive degrees from Cambridge (this policy held until 1948), where she had actually done her work, Scott took another set of examinations to meet the requirements for a doctorate from the University of London, which had begun granting degrees to women in 1876. She received a B.Sc. and a D.Sc. in 1882 and 1885, respectively. Both were First Class, the highest level possible.

While pursuing her graduate work, Scott became Girton College's first mathematics instructor. Before she was hired, Girton students had to either study with tutors who tolerated women or obtain special permission to attend lectures, sitting behind a screen at the back of the room so as not to distract the men. Obviously, this arrangement presented special disadvantages in mathematics. No doubt Scott's students were grateful for the privilege of studying directly with someone who knew the subject matter.

When Scott received her doctorate, there was only one woman professor in all the universities of Europe: **Sofya Kovalevskaya**, who was a mathematician at the University of Stockholm. Girls' high schools were being founded in England, providing jobs for many of Scott's classmates, but she aspired to become a research mathematician. Bryn Mawr College in Pennsylvania opened during that year with the goal of providing education for women equal to the best available for men. Scott ventured across the Atlantic Ocean to America and became one of the two women among the seven professors on its founding faculty. She was a pioneer in many aspects of her life, even in the way she wore her hair—bobbed short in 1885, a practice that was still highly controversial when she retired many years later.

She enjoyed aspects of her new country and welcomed the transition from lecturing under the shadow of severe examinations to lecturing in freedom to eager, but not specialized, students. For the first few years at Bryn Mawr, Dr. Scott was the only faculty member living in the main college building. Later she rented a house from the college and was known for her beautiful garden, often offering bouquets to passersby.

In suggesting the mathematical preparation for students entering Bryn Mawr, 27-year-old Dr. Scott set a precedent for over a century to come: algebra through quadratic equations and geometric progressions and plane geometry. She also required solid geometry and trigonometry in college for those who had not taken those courses previously. She believed in the evolution of intellectual ideas and expressed disapproval when the collegiate text she wrote was reprinted thirty-two years later, because she felt that it was already out of date.

Responsible for deciding which applicants were worthy of Bryn Mawr's demanding program, she soon tired of making up and grading entrance examinations. Her letters in the Bryn Mawr archives indicate that she urged her counterparts in other U.S. colleges to pool their resources and offer common exams for aspiring secondary school students. In 1901 the College Board (now responsible for the Scholastic Achievement Test, or SAT) was organized, and she served as its first chief mathematics examiner in 1902 and 1903.

Scott took an active role in the developing mathematical community in the New World. She participated in the founding and growth of the New York Mathematical Society, which later became the American Mathematics Society (AMS), serving as the only woman on its first board in 1894. She became vice president in 1905, culminating a decade in which women presented the same percentage of research papers to the AMS as they did in the 1970s. In mid-century, after her leadership ended, women were far less visible than they were at the turn of the century. The AMS remains the United States' major professional organization for research mathematicians, and only recently have women played a more significant role in its activity than they did in Charlotte Scott's time. In 1899 she became coeditor of the *American Journal of Mathematics*, the oldest surviving mathematics journal in this country. She remained coeditor until her retirement in 1926. In that position she affected the direction of mathematical research throughout the United States.

Meanwhile, she herself did research that was published not only in American journals but also in those of England and the European continent. Her research was primarily about algebraic curves of degrees higher than two, connecting algebra to geometry. Many high school students study curves of second degree: parabolas, circles, ellipses, and hyperbolas. The situation is much more complicated if a "3" appears in the exponent, and the complexity increases rapidly as the exponent grows.

Scott's clear delineation between proofs and examples, however, had an even greater impact on twentieth-century mathematics. Until Scott's time, most mathematics was used to solve specific problems of physics. Although she also solved particular problems, she was one of the first to prove theorems abstractly, a trend that accelerated rapidly by the 1920s. Recent mathematicians have begun to expand on her contributions and those of her doctoral student Virginia Ragsdale.

Along with a steady stream of undergraduates and master's degree candidates, Charlotte Scott mentored doctoral candidates, each of them for many years. Seven completed their Ph.D. work under her supervision; six were listed in the AMS membership roll in 1916. Marguerite Lehr, who began her graduate work in 1918, became Scott's last Ph.D. student in 1925 and succeeded Scott when she retired; Lehr remained on the Bryn Mawr faculty until her own retirement in 1964.

As early as 1884 the recommendation from Girton to Bryn Mawr described Charlotte Scott as "decidedly hard of hearing" but maintained that this deficit had not prevented her from being an able teacher. By the time Marguerite Lehr arrived on campus in 1918, Scott was totally deaf. She still could lecture perfectly, but a graduate student would answer most of the undergraduates' questions, relaying the hard ones to Professor Scott through lip reading. Her students became accustomed to sitting up close, facing her carefully for all conversation. Although she could not carry on casual conversations with her students, she took a personal interest in them, even entertaining them in her home on occasion.

Scott's supervisor, Bryn Mawr president M. Carey Thomas, was by all accounts a hard taskmaster. Each had been the first woman in her own country to earn a doctorate. They were only a year apart in age, but Thomas's biographer reports that the lack of warmth between them disappointed Scott. A letter from Thomas to Scott in 1912 reads, "I am sorry you thought I spoke with scorn about trigonometry. I did not. In point of fact, it was . . . the only thing I ever failed. . . . I only meant that to teach trigonometry . . . seemed to me like a waste of your great teaching ability."[1]

In 1922 the AMS met at Bryn Mawr to honor Scott. Her students, her colleagues, and the worldwide mathematics community gave speeches for and about her. Alfred North Whitehead, an extremely well known mathematician, made his first trip to this country specifically to give the address on relativity and gravitation. A faculty member rhapsodized,

"Her counsel is sought on all important matters. As chairman of various committees she has arrayed a body of information which is a monument to her creative wisdom."[2] There were many accolades reported in the Bryn Mawr *Bulletin*, but none more important than "the bulk of the company was made up of Miss Scott's own students—of persons, that is to say, who have consciously or unconsciously come to associate the divine science with . . . such things as perfect integrity, high courage, and the sense of beauty."[3]

Notes

1. Isabelle Maddison & Marguerite Lehr (1932) *Charlotte Angus Scott: An Appreciation*. Bryn Mawr Alumni Bulletin, v. 12, pp. 9–12.
2. Ibid.
3. Ibid.

Selected Works by Charlotte Angas Scott

(1892). The Nature and Effect of Singularities of Plane Algebraic Curves. *American Journal of Mathematics* 14, pp. 301–25.
(1897). On Cayley's Theory of the Absolute. *Bulletin of the American Mathematical Society* 3, pp. 235–46.
(1898). On the Intersections of Plane Curves. *Bulletin of the American Mathematical Society* 4, pp. 260–73.
(1899). A Proof of Noether's Fundamental Theorem. *Mathematische Annalen* 52, pp. 592–97.
(1901). Note on the Geometrical Treatment of Conics. *Annals of Mathematics* 2(2), pp. 64–72.
(1907). *Cartesian Plane Geometry, Part I: Analytical Conics*. London: J. M. Dent.

Selected Works about Charlotte Angas Scott

Kenschaft, P. C. (1982). Women in Mathematics around 1900. *Signs* 7(4), Summer, pp. 906–9.
———. (1983). Students of Charlotte Scott. *Mathematics in College* (Winter), pp. 16–20. Reprinted in *A Century of Mathematics in America* (Part 3, pp. 241–52). Providence, RI: American Mathematical Society.
———. (1987). Charlotte Angas Scott. In Louise Grinstein & Paul Campbell, Eds., *Women of Mathematics*. Westport, CT: Greenwood Press.
———. (1987). Charlotte Angas Scott (1858–1931). *College Mathematics Journal* 18(2), pp. 98–110.
———. (1987). Why Did Charlotte Scott Succeed? *Newsletter of the Association for Women in Mathematics* 17(2) pp. 2, 4–9.

PATRICIA CLARK KENSCHAFT

MARJORIE WIKLER SENECHAL

(1939–)

Birthplace: Missouri

The mathematical world of Marjorie Senechal, professor of mathematics at Smith College and a leading researcher on tilings and quasi-crystals (areas of geometry), is very visual. On a typically gloomy New England day in 1992, several high school students knocked on the door of Senechal's office at Smith College. Inside, the gloom gave way to a wonderful world of geometric toys and mathematical puzzles spread around on every surface, filling the corners and beckoning from every direction. Murmurs of "Let me try that!" or "How do you think this works?" could be heard for the next hour and a half as students engaged in playful mathematics and heard anecdotes about how these objects related to the world of research mathematics inhabited by Senechal and her colleagues. At least one of those students has decided to major in mathematics as she embarks on her college education.

Senechal entered the world of mathematics through a combination of avoidance of situations and discoveries of her talents. Her growing years in Lexington, Kentucky, in the 1940s and 1950s offered her little in the way of inspiring social relationships—except for her adult friends and her father, who was a dedicated research physician. Her academic talents were recognized by the dean of girls at her school, and she was offered the opportunity to begin college at the University of Chicago after her eleventh grade year. She began as a pre-med student but quickly discovered that she had a talent for and interest in mathematics. Mathematics also appealed to her because she would not always be tied to a lab or office; she would be able to do some work at home, thereby making it more feasible to eventually have a family. She has been heard to say that math suits her well because she can never know it all and therefore is never in any danger of being bored.

She finished her undergraduate degree in mathematics at the University of Chicago in 1960. She then attended the Illinois Institute of Technology, receiving her M.S. in 1962 and Ph.D. in 1965, both in mathematics. During the time she was a doctoral student she married Lester Senechal, also a mathematician. They moved to Arizona, where her husband was offered a faculty position. While there, she was able to finish her Ph.D. work in absentia but could not move ahead with her career because spouses of faculty members were prevented from working at

Marjorie Senechal. Photo courtesy of Marjorie Senechal.

the same institution. These laws have changed in most places, but it was common at the time Senechal was starting her career. She describes watching many faculty wives with Ph.D.s being closed out of a career owing to these nepotism laws.

The Senechals left Arizona in 1965 to travel to Brazil, where they taught for seven months supported by Fulbright Scholarships. This trip was the first in a long series of international connections, which continue to this day. After returning from Brazil, Senechal and her husband moved to Massachusetts and she began her long teaching career at Smith College in Northampton, where she is currently Louise Wolff Kahn professor of mathematics. Along the way she and Lester Senechal were divorced and she married her present husband, Stan Sherer, a photographer, in 1989. She has two daughters and a stepson.

Senechal's Ph.D. work was in the area of number theory (the study of numbers, their properties, and their relationships) and complex variables. As she moved further into the world of research, she found that she couldn't define her own questions and her own work; her research lacked her own creative input. She was also disturbed by the ways in which she could not make her work accessible to her students, most of whom were undergraduates. She began to familiarize herself with other areas of mathematics, particularly the geometry of numbers, by browsing through the library. Her colleague **Doris Schattschneider** describes her as fascinated by structure. She began to become interested in the ways in which mathematics relates to the growth of crystals and to symmetry. At this point she met Dorothy Wrinch, a mathematician and chemist who was studying crystal growth. Senechal found herself defining her own questions in a satisfying manner, and soon she shifted most of her attention to this new area of mathematics. Her mathematical research helps crystallographers understand the geometrical constraints and possibilities of the solid state of chemical compounds.

In 1975 she took her first sabbatical to Holland and came into contact with researchers doing highly important work in crystallography. Her new mathematical interests were solidified, and from that point on she found herself asking (and answering) some of the most important questions relating to crystallography and symmetry. Following this sabbatical she published a paper on the classification of color symmetry groups, which brought to the forefront a solution to a major mathematical problem of that time. Her clarification and discussion of this solution have stimulated much important mathematical work.

Motivated in part by her own daughter's interest in learning Russian, Senechal became an exchange scientist at the Academy of Sciences in the Soviet Union in 1979–1980. This community of colleagues, particularly the mathematicians and crystallographers associated with Deloné, a leading researcher, soon became very important to her. Now Senechal was firmly grounded in an international community of researchers that would take her overseas many more times. Since 1992 more than one-third of her presentations have taken place overseas. She has been responsible for more than fifteen international gatherings of mathematicians in the United States, including the Symmetry Festival at Smith College in 1973 and the Shaping Space Conference at Smith in 1984. Her favorite conference was the Regional Geometry Institute at Smith College in July 1993, because, as she says, "It was interdisciplinary, unpredictable, and full of communications across a wide variety of groups—students, secondary school teachers, undergraduate teachers, and researchers." Communication between anyone and everyone, using many modes, lasted all day and all night and produced many creative ideas.

Senechal has a fundamental orientation toward communicating across disciplines and among diverse groups of people. Thus she speaks many languages, which has enabled her to travel and work in other countries, particularly Russia and France. Traveling is not only an integral part of her work life but an important part of her relationship with her husband, Sherer. In 1994 they traveled to Albania to do a photo-essay of that country.

Senechal's work in crystallography has branched into the area of tilings. (A tiling is the repetition of one shape, or several shapes, that can be repeated to completely cover the plane.) Her current work involves quasi-crystals. A recent sabbatical was spent working with a group of colleagues in France and completing an introductory book on quasi-crystals. Her goal is to learn something new about mathematics each time she takes a sabbatical. She has been a prolific writer, producing almost fifty articles and ten books. She has also been the recipient of numerous grants and awards, including the Carl B. Allendoerfer Award of the Mathematical Association of America in 1982. She was invited by the National Academy of Sciences to give the keynote address to the U.S. Olympiad Team in 1994.

It is unusual for a researcher of this stature to maintain a strong commitment at an undergraduate, teaching-oriented institution, but Senechal has achieved just this. She is described as an inspiration by many of her students. She believes in getting students involved in a professional community as soon as possible and has been committed to involving students in the many conferences she organizes and attends. In spite of her deep enthusiasm for mathematics, she says she is "not a missionary." Her primary goal with students is to help them find out who they are and where their strengths lie. Her commitment is evidenced by the broad array of committees on which she sits and the professional societies to which she belongs.

Although one senses that mathematics is as much a hobby as work for her, Senechal has some non-mathematical pursuits; these include traveling, gardening, bicycling, and reading. She has held the post of president of the Northampton, Massachusetts, chapter of the League of Women Voters. An unfulfilled goal is to learn to sculpt marble.

Marjorie Senechal continues to contribute to the mathematics community through her research, writing, and gathering of scholars. She inspires both her students and colleagues with her curiosity, creativity, and willingness to spend time being a mentor.

Note

The information included in this biography is based on an interview conducted at Smith College in 1993 by the author.

Selected Works by Marjorie Senechal

(1975). Point Groups and Color Symmetry. *Zeitschrift fur Kristallographie* 142, pp. 1–23.

(1977). A Prophet without Honor, Dorothy Wrinch 1894–1976. *Smith Alumnae Quarterly* (April), pp. 18–23.

(1977). *A Workbook of Common Geometry* (with G. Fleck). Amherst, MA: University of Massuchusetts Press.

(1983). Coloring Symmetrical Objects Symmetrically. *Mathematics Magazine* 56(1), pp. 3–16.

(1988). *Shaping Space: A Polyhedral Approach* (with G. Fleck, Eds.). Boston: Birkhauser.

(1990). Quasicrystals: The View from les Houches. *Mathematical Intelligencer* 12(2), pp. 54–64. (with Jean Taylor).

(1991). *From Symmetry to Disorder: A Personal Odyssey. Five College Ink*, vol. 3 (Spring), pp. 3–7.

(1994). *The Cultures of Science.* Commack, NY: Nova Science Publishers.

(1995). *Quasicrystals and Geometry.* London: Cambridge University Press.

CHARLENE MORROW

LESLEY MILMAN SIBNER
(circa 1940–   )
Birthplace: New York

Lesley Sibner, presently a noted mathematical researcher, did not have a particular affinity for mathematics in her youth. In fact, she found high school geometry extremely boring. As an aspiring actress, she was generally not attracted to academic subjects even though she did well in school.

Lesley grew up in New York City. Her father, Isador Milman, was a high school history teacher; her mother, Charlotte, was an elementary school teacher. Leslie had no siblings. When she graduated from high school, she chose to go to Carnegie Tech University because it had a very good drama program. She was so interested in the theater, in fact, that in the midst of her undergraduate education she decided to return to New York City to pursue a career in drama. She did win some parts in summer stock productions and on TV, and like many aspiring young actresses she had to support herself by waiting on tables and being a salesgirl.

With encouragement from her father Sibner decided to return to college, attending City College in New York City. At Carnegie Tech she had concentrated on subjects such as fencing and foreign language interpretation and pronunciation—subjects potentially useful to an aspiring actress. At City College as a fine arts student, she had to take many

Lesley Sibner. Photo courtesy of Lesley Sibner.

additional required courses; among them was calculus. She fell in love with the subject and has explored and created extensions of calculus ever since.

Lesley recalls her calculus teacher, a woman who loved mathematics and was knowledgeable and enthusiastic about the subject, although not a research mathematician. This teacher recognized Sibner's talent and encouraged her to continue, recommending that Lesley read Courant's *Differential and Integral Calculus*. She not only read it but found pleasure in working out the problems. She immediately changed her major to mathematics and, on the advice of the same teacher, also took physics. Here she met her future husband, Robert Sibner, who as a New York University mathematics graduate student was teaching a physics course at City College.

After earning her B.A. from City College, Lesley went on to graduate school at New York University, receiving a scholarship and soon earning a Ph.D. In graduate school she had two major professors; one was a woman, **Cathleen Morawetz**. The other was Lipman Bers, a man who was well known for being comfortable with intellectual women and extremely supportive of female graduate students.

Sibner's mathematical research is in the area of partial differential equations (PDE), a topic that students begin to study in advanced calculus courses. When beginning mathematical research, a mathematician first looks for an interesting problem—one that has been suggested by a colleague or one that she has uncovered herself. When and if she solves it, she reports her findings to the community by writing and publishing a paper about the solution in a professional journal, or giving a talk about it at a professional meeting. Sometimes even if she has been unable to solve a problem, she may share what she has tried so far and then continue to work with her colleagues to explore the problem further. Research becomes exciting when a problem solved by one mathematician stimulates new ideas, new problems, and new solutions by others. In this way, there is much intellectual exchange between colleagues.

Mathematicians at universities also teach. As a tenured faculty member, Lesley Sibner is now able to teach many more courses that really interest her, and she enjoys this aspect of her work. She has very few women students in her classes, however, because Brooklyn Polytechnic University (where she is currently a professor of mathematics) is viewed primarily as an engineering institution. Over the years this image has changed little, which makes the recruitment of women students difficult. Sibner has served as major adviser to several Ph.D. graduate students, all men. While at the University of Pennsylvania as a visiting professor, Sibner had the opportunity to serve as a mentor for a young woman, Janet Talvacchia, and they wrote a paper together. Talvacchia is now a tenured professor at Swarthmore College. Sibner also cites a colleague, **Karen Uhlenbeck**, as the most important influence on her work—though she adds that Uhlenbeck, unlike herself, works in many different areas of mathematics. She says Professor Uhlenbeck is the most brilliant mathematician she has known.

Sibner does a significant portion of her work in collaboration with her husband, Bob. Although he began working in a different area of mathematics, their areas have merged as they have spent more time working together. There have been both benefits and disadvantages to their collaboration. On the positive side, Sibner says that working together is a natural thing to do. She enjoys the close interaction with another mathematician and feels that it has been productive for them both. Over the years Sibner has also collaborated with people other than her husband, as well as having worked alone. On the other hand, her work with Bob may be indirectly responsible for the delay in Lesley's being promoted above the level of associate professor. When considering promotions, the decision-making committee could always attribute the work done in their joint papers to the *other* person. Both Sibners were finally promoted to professor status, and, equally important, they still enjoy working together.

Sibner has received many honors during her career, including invitations to speak at prestigious conferences in the United States and abroad. She has served as a reviewer for the National Science Foundation. She has also been very active in professional organizations, such as the American Mathematical Society, serving as an officer and program chair for conferences. One particularly important honor was being chosen as a Bunting Science Scholar at Radcliffe College. The Bunting Institute was named after Alice Bunting, who was the first president of Radcliffe. Although most Bunting Scholars are involved in feminist studies, a science scholarship program funded by the Office of Naval Research is also included. Sibner was on a sabbatical leave at Harvard in 1990 when she heard about the program, applied, and was accepted.

As a Bunting Scholar, Sibner's professional duties involved being part of the mathematics department at Radcliffe. She recalls the weekly brown bag lunches at which people talked about their work. Evening social events with women from other disciplines—architecture, literature, politics—extended connections between the Bunting Scholars. Sibner found her year in this all-female environment to be very powerful. One important consequence has been the development of a network of colleagues across disciplines, who continue to help each other in any way they can. Her own longstanding love of theater provided a basis for friendship with a professor at Brown University, a playwright whose plays have been produced on New York's Off Broadway. The group of women was diverse, which added to the richness of the experience. She met Beverly Manley, a history scholar who is the former wife of the president of Jamaica. And then there was the director of the Institute, Dr. Florence Ladd, a black woman whom she describes as "an incredible human being!" Sibner found that her wide range of interests was significantly enriched by the breadth of the program.

The Sibners currently live in New York City's Greenwich Village. She emphasizes that she loves to live in New York because of the diversity of her interests. She plays tennis whenever she can, all year round, and spends a lot of time on the audience side of the footlights. She works a great deal of the time and loves to learn about new things, such as the exciting new field called wavelets.

Note

This biography is based on an interview by the author that took place at the Julia Robinson Celebration of Women in Mathematics Conference in Berkeley, California, in July 1996.

Selected Works by Leslie Sibner

(1987). (with T. H. Otway). Point singularities of coupled gauge fields with low energy, *Comm. Math. Phys.* 111, 275–279.

(1988). (with R. J. Sibner). Singular Sobolev connections with holonomy, *Bulletin of the AMS* 29, 471–473.

(1989). (with R. J. Sibner and K. Uhlenbeck). Solutions to Yang-Mills equations which are not self-dual, *Proc. Nat. Acad. Sci.* 86, 8610–8613.

(1990). Examples of Non-Minimal Critical Points in Gauge Theory. *Proceedings of the AMS Summer Institute on Differential Geometry.*

(1992). (with R. J. Sibner). Classification of Singular Sobolev Connections by Their Holonomy, *Communications in Mathematical Physics* 144, pp. 337–50.

(1994). (with J. Talvacchia). Existence of Non-Minimal Critical Points for the Yang-Mills-Higgs Functional over R3 with Arbitrary Positive Coupling Constant, *Communications in Mathematical Physics.* 162, pp. 333–51.

JOAN ROSS

MARY FAIRFAX GRIEG SOMERVILLE
(1780–1872)
Birthplace: Burntisland, Scotland

Mary Fairfax Grieg Somerville was one of the most famous women in Europe during the mid-nineteenth century. Renowned philosophers lauded her contributions to the advancement of the physical sciences, and her life demonstrated that a "normal" woman was capable of understanding the complex mathematics used to explain physical phenomena.

For three years Mrs. Somerville researched and wrote an English rendition of the French mathematical genius Laplace's *Mechanique celeste*, working in between the constant interruptions of running a household which included two teenage daughters. She undertook the project on the condition that no one would know, and if the result was not of sufficient quality it was to be secretly burned. But the reviewers considered her manuscript too important for a treatise, so she published it as her first book, *The Mechanism of the Heavens* (1831). The fact that a woman had written a book few learned men could completely understand earned Mrs. Somerville a reputation as a brilliant mind. Cambridge University used it as a textbook for advanced mathematics students. Her achievement inspired many and brought to the fore the issue of women's education.

Mary Fairfax was born in her aunt's home in southern Scotland on

Mary Somerville. Illustration courtesy of Culver
Pictures, Inc.

December 26, 1780. Her mother was returning to their village near Edinburgh after seeing off Mary's father, a distinguished admiral in the
British navy, on a long voyage from London. The Fairfaxs were a family
of the gentry, accepted in upper social circles but not well off financially.
In her father's absence young Mary Fairfax and her older brother were
raised by their indulgent, easygoing mother who allowed them to spend
carefree days exploring the garden, beach, and countryside near their
home.

Life changed drastically when Admiral Fairfax returned home to find
that his 9-year-old daughter could hardly read, let alone write, speak
properly, or work with numbers. Mary disliked having to read aloud
from the Bible to her father each day, but she enjoyed learning about
plants while helping him tend the garden. Soon Mary was sent to a
boarding school in Edinburgh, where she learned posture, grammar,
spelling, and arithmetic. She didn't take well to the extremely tedious
and inefficient teaching method in her new school, but the experience
fueled her desire to set her own course of study. Mary likened herself
to a caged wild animal given its freedom when permitted to return home
after her only year of formal education.

Mary quickly and ably learned all the skills considered desirable for young ladies—sewing, needlepoint, piano, drawing, French, cooking, and dancing—but was criticized for reading so much in her spare time. She was of the opinion that since women were given a desire for knowledge, it was only just to allow them to acquire it. Intrigued by the algebra problems she noticed in a fashion magazine and her drawing teacher's remark that Euclid's *Elements of Geometry* was the foundation not only of perspective, but of astronomy and all mechanical science, Mary talked her younger brother's tutor into obtaining books on these subjects for her. She secretly studied well into each night, because mathematics and other academic studies were considered unhealthy for the female mind. When her family caught on, Mary's candle was taken away as soon as she went to bed. She persevered and relied on her excellent memory to rework the first six books of Euclid as she lay in bed at night until she was confident she understood it all. Mary had found her life's passion.

Wintering with her mother in Edinburgh, Mary's days were filled with the active social life of a beautiful debutante; she continued to enjoy entertainment and social gatherings throughout her long life. When they returned home Mary began her habit of rising early and studying mathematics or classics until breakfast. When she grew overly tired and found she was struggling, Mary would play piano or read poetry or novels to clear her mind and resume her studies when her mind was fresh.

At age 24 she married Samuel Grieg and moved to London. He tolerated her studies of trigonometry, conic sections, astronomy, Newton's *Principia* (principles of physics), and French but had a low opinion of women's capabilities and no interest in science. Three years later Mary returned to her childhood home, a widow with two young sons.

The inheritance Mary Grieg received from her husband provided her the financial independence to assertively resume her studies. She began solving puzzles in a mathematical journal and won a silver medal for one of her solutions. The editor of the journal became the first person to sympathize with her desire to learn. He gave her a list of the books she needed to read to fill in and update her education, including works on calculus, algebra, astronomy, and probability.

Mary purchased this "treasure" (that is, the recommended books) one year after her marriage to her cousin, Dr. William Somerville, not a favorite in the family because of his liberal principles, the very quality that was attractive to her. In him she found a supportive partner who considered her great intelligence an asset to both their lives. The Somervilles had three daughters, who experienced none of the educational limitations Mrs. Somerville had endured.

In London, Dr. Somerville joined several scientific societies popular among the gentry and Mrs. Somerville furthered her education by attending Royal Institution lectures on practical applications of science. When the seriousness of her intellectual pursuits became evident, Mary

Somerville was warmly accepted into the philosophers' (men interested in advancing the natural sciences) inner circle. Most philosophers at that time were self-taught or taught by masters—no degree in science was necessary for acceptance. Research was primarily funded with inheritances, so a woman such as Mary Somerville did not threaten the group's economic security.

Discussion about scientific ideas and discoveries took place in the salons of the inner circle. Somerville impressed others with her keen intelligence, natural modesty, and self-assurance. She made a point of demonstrating that her mathematical and scientific pursuits did not interfere with her ability to raise a family, her skills as a hostess, or her culinary talents. Visiting philosophers were often introduced at these intellectual socials to share the latest research and news from other countries. When she made her first trip to the continent, she and her husband were welcomed in the same manner. She retained her love of travel, and as her husband's health began to fail they moved to Italy to benefit from its milder climate.

In 1835 scientists joined the ranks of poets, historians, and soldiers when the British government decided to acknowledge their contributions to the kingdom. Mary Somerville was one of those honored with a monthly pension. Subsequently, several scientific societies in Europe and America granted her honorary memberships.

Somerville found mentors among the most successful English philosophers and started conducting her own experiments. She looked for a relationship between light and magnetism. Her colleagues admired her simple apparatus that made use of household items and her careful application of the scientific method. Her discovery that violet light permanently magnetized a steel needle was the first research by a woman presented to the Royal Society (by her husband, since women could not become members) and the first paper published in *Philosophical Transactions*, along with Caroline Herschel's astronomical observations. Somerville's paper was well received in Britain and abroad, although her result was proved inaccurate three years later.

In Edinburgh, Somerville had studied the new French analysis with which few philosophers in London were familiar. This was an advanced form of algebra using calculus, periodic variations (as seen in astronomy), and probability methods. She went on to study Laplace's *Mechanique celeste*, which applied the laws of gravitation to astronomy in order to predict celestial events. Laplace himself recognized her as one of his most able readers; in recognition of this fact, Somerville received a lock of his hair after his death in 1827. Shortly thereafter she was asked (after receiving the approval of her husband) to write an English rendition of Laplace's *Mechanique celeste*. The resulting book, *The Mechanism of the Heavens*, contained a Preliminary Dissertation meant for the general public. It also served to introduce French analysis techniques and the materials and methods of French astronomy to English philosophers. The body of the book contained lucid, detailed translations of Laplace's works, including all his analysis. She supplemented the original text with diagrams and figures to further clarify difficult topics, and with experimental results of other philosophers that supported his theories. The master of Trinity College, Cambridge University, honored her with a poem that complimented Somerville's ability to bring clarity to the most complex ideas.

Her accomplishment came at a time when many philosophers were lamenting the fact that British science was lagging behind that of the rest of Europe. Many of her mentors had since passed away, and Mrs. Somerville became a mentor to several young philosophers and to the daughter of a friend. Due to the interest her book created, the Preliminary Dissertation was published on its own in the following year.

Somerville immediately started working on a new book, *On the Connexion of the Physical Sciences* (1834). She wrote it for a general audience by including no mathematical equations and a very large Explanation of Terms section. In the midst of a struggle among philosophers trying to distinguish the science disciplines from each other, her categories for the physical sciences (astronomy, electricity and magnetism, matter, sound, light, and heat) became the accepted definition for the next fifty years. She described the latest scientific achievements and revealed how the various disciplines relate to and depend on each other. More than half the experimental work included in the book was conducted on the continent (it was mostly written in Paris), again filling a gap in British philosophy circles. One reviewer of her work first proposed using the word "scientist" to describe those seeking knowledge and understanding of the natural world. The book was a huge success.

Although she loved abstract mathematics, Somerville never published her work in this area. She went on to publish a review of works explaining the reappearance of Halley's comet in 1835 and the results of her continued experiments on light. Somerville published two other books, *Physical Geography* (1848) and *On Molecular and Microscopic Science* (1869). *Physical Geography* was ahead of its time in proposing a regional approach to the study of geography rather than supporting the prevalent bias toward national or political lines. The book went through seven editions and was often used as a textbook. Somerville started writing *On Molecular and Microscopic Science* in her eighty-fifth year. Charles Darwin provided some of the illustrations, but she didn't include his ideas on evolution because she felt they needed further investigation.

Mary Somerville actively promoted opportunities for women's education and the women's suffrage movement. She left her treasured book collection to the Ladies College at Hitchen, now Girton College, Cambridge.

She completed her autobiography during her last year. She enjoyed investigating the properties of a new algebraic structure known as quaternions, a precursor to matrices, until the day she passed away at nearly 92 years of age on November 29, 1872, in Naples, Italy. After her death, Somerville College at Oxford University was named in her honor.

Selected Works by Mary Somerville

(1826). On the Magnetizing Power of the More Refrangible Solar Rays. *Philosophical Transactions of the Royal Society of London* 116(1), pp. 132–39.
(1831). *The Mechanism of the Heavens*. London: John Murray.
(1845). 'On the action of the rays of the spectrum on vegetable juices,' ... *Abstracts of the Papers Communicated to the Royal Society of London from 1843 to 1850, Inclusive* 5, 569.
(1848). *Physical Geography*. London: John Murray. 7th ed., 1877.
(1869). *On Molecular and Microscopic Science*. London: John Murray.

Selected Works about Mary Somerville

Hope, Eva. (1886). *Queens of Literature of the Victorian Era*. London: W. Scott.
Patterson, Elizabeth Chambers. (1983). *Mary Somerville and the Cultivation of Science, 1815–1840*. The Hague: Nijhoff.
Somerville, Martha, Ed. (1873). *Personal Recollections from Early Life to Old Age of Mary Somerville, with Selections from Her Correspondence*. London: John Murray.
Tabor, Margaret Emma. (1933). *Pioneer Women*. London: Sheldon Press.

BARBARA TERMAAT

PAULINE SPERRY
(1885–1967)
Birthplace: Massachusetts

In 1950 Pauline Sperry, a member of the mathematics faculty at the University of California in Berkeley, was fired for refusing to sign a loyalty oath. Two years later the California Supreme Court declared the oath unconstitutional and Sperry was vindicated, but by then her formal teaching career had ended.

Pauline Sperry was born on March 5, 1885, in Peabody, Massachusetts. Her parents were Willard G. Sperry, a Congregational minister from

Pauline Sperry. Photo courtesy of Bancroft Library,
University of California, Berkeley.

York Beach, Maine, and Henrietta Leoroyd. Her early religious upbring-
ing prepared her for her later strong convictions as a member of the
Society of Friends and as a secret philanthropist.

In 1906 Sperry, 21 years old, received a B.A. degree from Smith College, having been honored by election to Phi Beta Kappa. She sang in
the Choral Choir and was a member of the mathematics club during
college. After graduation she taught for one year at Hamilton Institute,
a private school in New York City. In 1907 she returned to Smith on a
fellowship to do graduate work in mathematics and music, earning a
master's degree in 1908. Sperry remained at Smith as a mathematics
instructor until 1912. During these years she taught plane, solid, and
spherical trigonometry as well as analytic geometry. The academic year
1912–1913 was a busy one for Sperry: She was granted a traveling fellowship from Smith College, attended Olivet College, and began graduate work at the University of Chicago.

In the following year she matriculated at the University of Chicago, where she earned a second master's degree in 1914. Her thesis was entitled *On the Theory of a One-to-One and One-to-Two Correspondence with Geometrical Illustrations*. For her doctoral work Sperry studied under the guidance of Ernest Julius Wilczynski. Professor Wilczynski had created a new school of geometers known as the American School of Projective Differential Geometers. Sperry's dissertation was entitled *Properties of a Certain Projectively Defined Two-Parameter Family of Curves on a General Surface*. For a short time after her presentation of this work to the mathematics community, there was a curve known as Sperry's Curve.

During the academic year 1915–1916 she held a teaching fellowship at Chicago while finishing her doctoral studies. She was elected to the honor society, Sigma Xi, before returning to her beloved Smith College for another year after completing her doctorate in 1916. Following her year of teaching at Smith in 1917, Sperry moved only twice more in her life: first to teach at the University of California in Berkeley, then twenty-three years later to take up the life of an activist for humanitarian causes and an advocate for civil rights in Carmel, California.

At Berkeley in 1923, Sperry was the first woman promoted to assistant professor in the mathematics department. In 1932 she was the first woman promoted to associate professor. She held this position until she was fired in 1950 for political reasons. Known locally as a great educator, she had taught a variety of courses including one on navigation; her Ph.D. work had been in both mathematics and astronomy. As an active and involved member of the academic community, Sperry, with her housemate Alice Tabor, established the Women's Faculty Club at the university. In 1926 and again in 1928 she published two trigonometry textbooks, although she published no further research articles after her dissertation.

In 1950, along with about eighteen other faculty members, Sperry refused, as a matter of principle, to sign a loyalty declaration required by the Board of Regents of the State of California. A person who refused to sign such an oath was automatically suspected of being a Communist and not only subject to losing her or his job but placed on a list that would make it impossible to find another job. Berkeley had been chosen as one of the first test cases for this oath. Sperry urged her colleagues to learn of the oath's brief but volatile history since 1949, when the Regents assumed a controversial position with regard to tenure and academic freedom. The concept of requiring an oath to promote patriotism in educational institutions had been an issue in California in the 1930s and 1940s. A few of the powerful Regents had been particularly active in seeking out Communists. Although Sperry was one of the litigants who won their case in appellate court, this struggle marked the termination of her thirty-four years as a teacher.

Quakers (members of the Society of Friends) have a well-established tradition of taking no oaths whatsoever. Sperry, although a Quaker, was not granted exemption from taking the oath. She was prohibited from teaching and received no salary. She knew that she was placing her academic career on the line, but this was a risk she was willing to take: to defend academic freedom at a time when national and state authorities were systematically removing opponents of cold war hysteria from employment. Two years after she was fired, the California Supreme Court declared the loyalty oath unconstitutional and ordered reinstatement of the faculty members who had refused to sign it. Sperry was given the rank of associate professor emerita and four years later she received the two years' pay she had lost upon being fired.

After leaving Berkeley, Sperry remained politically active—both with the Quakers and the American Civil Liberties Union, as well as the League of Women Voters. Sperry's responsibilities as a Quaker included serving on the Executive Council of the Friends Committee on Legislation of Northern California, the Fellowship of Reconciliation, the Friends Service Committee, and the Committee for a Sane Nuclear Policy. She also wrote and published poetry denouncing killing.

As a humanitarian, Sperry, with characteristic modesty and generosity, founded and maintained the Step-by-Step School in Port-au-Prince, Haiti, to feed and teach starving children. In 1965 she published "Formula for Happiness at Eighty" in the *Smith Alumnae Quarterly*. In this essay, setting out her belief that everyone should be "bold enough to ask the right questions and brave enough to face the answers about the untouchable subject, money," she described how she had learned to give away all her money. She told about those to whom she had secretly given, and how she did so with her stated ultimate goal, to "Give 'til it hurts!" (Sperry, 1965, pp. 154–155).

Selected Works by Pauline Sperry

(1918). Properties of a Certain Projectively Defined Two-Parameter Family of Curves on a General Surface. *American Journal of Mathematics* 40, pp. 213–24. Doctoral dissertation, University of Chicago.

(1926). *Plane Trigonometry and Tables* (with H. E. Buchanan). Richmond: Johnson Publishing.

(1928). *Short Course in Spherical Trigonometry*. Richmond: Johnson Publishing.

(1931). Bibliography of Projective Differential Geometry. *University of California Publications in Mathematics* 2, pp. 119–27.

Selected Work about Pauline Sperry

Rodenmayer, Robert. (1966). *How Many Miles to Babylon*. New York: Seabury Press. A chapter is devoted to Pauline Sperry and the resilience of the human heart.

(1965). Formula for Happiness at Eighty. *Smith Alumnae Quarterly* (Spring), pp. 154–55.

FLORENCE FASANELLI

ALICIA BOOLE STOTT
(1860–1940)
Birthplace: Ireland

Alicia Boole Stott was a nineteenth-century mathematician—no small feat for a person from a family with little money. She worked on polytopes (i.e., polygons in the fourth or higher dimensions), an area not generally studied until college—and Alice, as her friends called her, didn't even go to high school, let alone college. Little has been written about her life, but she contributed to a field that is becoming more and more important with the advent of computers, and it is impressive that she was able to do research at all.

To begin to understand her work, imagine a lake on a clear, still day. A little girl is fishing from a dock that extends out into the lake. Her line is in the water, and there's a round bobber sitting on the surface. She hasn't had a nibble yet, and in hopes of encouraging any lurking fish, she twitches the line a little every once in a while, lifting the bobber and line just a little way out of the water. Now imagine that you are a small water strider zipping back and forth on the lake looking for lunch, and that you can only see things right on the surface of the water. As the girl lets the fishing line down, you see a black dot as the line drops through the water, and then a small curved line as the bobber hits the water. The line keeps getting bigger until the bobber is floating on the lake, and then just sits there. If you, the water strider, were curious and skated all the way around the bobber, the curved line would look like a circle. (This scene is patterned directly after *Flatland* [Abbott, 1991], which is well worth reading!)

Whereas the little girl on the dock can see the 1-dimensional fishing line and the 3-dimensional bobber, the water strider can only see the part that's intersecting the surface of the water. It sees the fishing line as a point, which is 0-dimensional, and the bobber as a curved line or circle, which is 2-dimensional. Those of us who live in a 3-dimensional world have a hard time imagining what the fourth or even fifth dimension might look like, just as the water strider has no conception that the line it sees is actually part of a 3-dimensional sphere.

There are actually many different ways to think about the higher dimensions. The fourth dimension is often specified as time. In her popular book *A Wrinkle in Time* (1962), Madeleine L'Engle described the tesseract, or wrinkle in time, as the fifth dimension. The characters Meg, Charles, Calvin, and Mr. Murray use tesseracts to travel through otherwise impossibly huge expanses of space. Higher dimensions can also be defined without using time. To use another idea from *Flatland*, if you take a 0-dimensional point and move it in one direction, you get a 1-dimensional line. Take the line and move it in a perpendicular direction to draw a 2-dimensional square. Find a perpendicular direction to the square, and move along that axis to make a 3-dimensional cube. Logically, if you now move the cube along a perpendicular axis, you trace out a 4-dimensional hypercube, and you should be able to keep repeating the process for successively higher dimensions.

Many mathematicians and scientists work with higher dimensions even though they can't visualize them. They use symbols to describe what they can't actually see. A position in one dimension is a point on a line and is defined with one number, some value of x. In two dimensions, a position is described by two numbers that are plotted on an x-y coordinate system. In three dimensions, a position on a coordinate system of three axes is defined by three numbers: x, y, and z. If a box is sitting in a 3-axis coordinate system, its length would be plotted on the x-axis, height on the y-axis, and width on the z-axis, which is visualized as projecting out of the plane of the paper at right angles. In four dimensions, a point can be defined with a series of four numbers, and in the fifth dimension five points are required; but it's hard to imagine being able to visualize an object in either of those dimensions. Remarkably, Alice Boole Stott was apparently able to visualize objects in the fourth dimension. She was fascinated by patterns in space, and she did original work in the field of polytopes that was published and is still cited in books and articles on polygons.

Alicia Boole was born in Ireland in 1860, a time when women were excluded from most academic institutions, both as students and as faculty. The women of her time who did become professional mathematicians had private tutors and/or were sent to the few schools that would admit women. Alice, however, received no education at all past the age of 16 and was never able to attend a school or university.

Her father, George Boole, was a famous mathematician. Much of his work was in logic, and he invented Boolean algebra. His work laid the foundation on which today's computer world is based, since Boolean logic and binary notation are used to translate words and numbers into electrical impulses. Like Alice, he received very little formal education, largely because his family couldn't afford to send him to school. Also like Alice, he was incredibly self-sufficient and resourceful; and being a man, it was much easier for him to be accepted in professional circles even though he had no conventional training. George Boole taught himself five languages while still a teenager; he opened a school at the age of 20 and started to study mathematics at that point. Boole subsequently received a professorship at Cork University in Ireland and published several books that are still very important in mathematics and physics. His most notable publication is *Laws of Thought*, which was reissued as the second volume of *Collected Logical Works*. His life and work are discussed in Patrick Barry, ed., *George Boole: A Miscellany* (Cork, Ireland: Cork University Press 1969).

It would be easy to assume that having a mathematical genius for a father, a daughter could easily learn from him instead of going to school. However, when she was only 4 years old Alice's father died from pneumonia after being drenched on his way to an evening lecture. Her mother, Mary Everest Boole, was left with very little money and five daughters: Mary, Margaret, Alice, Lucy, and Ethel. Mrs. Boole was the daughter of a minister and the niece of Sir George Everest, after whom Mount Everest was named, but apparently her relatives weren't able to support her and her family of five. She moved to London to take a job as a matron at Queens College, leaving Alice in Ireland with her maternal grandmother and great-uncle. Alice joined her mother and sisters in London when she was about 10 years old, moving into their poor, crowded household. Her mother was an invalid at this point, and Alice's life must have been very difficult (Coxeter, 1963; 1987).

In spite of her illness, it may have been Mrs. Boole herself who helped Alice acquire the basic knowledge that made it possible for her to launch her own research into polytopes without the help of a formal education. Mrs. Boole was something of a scholar in her own right. After her children were grown she wrote several books, including *Preparation of the Child for Science* (1904), which has a chapter entitled "The Cultivation of the Mathematical Imagination." In this chapter she presented her ideas on how to teach mathematics to children. Although her writing contains many philosophical ideas that are not always easy to understand, it is clear that she considered it important to use ideas and terms accurately. She believed that even very young children should be taught to think logically and be exposed to natural phenomena, such as a swinging pendulum, which can provide an intuitive basis for understanding ideas in mathematics and science. She recommended that geometry be taught by helping students discover the basic axioms and principles themselves. She gave examples of concrete ways to elicit the idea of a line, a tangent, and a circle, as well as a way to discover the Pythagorean formula. She believed in guiding young minds toward creating their own systems for organizing ideas, and in letting them make their own discoveries.

The turning point in Alice's intellectual life came when she was about

18 years old. Mrs. Boole liked to spend time having intellectual discussions with the well known scientist James Hinton and a group of his friends. Hinton had a son, Howard, who was a teacher. Howard came to visit one day and brought a collection of small, wooden cubes with him, planning to teach Alice and her sisters about fourth-dimensional hypersolids. Most of the girls got little or nothing out of it, but Alice was fascinated. This experience marked the beginning of her mathematical studies.

As an adult Alice was a housewife and a mathematician, although she never held an academic position. She married an actuary, Walter Stott, with whom she had two children. Although much of her energy went into raising her children, she still managed to do research. Her husband became aware of a mathematician in the Netherlands, Professor Pieter Hendrik Schoute at the University of Groningen, who was doing work similar to hers. Stott was adept at visualizing figures in hyperspace and had prepared pictures of her work, which she sent to Schoute. He was very impressed, and they subsequently collaborated for many years. She was the more imaginative in her geometric visualization, and he brought more conventional mathematical skills to the partnership. Schoute arranged for her work to be published in two papers. After his death the University of Groningen conferred an honorary degree on Stott. She also worked with Professor H. M. S. Coxeter, an expert on polytopes at the University of Toronto, who cites her work in his own publications. In 1935, when she was 75 years old, Stott was still corresponding with Coxeter.

In the 1990s many scientists work with systems of higher dimensions. Whenever an ecologist tries to understand an organism living in an ecosystem, important variables that affect the organism—such as temperature, rainfall, pH, biomass of prey, or number of predators—must be identified. Each of these variables can be thought of as one axis in an n-dimensional hypervolume. Computer models are written that attempt to track each of the relevant variables. This is how estimates of population size are made so that, for example, a fisheries biologist can predict how much fishing can be done on a particular species without driving it to extinction. Work is also being done on polytopes today using computers to draw and redraw figures moving through space, so that even those of us who can't visualize the fourth dimension on our own can get an impression of what it looks like. These ideas have been used in the development of CAT scans, which are used to track the growth of tumors. Several other applications of polytopes are discussed in the introduction to the 1991 edition of *Flatland*.

It is most fitting that Alicia Boole Stott's pioneering work on polytopes and her father's invention of Boolean logic have come together in our modern world to produce new thinking about higher-dimensional phenomena and computer environments for their visualization.

Selected Works about Alicia Boole Stott

Abbott, Edwin A. (1991). *Flatland*, 6th ed. Princeton, NJ: Princeton University Press.

Coxeter, H. M. S. (1963). *Regular Polytopes*, 2nd ed. New York: MacMillan.

———. (1969). *Introduction to Geometry*. New York: John Wiley and Sons.

———. (1987). Alicia Boole Stott. In Louise Grinstein and Paul Campbell, Eds., *Women of Mathematics*. Westport, CT: Greenwood Press.

Hutchinson, G. E. (1965). *The Ecological Theater and the Evolutionary Play*. New Haven: Yale University Press. (Possibly the most accessible treatment of the n-dimensional niche idea.)

———. (1978). *An Introduction to Population Ecology*. New Haven: Yale University Press.

Stott, Alicia Boole. 1900. *On Certain Section of the Regular Four Dimensional Hypersolids*. Verhandlingen der Koninklijke Akademie van Wetenschappen (Amsterdam) (1. Sectie) 7(3): 5 plates.

Stott, 1910. *Geometrical Deduction of Semiregular from Regular Polytopes and Space Fillings*. Verhandlingen der Koninklijke Akademie van Wetenschappen (Amsterdam) (1.Sectie) 11(1): 3 plates.

LOUISE ROSLANSKY GROSSLEIN

OLGA TAUSSKY-TODD
(1906–1995)
Birthplace: Olmutz (now called Olomouc), Czechoslovakia

Olga Taussky-Todd was the first woman to teach at the California Institute of Technology (Caltech) under a formal appointment and the first woman named to full professor at that institution. As a mathematician working during the era when there was an increased awareness of the critical need for outstanding role models for women in mathematics and science, Taussky-Todd was particularly sought after as a speaker. She was both an outstanding mathematician and an inspirational role model.

Born Olga Taussky on August 30, 1906, she was the middle of three sisters. Her father was an industrial chemist who also wrote for newspapers. He had hoped that his daughters would choose careers in the arts, but they all seemed more interested in science. Taussky-Todd de-

Olga Taussky-Todd. Photo courtesy of California Institute of
Technology.

scribes her mother as "a country girl. . . . She was not an educated
woman, but she was intelligent and practical. She had a mind of her
own."[1] Shortly before Olga's third birthday the family moved to Vienna,
where they stayed until about the middle of World War I. They then
moved to Linz, Austria, where her father became director of a vinegar
factory.

Olga did not learn to read, write, or count until she entered school.
Although she was a very good student, she was not a top achiever in
arithmetic. By the time the family moved to Linz, however, she was
doing well in grade school arithmetic. She also enjoyed composing music
and writing poetry. In fact, writing poetry was something that Taussky-
Todd continued to do throughout her life.

In her 1985 autobiography Taussky-Todd wrote, "The work at school
was really not that difficult if one applied oneself to it, but it was so
uninteresting that you could not wish to apply yourself. I felt there was
another mathematics."[2] This other mathematics was the one that she was

experiencing outside of school with her father at his vinegar plant. He would arrange mathematically related chores for her. For example, the workmen had to send quantities of vinegar to the local grocers at legal acidity levels. When the vinegar produced in the factory exceeded this level, water would be added. Sometimes several types of vinegar were added in addition to the water. The workmen had a fairly good idea of the proportions in question, but Olga's father challenged her to work this out for herself. "This leads to a diophantine equation to be solved in positive integers. I apparently managed this all right and produced a little table with colored pencil entries which was posted up in the relevant room."[3] Another mathematical chore involved rearranging her father's magazines in chronological order. She claimed that after that, she could not pass by disarranged periodicals in a library without putting them back in order. Olga's relationship with her father played a significant role in the development of her mathematical interests.

Another important person in Olga's life was Resa, the wife of one of the four brothers who owned the vinegar plant. Olga tutored Resa's daughter in mathematics. Even though Resa's husband was very well-to-do, Olga was told by her father not to accept any payment. Resa did, however, give her very expensive books—books she had heard of in school but never dreamed of possessing. Olga and Resa remained good friends for decades.

At age 14 Olga transferred to high school (called *Mittelschule*) and at 15 to the *Gymnasium*. She studied Latin for eight hours a week at the one school that girls could attend, but she would have preferred to study more science or mathematics had it been possible. Gradually she became more and more oriented toward mathematics. "I later found that the yearning for and the satisfaction gained from mathematical thought brings the subject near to art."[4] During this time, as she was growing into womanhood, the war came to an end and Austria was left in poverty.

Before World War I, careers for women were very limited—typically to teaching in girls' schools or working as secretaries, as shop assistants, in domestic service, as dressmakers, or as nurses. After the war even greater training for teachers was required than before, perhaps even a doctoral degree for a job in the better high schools. Schools expected students, including girls, to be very serious; cosmetics and hairdos were out. When Olga was in her last year at the government school, the Austrian government ruled that all pupils in their final year must write an essay on a topic of their own choosing. Olga decided that her subject would be mathematics, but she had no idea what topic to choose. Finally, she wrote an essay entitled "From the binomial to the polynomial theorem." Among other things the paper described Pascal pyramids of all dimensions, instead of the Pascal triangle that is usually studied. This experience gave her a great deal of confidence to go forward with mathematics. Fortunately, in spite of her father's death and her family's ensuing financial straits, she was allowed to enroll at the University of Vienna, studying mathematics and also taking a major in chemistry. Olga later dropped chemistry when she found that both her sisters were studying the "family subject."

As seems to be the case with many aspiring mathematics majors, Olga had no idea what it meant to study mathematics when she entered the university in the fall of 1925, but she did have the opportunity to be the student and advisee of Philip Furtwanger, a famous German number theorist. Furtwanger, who was nearly 60 years old and having difficulty walking, needed an assistant to write on the blackboard for him, a position that Olga was able to fill. At the end of her second year at the university, and after taking his course in algebraic number theory, Olga asked Professor Furtwanger if she could write a thesis on number theory. She did so and thus determined the direction of her future work. At times, she said, she felt she was "married to number theory."[5] After receiving her doctorate in 1930, Olga supported herself by tutoring. Her teachers, impressed with her work, pushed her to give papers at congresses in front of world-famous mathematicians. She did agree to give these papers, terrified though she was.

Through the efforts of Richard Courant, a world-renowned mathematician, Olga was fortunate to receive an appointment at Göttingen, a prestigious German university, helping Courant with the editing of an edition of Hilbert's papers on number theory. There she also worked with **Emmy Noether** and developed a friendship with her.

Taussky-Todd subsequently moved back to Vienna and spent time tutoring and involving herself in the mathematics department at the university. Eventually she obtained a formal appointment, which paid a small stipend. While working in Vienna Taussky-Todd felt that she had her first break in her work in number theory when she proved an important theorem concerning associative division algebras. While waiting to hear about a science fellowship for which she had applied, she was offered and accepted an appointment in the mathematics department at Bryn Mawr, a women's college in Pennsylvania. Although she had felt that her chances were remote, she was also awarded the three-year Girton College fellowship, which gave her great professional freedom. (Girton College is a part of Cambridge University in England.)

She spent the first year of her fellowship at Bryn Mawr because she had already accepted the offer there, but then went to England as a fellow at Girton College. During the year at Bryn Mawr she worked with Emmy Noether, who was by now a professor there. Taussky-Todd often accompanied Noether on her trips to Princeton and several times met Albert Einstein, who was then a resident at the Institute for Advanced

Studies in Princeton. When she went on to Girton, Taussky-Todd was
able to do some significant and satisfying work, in which she was aided
by discussions with B. H. Neumann, an eminent mathematician. Later
she became a junior faculty member at Westfield College, an undergraduate women's college that is part of the University of London.

At a mathematics seminar in London Olga met Jack Todd, an Irish
mathematician. They were married a few months later in September 1938
on the day that Britain's Prime Minister Neville Chamberlain returned
from Munich with his "peace in our time" pact. Unsure that peace would
hold, Olga and Jack decided to help dig trenches in suburban London
instead of taking a honeymoon. World War II broke out the year after
Olga and Jack were married, and they both went to work for the British
government. In 1947 the couple went to the United States to work for
the National Bureau of Standards field station at the University of California at Los Angeles (UCLA) Institute for Numerical Analysis. Large-
scale computers were under construction at this time, and the Institute
was developing uses for them. During the year in California, Olga
Taussky-Todd wrote six theoretical papers and spoke at several universities on various topics in number theory as well as matrix theory and
its computer applications. The couple returned to England upon completion of their California assignment, and Jack was soon invited back
to the National Bureau of Standards headquarters in Washington, D.C.,
to head the Computation Laboratory. Olga was given a staff consultant
position. They worked for ten years at the Bureau and became recognized as experts in the new field of high-speed computer programming
and analysis.

In 1957 Jack and Olga returned to California, this time to Caltech—
Jack as a full professor, and Olga as a research associate. In 1963 Taussky-
Todd was granted tenure; in 1971 she became a full professor. Her professional work, for which she is well known, includes more than two
hundred scientific papers. Matrix theory was one of Taussky-Todd's major subject areas. In "How I Became a Torchbearer for Matrix Theory"
(1988) Taussky-Todd passionately describes her work.

In 1976 Caltech held a symposium in honor of Olga Taussky-Todd.
One outcome of the symposium, which was attended by mathematicians
from across the country, was a volume of the journal *Linear Algebra and
Its Applications* dedicated to Taussky-Todd, its founding editor. She also
served as editor of the *Journal of Number Theory, Linear and Multilinear
Algebra*, and *Advances in Mathematics*. The *Los Angeles Times* named
Taussky-Todd Woman of the Year in 1964. Between 1964 and 1972 she
served on the Los Angeles Mayor's Committee on Space. In 1971
she received the Lester R. Ford Award for the outstanding article in
the *American Mathematical Monthly* during 1970. She was the second
woman ever to receive this prestigious award, following Margaret W.

Maxfield in 1968. In 1988 the University of Southern California awarded Taussky-Todd an honorary doctorate that "she greatly prizes, as she does the Golden Doctorate that her alma mater, the University of Vienna, awarded her in 1980 in recognition of her achievements in research and in teaching."[6] In 1985 Taussky-Todd was awarded the Golden Cross of Honor Class of the Austrian Republic and a corresponding membership in the Austrian Academy of Sciences. She served as vice-president of the American Mathematical Society (AMS) during 1986–1987 and on the AMS Council for six years.

During their long marriage Olga and Jack enjoyed many mathematical discourses and attended many mathematics meetings together. They supported each other in the pursuit of their careers. Occasionally they coauthored papers. Taussky-Todd said, "My life and my career would have been so different if my Irishman had not come along."[7] Taussky-Todd expressed pride in her life's work as a torchbearer for matrix theory and was happy that many of her former graduate students are carrying on work in this area.

Taussky-Todd was not only a first-rate mathematician and teacher; she was a mentor for younger women mathematicians. When **Marjorie Senechal** was presenting a paper at an AMS meeting for the first time in 1962 and feeling quite alone and far from home, Taussky-Todd turned the experience into a pleasant one by coming up to Senechal, all smiles, introducing herself, and saying, "It's so nice to have another woman here! Welcome to mathematics!" Senechal said that it made a great impression on her that a leading mathematician was also such a lovely human being.[8]

The year 1990 found Taussky-Todd, then well into her eighties, working in her large corner office on campus and still pursuing her primary interest, number theory. She died on October 9, 1995, one year short of her ninetieth birthday.

Notes

1. Olga Taussky-Todd, "Olga Taussky-Todd: An Autobiographical Essay," in D. J. Albers and G. L. Alexanderson, eds., *Mathematical People* (Boston: Birkhäuser-Boston, 1985), p. 311.

2. Ibid., p. 313.

3. Ibid., p. 312.

4. Ibid., p. 313.

5. Ibid., p. 317.

6. Laura Marcus, "A Mathematical Match: Olga Taussky-Todd and Jack Todd," *On Campus* (California Institute of Technology), 1990, p. 4.

7. Ibid.

8. C. Davis, "Remembering Olga Taussky-Todd," *AWM Newsletter* 26, no. 1 (1996): 9.

Selected Works by Olga Taussky-Todd

(1979). Number Theory. In Ernest Robson and Jet Wimp, Eds., *Against Infinity: An Anthology of Contemporary Mathematical Poetry* (p. 69). Parker Ford, PA: Primary Press.

(1981). My Personal Recollections of Emmy Noether. In J. W. Brewer and M. K. Smith, Eds., *Emmy Noether: A Tribute to Her Life and Work*. New York: Dekker.

(1985). Olga Taussky-Todd: An Autobiographical Essay. In D. J. Albers and G. L. Alexanderson, Eds., *Mathematical People* (pp. 310–36). Boston: Birkhäuser.

(1988). How I Became a Torchbearer for Matrix Theory. *American Mathematical Monthly*, 95 pp. 801–12.

Selected Works about Olga Taussky-Todd

Davis, C. (1996). Remembering Olga Taussky Todd. *AWM Newsletter* 26(1), pp. 7–9.

Kenschaft, Patricia Clark. (1991). *Winning Women into Mathematics*. Washington, DC: Mathematical Association of America.

Luchins, Edith H. (1987). Olga Taussky-Todd. In Louise Grinstein and Paul Campbell, Eds., *Women of Mathematics*. Westport, CT: Greenwood Press. (Contains an extensive reference list of Taussky-Todd's mathematical writings.)

Marcus, Laura. (1990). A Mathematical Match: Olga Taussky-Todd and Jack Todd. *On Campus* (California Institute of Technology), pp. 4–8.

Pinl, M., and Furtmuller, L. (1973). Mathematicians under Hitler. In *Leo Baeck Yearbook* (Vol. 18, pp. 129–82). London: Secker and Warburg.

Redheffer, R. (1966). Remarks on a Paper by Taussky. *Journal of Algebra* 2, pp. 42–47.

Schneider, H. (1977). Olga Taussky-Todd's Influence on Matrix Theory and Matrix Theorists. *Linear and Multilinear Algebra* 5, pp. 197–224.

LYN TAYLOR

JEAN TAYLOR
(1944–)
Birthplace: California

Jean Taylor, professor of mathematics at Rutgers University, works in a world described by mathematicians as "minimal surfaces." Examples of minimal surfaces appear all around us. Think about the following experiment, which you may have tried as a young child. Take a plastic or wire wand, bend it to form a triangle at one end, and dip it into a bucket

Jean Taylor. Photo courtesy of Jean Taylor.

of soapy water. When you remove the wand, what shape will the resulting bubble form? If you guessed a sphere, you are right. But why a sphere? And what shapes occur when two bubbles are joined together? Does the behavior of soap bubbles extend to other materials and physical processes, such as metals and crystal growth? These questions have intrigued Jean Taylor for the past two decades and form the basis of her widely recognized work in the mathematics of optimal form.

Taylor, born in San Mateo, California, on September 17, 1944, became interested in mathematics through an unlikely sequence of events and experiences, both as a child and as a college student. Her first recollections of mathematics go back to elementary school in Sacramento, California, when she was doing two-digit multiplication. She was asked to multiply 40×26, and she proceeded to rewrite the problem as 26×40 to make the computation easier. As she was about to begin multiplying, the principal walked in, looked at her rearrangement, and proclaimed that she could not change the problem. To Taylor's amusement and dismay, she realized that despite her protests she would be forced to do the problem the principal's way. Her introduction to mathematics, unfortunately, did not inspire her initially. She knew she was good at it but did not find it particularly interesting.

In eighth grade Taylor took the Kuder Inventory Personal Preference Test, which tries to help students identify potential career areas. It suggested that she had a preference in the literary, scientific, mechanical, and computational areas. It was Taylor's first indicator that she had potential interest in mathematics. However, since she did well in most of her classes, and since her academic talents were widespread, she did not particularly think of mathematics as a major interest. In fact, she initially did not find the subject exciting.

But in ninth grade her view of mathematics changed. At Joaquin Miller Junior High School in Sacramento, Taylor took algebra, the first mathematics course she found really interesting. She received more encouragement to major in chemistry, however, from a high school chemistry teacher. Taylor had never thought about chemistry as a major but decided to consider it because the teacher had shown enough interest in her to suggest it. Taylor later commented, "That experience reminds me of the effect that teachers have on students."

It had never occurred to Taylor to consider attending college on the East Coast; however, she was influenced by a professor from Harvard who was a speaker at a church camp she attended one summer. She was intrigued by his talk, especially when he claimed that one couldn't *not* believe in something unless there was the possibility of believing in it. Taylor went up to him after the speech to challenge his assertion and told him that she didn't believe that the moon is made of green cheese. He found her comments interesting and suggested she consider going to Radcliffe for her undergraduate education. Although she did not attend Radcliffe, his suggestion provided the impetus for Taylor to leave the West Coast and to major in chemistry at Mount Holyoke College in Massachusetts. (Mount Holyoke is a women's college with an impressive record in producing students who later earn Ph.D.s in chemistry.) Taylor did, indeed, find the chemistry department a very exciting place. She worked on independent projects in computing molecular orbiting; she did research in behavioral psychology; she was inspired by the people at Mount Holyoke who made their subjects come alive.

The turning point in her career came a few years later when she was a graduate student in chemistry at the University of California at Berkeley. Encouraged by some friends, she audited a course in differential geometry. It was taught by a mathematician named Chern, who talked about curves and surfaces. Taylor found the mathematics so fascinating that she talked with the professor about possibly switching her major to mathematics. He suggested she take the final exam, and she did. She performed so well that he helped her make the change. In 1968 she earned a master's degree in physical chemistry, and in 1971 earned a master's degree in mathematics from the University of Warwick in England. She earned her Ph.D. in mathematics at Princeton in 1973, spent the 1972–1973 academic year as an instructor at MIT, and then went to Rutgers as an assistant professor. Currently Taylor teaches a course in multivariable calculus and a graduate course in special topics in analysis, concentrating on the mathematics of surfaces and materials science.

Jean Taylor lives in Princeton, New Jersey, and has an incredibly active life outside of her mathematical pursuits. Her interests reflect her energy and sense of adventure: She hikes, kayaks, wind surfs, and flies airplanes. She is married to Princeton mathematician Frederick Almgren Jr. and is the proud stepmother of mathematicians Robert Almgren (assistant professor at the University of Chicago) and Ann Almgren (postdoctoral fellow at Lawrence Livermore National Laboratory). Her youngest daughter, Karen Almgren, took Galois Theory at Princeton University while she was in the eleventh grade. Says Taylor, "I consider these three mathematicians to be major successes of the creation of a good learning environment for mathematics by myself and my husband. We talk about mathematics as though it was the most interesting thing one can do. And it is!"

Taylor was always interested in why things have the shapes they do. In fact, this fascination was what drew her to chemistry originally: The shapes of molecules affected the way they acted. Her concentration in geometric analysis stemmed from her realization that the subject was entirely about shapes. Her early work dealt with the shapes of soap bubbles and soap films. Her later work concentrates on the shapes of crystals. In essence, she develops mathematics to describe the shapes of crystal materials, making use of a concept known as the Wulff construction.

One of the reasons that the soap bubble is round is that the bubble has the smallest surface area for the volume it occupies. Surface area is part of the total energy system, which always gravitates toward a reduced energy state, a basic physical principle. The same minimum-energy principles that dictate the behavior of soap bubbles are at work in the formation of crystals. However, with crystals, force patterns along the surface can be different at different places. Taylor studies mathematical functions that reveal what the energy is per unit area in each direction, and then tries to find the shape that has the minimum energy.

Taylor's interest in this work began in the fall of 1970, when she attended the International Congress of Mathematicians in Nice, France. This happened just before Taylor was to return to the United States to begin her doctoral work at Princeton. Frederick Almgren, who was to become her husband three years later, gave a talk on geometric measure theory at the Congress. It was from Almgren that Taylor learned of an unsolved problem about length and smoothness of soap-film triple junction curves. At that moment she knew it was to be her thesis problem, even before she arrived at Princeton. Taylor spent two years working on the solution, which she published in the journal *Inventiones Mathematicae*.

Taylor's next focus became clusters of bubbles rather than soap film. She spent time examining a body of mathematics known as Plateau's rules, using geometric measure theory and the work of previous mathematicians who were only able to make assumptions about curves of soap-bubble clusters. In 1976 she completed her proof, which appears in the *Annals of Mathematics*.

Taylor's current interest in crystals has introduced her to the world of materials science, which overlaps with her mathematical work in describing how soap bubbles behave. Because some materials consist of bunches of little crystals that behave at times like a froth of soap bubbles, materials scientists were interested in what Taylor had to say about them. Steel is a good example of a material that is made up of many little crystals. Because many tons of steel are cast every day, materials scientists are interested in the surface energy created by these crystals and how it affects the shape the crystals assume when they solidify.

Taylor now spends time at meetings of materials science societies; she realizes how much effort it takes to learn how to talk to people in other fields, but she finds it worthwhile and interesting. One activity in which she has been involved is a committee sponsored by the National Academy of Science that produced the document *Mathematical Research in Materials Science—Opportunities and Perspectives*. In addition, she serves on the Board of Directors of the American Association for the Advancement of Science (AAAS), is a vice-president of the American Mathematical Society (AMS), is a member of the Joint Policy Board for Mathematics, and is an advisor for *M*, a television series being produced by WQED. She has been an invited speaker at conferences in Germany, China, Greece, Australia, Japan, and Brazil. As a woman who is widely recognized for solving historical problems in optimal form, Taylor continues to chart unknown territories in the mathematics of minimal surfaces.

Note

The information included in this biography is based in part on an interview by the author.

Selected Works by Jean Taylor

(1973). Regularity of the Singular Set of Two Dimensional Area Minimizing Flat Chains Modulo 3 in R3. *Inventiones Mathematicae* 22, pp. 119–59.

(1976). The Geometry of Soap Films and Soap Bubbles (with F. Almgren Jr.). *Scientific American* (July), pp. 82–93.

(1976). The Structure of Singularities in Soap-Bubble-Like and Soap-Film-Like Minimal Surfaces. *Annals of Mathematics* 103(2), pp. 489–539.

(1986). (with J. Cahn). A Cusp Singularity in Surfaces That Minimize an Anisotropic Surface Energy, *Science* 233, pp. 548–51.

(1987). (with E. Bombieri). Quasicrystals, Tilings, and Algebraic Number Theory: Some Preliminary Connections. In M. Mendè's France (Ed.), The Legacy of Sonya Kovalevskaya, *Contemporary Mathematics* 64, pp. 241–64. Providence, RI: American Mathematical Society.

(1991). On the Global Structure of Crystalline Surfaces. *Discrete and Computational Geometry* 6, pp. 225–62.

(1992). Geometric Crystal Growth in 3D via Faceted Interfaces. In Jean E. Taylor, Ed., Computational Crystal Growers Workshop, *Selected Lectures in Mathematics* (pp. 111–13 plus video 20:25–26:00). Providence, RI: American Mathematical Society.

(1992). (with J. Cahn and C. Handwerker). Geometric Models of Crystal Growth. *Acta Mettalurgica et Materialia* 40, pp. 1443–74.

(1994). Surface Motion by Surface Diffusion (with J. W. Cahn). *Acta Mettalurgica et Materialia* 42, pp. 1045–63.

(1995). Surface Motion Due to Surface Energy Reduction. *Notices of the American Mathematical Society*, pp. 38–40.

FAYE NISONOFF RUOPP

CHUU-LIAN TERNG
(1949–)
Birthplace: Hualian, Taiwan

Chuu-Lian Terng is a professor of mathematics at Northeastern University in Boston. She is recognized in the international mathematics community as an outstanding researcher of differential geometry. In her bright sunny office overlooking the park, a large chalkboard with an unfinished geometric equation—her "newest puzzle"—dominates the room as if it were a piece of visual art. It is the perfect symbol for a woman who sees mathematics as fun, as puzzles to be solved, as a way to explore and understand things we can't see with our eyes. For Terng, research is exciting because one doesn't always know what will happen. Although the equation on the board is pure research, the geometric ideas of mathematicians like Terng have been used to create important innovations, including CAT scans, that have improved our lives.

As a young child, Terng did not imagine a career in mathematics that

Chuu-Lian Terng. Photo courtesy of Chuu-Lian Terng.

would take her around the world. Yet it was her experience in a small town in Taiwan that best prepared her for a career in geometry. The oldest of four children, Terng was the only girl. In her community there was no social pressure for girls to be smart, but her warm and loving family did expect her to be a good student. Terng discovered her love for mathematics early, while attending the public elementary school next door to her house. By fourth or fifth grade, "I discovered that math was the thing I could do most easily, and I liked it."

Education in Taiwan is organized differently from education in the United States, and Terng feels this may have helped her in the beginning. In Taiwan, all public schools have the same curriculum and the expectation that all students will do well. Terng enjoyed being the brightest in her class, and her parents expected her to study hard. As they grew older, however, many of her friends were not as interested in studying and encouraged her to play after school. Although she enjoyed being with her friends, her grades went down and her parents required her to stay at home and study. This was not a punishment for Terng; she enjoyed the time she spent studying and reading. When she took the entrance exams for middle school, Terng became one of the few from her elementary school to be admitted to a prestigious middle school for girls.

In middle school, with no boys "for distraction," the young women excelled at academics, building their self-confidence and the feeling that they could try anything. Terng did especially well in math. Subsequently she attended the first-level high school. She did so well there that her entrance exams to college were waived and she entered the National Taiwan University to major in mathematics.

Her love for the "puzzle" and the excitement of solving mathematics challenges became her life focus. "Of course, mathematics is a challenge; it is something you must work at. But it is so much fun! To make sense of the world, to imagine new things, to ask new questions—and to do this with interesting people. I could not have asked for anything better!" She came to the United States for graduate study in mathematics, first in California and then at Brandeis University, near Boston.

One of the ways she learned and worked best was with a small, cooperative learning group of women students. The group met regularly to study together, to ask one another questions, and to support one another emotionally. They are still very good friends; they are all mathematicians now and live in different places, but they keep in touch and support one another. Terng's professors were very helpful also, assisting her in understanding the education system in the United States and mentoring her as a new mathematician. Terng feels that it was this group support and the mentoring that helped her keep going and succeed in her field.

As a professor of mathematics, Dr. Terng has taught in a number of colleges and universities throughout the country; she is now at Northeastern University in Boston, which is an urban campus and one of the few in the country with a co-op program focus. In a co-op program, students alternate taking classes with full-time employment at sites related to their area of interest. Such "real-world" experience enhances their studies. This excites Dr. Terng, as she can engage students in mathematical discovery by drawing on their experiences outside of class.

Her time at the university is divided between teaching and research, and she is constantly balancing the two. "It's exciting that with my graduate students I can try out puzzles and ideas that intrigue me. I don't need to have the right answer—like I don't have the answer to this problem (gesturing to the equation on her chalkboard), but teaching lets me share the excitement of discovery with my students. They learn that not all the questions are answered yet." Through her teaching she pushes herself to discover new challenges and shares the excitement of looking for answers.

In her mathematical research she studies the shape, geometry, and analytic aspects of surfaces and their higher-dimensional analogues. Although she often works by herself, Terng also enjoys collaboration, working jointly on mathematics problems or writing papers. Some of her colleagues live and work in other parts of the world. "We work in a number of ways, sharing ideas, sending papers and information back and forth. It's very nice to work with people who are interested in the same things." Travel has become an important part of her work; it has included trips to conferences and meetings in Germany, France, Belgium, China, England, and back home in Taiwan. She presents papers on her work in progress, meets with others doing similar work, and enjoys the camaraderie of being with other mathematicians.

Now well established in her field, Terng has taken on a new challenge: supporting the involvement of girls in mathematics. "For so long I was often the only woman, but I never thought too much about it because I had supportive colleagues." But as she looked around, she discovered that there were few women entering mathematics. It saddened her because she thinks that mathematics can be a good career field for women. She wanted to do something about it.

Doing something has meant becoming involved in a number of organizations and programs that focus on encouraging girls in mathematics. She has become a role model and a leader in the Association for Women in Mathematics, having just finished a term as president. For a long time Terng worked primarily in her own professional groups, but she is now working with women around the country to dispel the idea that mathematics is not for girls. She wants them to see how much fun it can be. She observes that often in this country girls are told they cannot do mathematics, but she knows that anyone who likes to solve puzzles, understand how things work, and see how things are related can find satisfaction in mathematics. "I do not know why here it is seen as something better for men—maybe we have to look at what we think men and women are so that we can change this."

For Terng, work and family have often blended. She met her husband while she was working on her doctorate; he was on the faculty. "I enjoyed listening to him as a professor and solving problems with him. This mutual interest is still at the center of our marriage. We can talk about mathematics together. We understand what each is working on and how much focus that takes." At times she and her husband have worked on projects together, coauthoring papers and presenting their findings.

When she leaves her work, she relaxes at home with her husband, solving another kind of puzzle—how to create a beautiful garden in her spare time. Passionate about the creative process of gardening, she especially likes peonies, hostas, and daylilies and has many different varieties. "It is so relaxing, so intriguing to work in the dirt, to plant and to see what happens. Of course, my husband sometimes needs to remind me to come in because it is getting dark. I love it so much I forget about time.''

Note

The information included in this biography is based on an interview by the author.

Selected Works by Chuu-Lian Terng

(1987). (with R. S. Palais). A general theory of canonical forms. *Transactions of the American Mathematical Society* 300, 771–789.

(1988). (with W. Y. Hsiang & R. S. Palais). The topology of isoparametric submanifolds in Euclidean spaces. *Journal of Differential Geometry* 27, 423–460.

(1989). Proper Fredholm submanifolds of Hilbert space. *Journal of Differential Geometry* 29, 9–47.

(1994). Hyperpolar Actions and k-Flat Homogeneous Space (with E. Heintze, R. S. Palais, and G. Thorbergsson). *Journal für de Reine und Angewardte Mathematik* 454, pp. 163–79.

(1995). Submanifold Geometry in Symmetric Spaces (with G. Thorbergsson). *Journal Differential Geometry* 42, pp. 665–718.

(1995). Polar Actions on Hilbert Spaces. *Journal of Geometric Analysis* 5, pp. 129–50.

KATHERINE HANSON

KAREN UHLENBECK
(1942–)
Birthplace: Ohio

Karen Uhlenbeck is a professor of mathematics at the University of Texas at Austin who has helped understand one of science's greatest mysteries: the fundamental properties of matter in the universe. She is one of only a few mathematicians who is acknowledged as an expert in theoretical physics.

Born on August 24, 1942, in Cleveland, Ohio, Karen is the oldest of four children. Her father was an engineer and her mother an artist, both first-generation college graduates. They imparted to her a love of nature; even now, in their eighties, her parents still hike and backpack. Uhlenbeck feels at home in nature and in her spare time can often be found in her garden or out in the wilderness. Because she had a difficult time dealing with her siblings, she chose a career where she imagined she could compete with herself and didn't have to work with others. Now,

Karen Uhlenbeck. Photo courtesy of Karen
Uhlenbeck.

however, she often works with others; she has found that she can learn
a great deal from other people and enjoy collaborative projects.

Uhlenbeck attended elementary and secondary school in New Jersey
and wasn't very interested in mathematics as a child or adolescent. She
believes that this is because one doesn't really understand what mathematics is until at least halfway through college. All her family were avid
readers, possibly because they lived in the country and there was little
else to do. During fifth grade Karen often read under her desk at school
and all night long at home. She was particularly interested in reading
about science, and when she was about 12 years old her father started
bringing home Fred Hoyle's books on astrophysics. She recalls, "I also
remember a little paperback called *One, Two, Three, Infinity* by George
Gamow, and I remember the excitement of understanding this very sophisticated argument that there were two kinds of infinities."

Because New Jersey did not have a state university that was open to
women at that time, the University of Michigan was her chosen under-

graduate college; there she enrolled in the honors program. Although she planned to major in physics, she had an exciting junior-level mathematics course that influenced her to become a mathematics major. In fact, there were three women in her freshman honors class at Michigan who are now Ph.D. mathematicians—unusual for that time. She, and others, speculate that this phenomenon of success (of women from the honors program during this period) was due to bright women *not* being sent to expensive, private colleges. They attended places like Michigan with honors programs instead. Karen feels that if they had been bright men, their fathers would have sent them to Ivy League schools.

In 1964 Uhlenbeck received her bachelor's degree in mathematics from the University of Michigan. She then spent a year studying math at New York University's prestigious Courant Institute. In 1965 she was married and moved to Massachusetts, where her husband was studying biochemistry at Harvard. She was able to attend Brandeis University under a National Science Foundation graduate fellowship; here she was a very good student and received a great deal of attention and positive feedback. She did not, however, learn to value her fellow students who were women. In fact, they were considered somewhat of a liability in that they could not help each other get ahead. It was better to cultivate the friendship of men, who could help establish connections with important mathematicians.

In 1968 Uhlenbeck earned her doctorate and taught for a year at MIT while her husband completed his doctorate in biophysics. There followed two years of teaching at the University of California at Berkeley, after which Karen started looking for a tenure track position in a mathematics department. Even though she had been an outstanding student and had had no difficulty finding temporary positions in highly respected mathematics departments, she now had difficulty finding a permanent job. All of a sudden she was told, "that people didn't hire women, that women were supposed to go home and have babies." The universities that were interested in her husband—MIT, Harvard, and Princeton—did not want to hire her, suggesting that nepotism rules prevented them from doing so. She recalls the dilemma she felt. She would rather that they had been honest and said they wouldn't hire her because she was a woman. "Conversely, I would have been just as offended if they did hire me because I was a woman. I wanted to be valued for my work as a mathematician, not because I'm a member of a particular group."[1] One positive influence in her life at that time was the support of her parents-in-law (her father-in-law was a well-known theoretical physicist), who valued intellectual pursuits highly. Their encouragement was crucial to her survival in mathematics.

Finally Uhlenbeck joined the faculty at the University of Illinois, Urbana, where both she and her husband were hired. She considers her husband's accepting this position a remarkably generous act because he could have had jobs at more prestigious universities such as MIT, Stanford, or Princeton. However, she did not like living in Urbana and felt out of place both professionally and socially. While there, she received a Sloan fellowship that allowed her to take time to rearrange her life and develop her mentoring relationships further. She was able to work with **Lesley Sibner**, who has served as a mentor, role model, and adviser to Uhlenbeck for many years. She also began to work with Jonathan Sacks and Bill Abikoff, two mathematicians whom she considers her first close mathematical contacts.

Much of what happened concerning women during those years is only now becoming more clear to Uhlenbeck. She began a career path in mathematics before the feminist movement and affirmative action programs were established. At first women seemed to be progressing well in their careers, but suddenly there was a lot of fuss about women being unwelcome. Initially this was bewildering, but then organizations such as the Association for Women in Mathematics began spotlighting roadblocks for women and noting the low number of women in tenured positions, especially at prestigious universities. The issues raised by these organizations clarified some of what had been happening to Uhlenbeck.

Several years later Uhlenbeck, now divorced, moved to Chicago, where she obtained a temporary position at Northwestern University; then she took an appointment at the University of Illinois, Chicago Circle campus. She established fruitful connections with mathematicians Bob Williams and S. T. Yau, whom she credits with establishing her definitively as a mathematician. In 1982 Karen took a professorship in the mathematics department at the University of Chicago, the same year she was awarded a prestigious MacArthur fellowship, which supported her work for five years. She was elected to the American Academy of Arts and Science in 1983 and the National Academy of Sciences in 1986. At present she is a professor of mathematics at the University of Texas at Austin. She is one of three women in the mathematics department there. She holds a Richardson Foundation Regents Chair in mathematics.

Uhlenbeck's research focuses on differential equations and is inspired by physics, particularly Maxwell's equations for electromagnetism. When considered in space-time, these equations yield partial differential equations with four-dimensional manifolds. A nonlinear study can yield important topological results. Her work is difficult to categorize because it spans many areas within mathematics as well as between mathematics and physics. She has variously been called a differential geometer, nonlinear analyst, and differential topologist. Uhlenbeck describes her work: "Very rarely does a physicist come to a mathematician with a question that the mathematician can answer. Instead, the mathematician sees the mess that the physicist uses and tries to figure it out."[2] By clarifying the extremely complex interrelationships of curved spaces in four dimensions (length, height, width, and time) with new equations describing the fundamental subatomic particles, she is helping to expand Einstein's theory of relativity.

Like many other mathematicians who work in extremely abstract areas, Uhlenbeck finds it difficult to describe her work in any depth to those who do not have advanced training in mathematics. She sees the role of mathematics as a process of abstracting ideas from their context and streamlining them. The ideas can then be applied in many different areas, such as economics or physics. She is clearly passionate about her work.

In 1995 Professor Uhlenbeck was the recipient of the Common Wealth Award for Science and Invention in recognition of her contributions. She is active in many professional organizations, including the Mathematical Association of America (MAA) and the Association of Women in Mathematics (AWM). She has served as vice-president of the American Mathematical Society (AMS).

As a professor who has taught many undergraduate students, Uhlenbeck is concerned about the way mathematics is taught and feels that not enough students are succeeding in the sciences. Although she is beginning to see more diversity in her large engineering classes—more women, Hispanics, and African Americans—she notices that most of the people coming into science are being trained somewhere other than the United States. She would, in particular, like to see more women enrolled in her classes, and for the past two years she has had a mentoring program for women in mathematics. She is now aware that she herself is an important role model for young women and takes this responsibility very seriously. She believes that motivation is the most important thing a teacher can inspire in students. Although she is optimistic about the future, she cautions that young people still experience discrimination, perhaps a much more subtle form than has been seen in the past.

Uhlenbeck's work is widely known in her professional community, and many of her colleagues consider her to be "the most eminent mathematician alive today."[3] She is a very popular speaker and is the author of numerous, highly respected publications.

Notes

1. Quoted in S. Ambrose, "Coming to Grips with Success: A Profile of Karen Uhlenbeck," *Math Horizons* (April 1996): 16.

2. "Professor Profile: Dr. Karen Uhlenbeck," *University of Texas Campus Newspaper* (University of Texas, Austin), 1994.

3. Susan Edeen, John Edeen, and Virginia Slachman, *Portraits for Classroom Bulletin Boards: Women Mathematicians* (Palo Alto, CA: Dale Seymour, 1990), p. 30.

Selected Works by Karen Uhlenbeck

(1996). (with R. Mazzeo and D. Pollack). Moduli Spaces of Singular Yamabe Metrics. *Journal of the American Mathematical Society* 9(2), pp. 303–44.

(1995). (with R. Mazzeo and D. Pollack). Connected Sum Constructions for Constant Scalar Curvature Metrics. *Topological Methods in Nonlinear Analysis* 6(2), pp. 207–33.

(1995). (with G. Daskalopoulos). Wentworth, Richard Moduli of Extensions of Holomorphic Bundles on Kähler Manifolds. *Communications in Analysis and Geometry* 3(3–4), pp. 479–522.

(1995). (with G. Daskalopoulos). An Application of Transversality to the Topology of the Moduli Space of Stable Bundles. *Topology* 34(1), pp. 203–15.

(1992). Instantons and their relatives. *American Mathematical Society Centennial Publications*, Vol. II (Providence, RI, 1988), 467–477, Amer. Math. Soc., Providence, RI.

(1992). On the connection between harmonic maps and the self-dual Yang-Mills and the sine-Gordon equations. *Journal of Geometry and Physics* 8(1–4), 283–316.

(1991). (with D. S. Freed). *Instantons and four-manifolds. Second edition.* Mathematical Sciences Research Institute Publications, 1. Springer-Verlag, New York.

(1989). (with L. M. Sibner, and R. J. Sibner). Solutions to Yang-Mills equations that are not self-dual. *Proceedings of the National Academy of Sciences of the USA* 86(22), 8610–8613.

(1986). (with S.-T. Yau). On the existence of Hermitian-Yang-Mills connections in stable vector bundles. *Communications in Pure and Applied Mathematics* 39(S), 257–293.

Selected Works about Karen Uhlenbeck

Ambrose, S. (1996). *Coming to Grips with Success: A Profile of Karen Uhlenbeck.* Math Horizons, pp. 14–17.

———. (1997). Karen Uhlenbeck. In S. Ambrose, K. L. Dunkle, B. B. Lazarus, I. Nair, & D. A. Harkus, Eds., *Journeys of Women in Science and Engineering: No Universal Constants.* Philadelphia: Temple University Press.

Edeen, Susan, Edeen, John, and Slachman, Virginia. (1990). *Portraits for Classroom Bulletin Boards: Women Mathematicians.* Palo Alto, CA: Dale Seymour. pp. 30–31.

Jackson, A. (1994). Karen K. Uhlenbeck. In A. Jackson, Ed., *Profiles of Women in Mathematics: The Emmy Noether Lecturers.* College Pack, MD: American Women of Mathematics.

Professor Profile: Dr. Karen Uhlenbeck. (1994). *University of Texas Campus Newspaper* (University of Texas, Austin).

LYN TAYLOR

MARION WALTER

(1928–)

Birthplace: Berlin, Germany

Marion Walter is a consummate question-asker. In fact, she is so good at asking questions that she has made a career of it and now is widely known for developing interesting ways for mathematics teachers to take the emphasis off "the answer" and put it on the posing of problems. She has inspired hundreds of students to see mathematics in the world around them and to use their environment to understand mathematics more deeply. A highly respected colleague, Bob Davis, has recently said that the current school reform movement could not have assumed its present form without the contributions that have been made by Marion Walter.

Marion, born on July 30, 1928, recognized at an early age that there was an advantage to being good at mathematics. At age 7, while Marion was still living in her native Germany, a teacher decided not to report her for refusing to say "Heil Hitler" because Marion was her best student in arithmetic. This refusal was a particularly risky venture for Marion, a young Jewish girl in the dangerous prewar climate. In 1939 Marion and her sister, Ellen, were put on a Children's Transport (a route by which many Jewish children managed to leave Germany) and sent to a boarding school in England. Marion was one the fortunate children whose parents also managed to leave Germany. Her parents, Erna and Willy, arrived in England later in 1939; but she was not able to spend much time with them, mainly due to the conditions in England during the war.

In school, Marion soon began learning how to solve linear equations. Because she understood only a little English, she did not benefit much from the teacher's explanations but instead had to figure out on her own how to solve the equations. In retrospect, she thinks this difficulty may have been an advantage. Math continued to be of interest to her all throughout school. Although she was told it was impossible, she spent hours trying to find a method for trisecting any angle using only compass and straightedge. Her teacher patiently read through many of Marion's long attempts in order to locate her errors. Later, Marion reflected that this exploration had not been a waste of time because, in the process, she learned plane geometry exceedingly well.

After Marion graduated from school in December 1944 at age 16, the only math teacher at her school resigned. Because it was impossible to

Marion Walter. Photo courtesy of Marion Walter.

quickly find a replacement during wartime, and because Marion had earned a mark of distinction on her Cambridge University School Certificate exam, the headmistress asked her to stay on to teach math. Marion taught there for two terms, enjoyed it, and was particularly proud of the fact that all the girls passed their school-leaving exams in mathematics. She had been leaning toward a career in art, but this early teaching experience prompted her to decide to become a mathematics teacher instead. Marion completed two years of college in England before leaving in 1948 for the United States with her sister and mother. Her father had died while the family lived in England.

In New York Marion attended Hunter College, majoring in mathematics and minoring in education, and graduated in 1950. Thereafter she began her teaching career at Hunter College High School and also taught at George Washington High School. Because it was not possible to obtain a permanent job without a master's degree, she began working on her master's in mathematics at New York University, attending classes in the evenings. Several semesters later she was invited to work as a research assistant (mainly doing computing work) at what became the Courant Institute, while completing work for her degree in the evening. Though she was reluctant to give up teaching, she accepted the position at the Courant because it cut down on commuting time.

In the summers of 1952 and 1953 Marion was awarded a National Bureau of Standards Summer Student Scholarship to study at the Institute of Numerical Analysis at UCLA, which was headed by the well-known mathematician D. H. Lehmer, husband of **Emma Lehmer**. Through a series of incidents, Marion almost missed this opportunity. The letter informing her of her interview for the position did not arrive until after the scheduled interview time. In the meantime, the interviewer told Professor Isaacson, for whom Marion was working, that the Institute did not employ women. Immediately Isaacson wrote a letter of recommendation directly to Lehmer, and Marion was awarded one of the five fellowships. During the following summer, when Marion was granted a second fellowship, **Olga Taussky-Todd** became Marion's mentor and encouraged her to work on her master's degree thesis.

Marion earned her master's degree in mathematics from New York University in 1954. She was encouraged, especially by Lipman Bers, to work toward a Ph.D., but she did not want to continue supporting herself by doing computer work. Instead she accepted a teaching assistantship in the mathematics department at Cornell University. After two years she decided to apply for a full-time college teaching position. She took a one-year appointment at Simmons College in Boston in 1956. At that time the mathematics department at Simmons was only a service department and did not offer a mathematics major. By the end of Marion's first year several of her students wanted to major in mathematics, and she was asked to create such a major. Over the years many of her students went on to mathematics-related careers. Although Marion enjoyed the teaching aspects of the position, administration did not appeal to her, and at the end of four years she stepped aside as department chair.

During her nine years at Simmons Marion worked on some interesting projects, had contact with creative people, and began to take courses toward a doctorate in education at Harvard University. In 1960 she earned a fellowship to attend the National Science Foundation Summer Program at Stanford, which she considers to be one of the highlights of her career. The mathematician George Pólya, famous for his work on problem-solving strategies, was one of her teachers there. From 1962 to 1968 she participated during the summer in the Elementary Science Study at the Education Development Center in Newton, Massachusetts. Her work there involved mathematics curriculum development, and she created her well-known Mirror Cards designed to give children experience with symmetry. Her first book, based on using a mirror to explore symmetry, and her 1985 book related to the Mirror Cards, each won an Honorable Mention from the New York Academy of Science Children's Book Award Program.

In 1965 she resigned from her full-time position at Simmons to concentrate on completing her doctorate at the Harvard Graduate School of Education (HGSE). In addition to her courses in the mathematics department and in the School of Education, she took several courses at the Visual Arts Center at Harvard that have influenced her work greatly. Marion earned her Ed.D. in mathematics education in 1967 and accepted an appointment at the HGSE, teaching prospective elementary and high school teachers. Noticing how often students planning to become elementary school teachers feared mathematics, she took on the challenge of helping them develop a more positive attitude. Many of her students did come to like mathematics better, and quite a few became math specialists.

During her time at Harvard, Marion began a number of successful collaborations. She and Stephen Brown, a fellow graduate student and then a colleague at HGSE, created a new course addressing the posing of problems and approaches to problem solving. Their work on this course over several years culminated in the 1983 publication of the book *The Art of Problem Posing*, which became widely known and used. Brown says of her work, "Marion has a flair for making mathematical ideas accessible to students, whether they think they are good in math or not. She has the ability to milk mathematical activities from almost anything, including things that other people would throw away."

While she was at Harvard, Marion formed a group called the Boston Area Math Specialists (BAMS) to provide monthly workshops for practicing teachers. BAMS continues to be active in contributing to mathematics education in Massachusetts. During two of these years she also served as a mathematics consultant to the project that eventually led to the *Sesame Street* television series for children.

In 1970 Marion's book *Boxes, Squares, and Other Things* was published. The exercises in this book lead children to abstract mathematical ideas by engaging them in spatial tasks and hands-on activities. This kind of approach is common practice now but was highly innovative at the time it was developed. Her booklet, which went out of print in 1985, was chosen as one of a few select books that the National Council of Teachers of Mathematics recently reprinted in celebration of its seventy-fifth anniversary. In testimony to the importance that boxes have played in her teaching, a student once wrote Marion a note that accompanied a gift, saying, "You are one of the few people who will probably enjoy the box as much (or more!) than the contents."

In 1972 the Harvard Master of Arts in Teaching program, in which

Marion taught, was abolished. Eleanor Duckworth, a former colleague at the Elementary Science Study, urged her to apply for a teaching position at the Atlantic Institute of Education and Dalhousie University in Halifax, Nova Scotia, and Marion was invited to Halifax to give a workshop as part of her interview. She went (perhaps more because she had always wanted to see the high tide at the Bay of Fundy), and she did accept a nine-month appointment. Subsequently Marion worked briefly in Israel as a UNESCO consultant for mathematics teaching, taught at the State University of New York in Buffalo, and gave many workshops for teachers and mathematics educators. She has also published several children's books with activities based on using mirrors.

In 1977 Marion accepted what began as a one-year teaching position in the mathematics department at the University of Oregon and ended with her retirement in 1994. Her highest priority was getting students to be enthusiastic about mathematics. Students in her classes quickly learned that they would not simply be listening to a lecture but would be actively involved in solving problems. Many of her students fondly remember her habit of answering their questions with questions. Walking into her office is like visiting a museum, with mementos, photographs, and postcards from all over the world. There are stacks of geometric objects—toys to play with and use to explore mathematical ideas.

Marion's strong interests in geometry, problem posing, and visual arts have provided the dominant themes for her work throughout her career. She has published more than 40 papers and given nearly 100 workshops and talks throughout the United States and in Canada, England, Denmark, Hungary, and Israel. Recently, while employing a problem-posing strategy, she conjectured a theorem that others subsequently proved and called the Marion Walter Theorem. It states that if the trisection points of the sides of any triangle are connected to the opposite vertices, the hexagon that is formed is one-tenth of the area of the triangle.

Though retired, Marion goes into her office regularly, concentrating on writing and exploring the overlap of mathematics and the visual arts. Photography is a hobby, although her photos often take on a mathematical theme. She has published photo-essays on the symmetry of hubcaps and manhole covers. She loves to dabble in art projects such as enameling and tile-making, and traveling has great appeal for her. One of her favorite hobbies, however, is collecting all manner of objects, strange and familiar, to use as a basis for her problem-posing activities. To Marion Walter, very little is regarded as unusable trash.

Note

The information included in this biography is based in part on an interview by the author.

Selected Works by Marion Walter

(1970). *Boxes, Squares, and Other Things: A Teacher's Guide to a Unit in Informal Geometry* (Reprinted in 1995). Reston, VA: National Council of Teachers of Mathematics.

(1971). (with Stephen Brown). Missing Ingredients in Teacher Training: One Remedy. *American Mathematical Monthly* 78(4), pp. 399–404.

(1980). Mathematizing with a Piece of Paper. *Mathematics Teaching* 93. (Reprinted in Finland and Germany.)

(1983). (with Stephen Brown). *The Art of Problem Posing.* Mahwah, NJ: Lawrence Erlbaum Associates. (2nd ed., 1990; published also in Japanese and Italian.)

(1985). The Day All Textbooks Disappeared. *Mathematics Teaching* 112, pp. 8–11.

(1985). *The Mirror Puzzle Book.* Norfolk, England: Tarquin Publications. (Published also in Chinese, Korean, and French.)

(1986). A Mathematical Memoir. *Mathematics Teaching* 117, pp. 14–16.

(1988). Constructing Polyhedra without Being Told How To. In M. Senechal and G. Fleck, Eds., *Shaping Space: A Polyhedral Approach* (pp. 44–50). Boston: Birkhauser.

(1993). (with Stephen Brown, Eds. *Problem Posing: Reflections and Applications.* Mahwah, NJ: Lawrence Erlbaum Associates.

CHARLENE MORROW

SYLVIA YOUNG WIEGAND
(1945–)
Birthplace: Cape Town, South Africa

"Crazy about running!" is one way algebraist Sylvia Wiegand, professor of mathematics at the University of Nebraska, describes herself. Most people would probably agree with that assessment, given her record of finishing 100-mile races. Running, however, is just one facet of Sylvia's life, which also includes mathematical research, family, friends, teaching, travel, and service to her profession. Wiegand finds that running "complements her academic pursuits nicely."

Wiegand never doubted that women have a place in mathematics. Most lists of noted women mathematicians include her paternal grandmother, **Grace Chisholm Young**. Young was a devoted mother to six children and taught each of them to play a musical instrument and to speak several languages. At the same time she wrote books, completed coursework for a medical degree, and—together with her husband, William Henry Young—produced a substantial amount of mathematical re-

Sylvia Wiegand. Photo courtesy of Sylvia Wiegand.

search that played a key role in the development of modern analysis. It was, as Sylvia puts it, a "glorious partnership." Another strong influence for Sylvia was her maternal grandmother, Agnes Dunnett, one of the first women medical doctors in England.

In her own parents Sylvia finds a study in contrasts. Laurence Chisholm Young, an eminent research mathematician and champion chess player, is direct and enjoys challenges. Sylvia's mother, Elizabeth Young (who died in February 1995), was extremely gracious and had hosts of friends. Sylvia, born on March 8, 1945, in Cape Town, South Africa, was 4 years old when Elizabeth brought their six young children to Madison to join her husband who had begun a long tenure at the University of Wisconsin. In 1995 the University of Wisconsin mathematics department hosted a celebration in honor of his ninetieth birthday.

Sylvia, the fourth child, traces some of her interest in mathematics to the mathematical puzzles that her father posed to his children. She recalls that her father was very proud of her whenever she came up with a correct answer. Although an older brother, who died at age 23, was a graduate student in mathematics, the other siblings chose other careers: journalism, teaching, and computer science. Sylvia is the only one of her generation to carry on the family mathematical tradition. (The new generation seems to be continuing that tradition: Sylvia's son, David Wiegand, recently graduated from Reed College with a degree in mathematics and won a national scrabble championship. Daughter Andrea has more of a literary bent; she has been writing poetry and stories since second grade.)

Sylvia was already advanced in mathematics by eighth grade, when she went to England during her father's sabbatical; she was even more accelerated on her return. Later, during her last two years at Wisconsin High School in Madison, she took several mathematics courses at the University of Wisconsin. Her father on occasion even entrusted her with the task of taking notes in his graduate classes there. As a teenager Sylvia thought that his set theory course was rather easy, but she realizes now that she probably missed a great deal of the subtlety.

Although her qualifications earned her a scholarship to Bryn Mawr, a prestigious women's college in Pennsylvania, Sylvia found the adjustment to college classes difficult at first and remembers that she asked more questions than anyone else. On the other hand, she says that Ethan Bolker and her other professors were fantastic, and that mathematics and physics majors were highly valued at Bryn Mawr. Using I. N. Herstein's widely respected text, *Topics in Algebra* (1964) may have decided her fate in choosing a career in algebra—she took great delight in working on the problems Herstein posed.

At a party during her first year in college Sylvia met Roger Wiegand, a senior mathematics major at Princeton. Roger chose the University of Washington for graduate school—influenced, he admits, by the proximity to mountains (he had started climbing as a 10-year-old) as well as by the excellence of the mathematics program. In 1966 Sylvia's college credits from Wisconsin enabled her to achieve the rare distinction of earning a degree from Bryn Mawr in only three years. Sylvia and Roger were married that same summer.

For the next year, while Roger was finishing his Ph.D., the two were graduate students at the University of Washington. When Roger was offered a position at the University of Wisconsin in Madison, Sylvia became a graduate student in mathematics there; her father was still on the faculty. Although this situation put extra pressure on her as her father's daughter and as the granddaughter of two famous mathematicians, Sylvia found an encouraging climate for women in the mathematics department at Wisconsin. She attributes that in part to the presence of **Mary Ellen Rudin**, a highly respected, enthusiastic, outgoing professor who served as a mentor to many women graduate students. When Professor Rudin was later offered an endowed chair at Wisconsin, she asked that it be named after Grace Chisholm Young, Wiegand's grandmother, whom Rudin had always greatly admired. Now Sylvia is herself a valued mentor to women graduate students. Her sister, Beatrice Nearey, says that "putting people at ease and enabling them to widen their horizons, as well as their intellectual curiosity," are the basic characteristics she associates with Sylvia.

After Wiegand completed her Ph.D. in Madison, she and Roger looked for positions together—a special challenge because they are both in the same field, commutative algebra. Fortunately, the University of Nebraska offered them the opportunity to work at the same institution. In a book about her grandmother, Wiegand wrote, "Most mathematicians need a supportive spouse as well as stimulating discussions about mathematics" (Wiegand, 1996). Her grandparents, Grace and William, found that in each other. And so have Roger and Sylvia, two generations later. They too have collaborated on mathematical research and inspired each other during less productive periods in their research careers. Sometimes Wiegand is asked if it would not be easier on their relationship if they spent more time working separately, and she says no. She finds working intensely on separate projects harder, because each person is less understanding of the pressures of the other's work.

Wiegand's research area, commutative algebra, was created and formalized in the late nineteenth and early twentieth century by the famous German mathematicians David Hilbert, Richard Dedekind, and **Emmy Noether** to provide a common language and a solid mathematical foundation for two other significant areas of mathematics: number theory and algebraic geometry. Wiegand's major recent research efforts have been the study of prime ideals in the Noetherian rings (named for Emmy Noether) and decompositions of modules. Roughly speaking, this means that she looks for patterns in objects that behave like the integer prime numbers (2,3,5, etc.), and she analyzes the smallest basic building blocks for structures called modules.

When she first began, Wiegand imagined that mathematical research would involve isolating herself. Experience has taught her that this is far from the truth. She recalls a piece of mathematical work that evolved out of a series of jogging sessions with a colleague. Wiegand has come more and more to appreciate the role of communication in mathematics. Students in her classes are encouraged to talk to each other about the mathematics they are learning. She devotes considerable time to committee work, which also demands good communication skills. As chair of the American Mathematical Society's (AMS) Policy Committee on Meetings and Conferences, Wiegand frequently organizes research sessions in commutative algebra, such as one held in San Francisco in January 1995. She has also organized and assisted with many programs to encourage younger women in mathematics and science. Sylvia was elected to the AMS Council for 1994–1996 and is the current president of the Association for Women in Mathematics for 1997 and 1998. She was awarded a National Science Foundation visiting professorship in 1993 and used it to spend the year at Purdue University, where she not only worked on her own research but arranged for many well-known women mathematicians to visit and meet with the graduate students.

When she was a child, Sylvia was interested in writing fiction and actually started an epic novel. Later she was editor of her high school newspaper. She still does a great deal of writing as a referee for professional papers, editor of two journals, and author of her own mathematical research papers and historical articles about her grandparents. She also frequently submits articles about the sport of running to the *Lincoln Track Club Newsletter*.

Spending time with each other and with their children is a priority for the Wiegands. Both enjoy cooking and parties. Family vacations, often combined with trips to conferences, typically involve highly challenging outdoor activities in beautiful mountainous places. David and Andrea started mountaineering even earlier than their father and are now accomplished climbers.

As for Sylvia, she is hooked on running. She hesitates, however, to call herself a competitive runner; she focuses less intensely on pursuing a particular time goal, more on enjoying the surroundings and the people. She completed the 100-mile mountainous Western States run; this course has a total of 18,000 feet of uphills and 23,000 feet of downhills and most of it takes place above 10,000 feet. With her family as support team, she was able to complete the 100-mile 1994 Leadville race within the cutoff time of thirty hours. She feels that long-distance running typifies one of her main strengths, perseverance. "I'm not fast, but I can keep going!" In one long-distance race, commentators paid no attention to her slow progress until about halfway when they realized she was the first woman and her pace hadn't changed for thirty miles. Sylvia has approached her mathematical work with that same persistence. She had some dry spells when her children were young and when her service activities were overwhelming, but her involvement in research persisted; currently she produces several research articles a year, totaling more than thirty at present. She is frequently invited to talk about her research, sometimes in exotic places such as Marseilles, Rome, and Morocco. To her surprise, some people who may not have taken her seriously at the beginning of her career are now on the sidelines cheering for her.

Note

The information included in this biography is based in part on an interview by the author.

Selected Works by Sylvia Wiegand

(1987). Grace Chisholm Young. In L. Grinstein and P. Campbell, *Women of Mathematics*, Westport, CT: Greenwood Press, pp. 247–254.

(1994). Bounds for one-dimensional rings of finite Cohen-Macaulay type (with R. Wiegand). *Journal of Pure & Applied Algebra* (93), 311–342.

(1995). One-Dimensional Rings of Finite Representation Type (with N. Cimen and R. Wiegand). In A. Facchini and C. Menini, Eds., *Abelian Groups and Modules*. Dordrect: Kluwer.

(1995). Prime Ideals in Birational Extensions of Polynomial Rings II (with W. Heinzer and D. Lantz). In D. Anderson and D. Dobbs, Eds., *Zero-Dimensional Commutative Rings*. New York: Marcel Dekker.

(1995). Prime Ideals in Polynomial Rings over One-Dimensional Domains (with W. Henizer). *Transactions of the American Mathematical Society* 347 (2), pp. 639–50.

(1996). Grace Chisholm Young and William Henry Young. In H. Pycior, N. Slack, and P. Abir-am, Eds. *Creative Couples*. New Brunswick, NJ: Rutgers University Press.

KATHLEEN SULLIVAN

GRACE CHISHOLM YOUNG
(1868–1944)
Birthplace: England

The life story of Grace Chisholm Young is inspirational. It is about persistence, dedication, and love for both work and family. It is even more remarkable because she was a mathematician who was born more than one hundred years ago—on March 15, 1868, in a town just outside London, England. At the time of her birth, her father was the Warden of the Standards in the British government, responsible for weights and measures. Her mother enjoyed music and was an accomplished pianist. Grace had an older brother and an older sister.

Education in England was quite different in the middle of the nineteenth century from education today. Until 1870 the law only required education for boys. In 1880 a law was passed that made education mandatory for all children until the age of 11. However, in special circumstances exceptions could be made so that a child would not have to attend school. One such exception was made for young Grace. She had suffered terrible headaches and nightmares as a very small child, and it was felt that she would be better off not attending school, staying at home instead and being educated by her mother. Because Grace's father

Grace Chisholm Young and son. Photo courtesy of Sylvia Wiegand.

was rather elderly when Grace was born and retired when she was still quite young, she was able to spend time with both parents during her early years.

Grace was the baby of the family and quite persistent in her ways. She was only taught things in which she was interested. With her mother, she studied music; with her father, she was able to explore and work in his workshop. However, her real love was mental arithmetic. She showed a very intense interest in mathematics at an early age.

When Grace was 10 years old her parents hired a governess to be her teacher and to work with her at home. She was an avid learner and at age 17 passed the Cambridge Senior Examination, but because she was a woman she was not allowed to enter Cambridge University; only men were permitted entry. She had dreamed of going to the university and studying medicine, but those dreams were not to be. In addition to being denied entry into Cambridge University because of her gender, her mother would not allow her to study medicine.

Finally, in 1889, when Grace was 21 years old she enrolled in Girton College, a part of Cambridge University that was dedicated to providing a university education to women. By this time Grace had decided she wanted to study mathematics. Although she received a partial scholarship from Girton, she still needed money to pay the rest of her tuition. She knew her father was supportive of her attending college and had the money to help her. He was happy to do so, for he knew Grace had great potential in mathematics.

While she was at Girton Grace met her future husband, William Young, who became her tutor in mathematics when her regular tutor was no longer able to work with her. Tutors at college were similar to teachers or instructors, rather than people who worked with students who needed extra help. Grace certainly didn't need extra help, as she did very well in her studies and wanted to continue studying mathematics as a graduate student. Unfortunately, she faced an all-too-familiar problem: Women were not yet permitted to enroll in graduate schools in England.

Grace was not deterred from pursuing her dream. She decided to go instead to Göttingen, Germany (one of the mathematics centers of the world), to study with Felix Klein, a well-known and respected mathematician. She still faced problems because she was a woman. She had to get special permission to be admitted; then, when her work was completed, she had to have approval of the government to take the examination for her degree. Fortunately, permission was granted and Grace Chisholm Young, at age 27, earned her doctorate. Although **Sofya Kovalevskaya** had been granted a doctoral degree from Göttingen in 1874, she was not officially a student at the University; thus Young became the first woman to officially earn a doctorate from a German university.

Having completed her degree Grace returned to England, dissertation in hand. In those days, copies of the dissertation were sent to people who would have an interest in that nature of work. A copy was sent to William Young, Grace's former tutor at Girton. William was grateful for the paper and wrote a thank-you letter in which he asked Grace if she would be interested in working with him on an astronomy book. They subsequently fell in love, were married, and moved to Switzerland—a long way from England and their families. They both felt that the environment in Switzerland would be more conducive to learning and that they would have many more opportunities to support their creative research efforts.

At this point in Grace's life, it would have been easy to give up her work and studies and devote herself to her husband and raising a family. However, this is not what she wanted. The two worked together writing scholarly papers and books. Because they were both accomplished mathematicians, it is difficult to determine who did most of the work. It may be that by working together they were able to achieve far more than either one would have accomplished alone. It is interesting to note that although William's name appeared on most of the papers, he often wrote that he would not have been able to complete the work without Grace.

Unfortunately, William never found a full-time, permanent professorship so that the family could settle down and live what some might call a "normal" life. William was never offered a job at a top university despite being respected by many of his peers. In 1922 he became president of the London Mathematical Society, and in 1929 he was president of the International Union of Mathematicians. Because he had no permanent position, William was forced to spend much of the year traveling to far-off places to teach, and this kept him away from his family. During his absences Grace raised the children alone and worked with William through correspondence. When William was home he was very demanding of Grace. She often became exhausted and slept for several days when he finally left again. Because his travels took him to many distant lands, and transportation was by boat or train, William was gone for very long periods of time.

Cecily Tanner, Grace and William's second child, once wrote that her father, although very bright, needed direction and stimulation, whereas her mother, also of great intelligence, was quite the opposite and had a lot of energy, initiative, and persistence. With these skills, Grace was able to promote William and his work to a much greater degree than he would have done alone. However, by doing this Grace allowed William's work to become the primary focus of their collaboration, whereas her own work took a back seat.

Grace and William had six children during the first eleven years of their marriage, and Grace was as devoted to them as she was to her work. She taught her children music and how to play a musical instrument, just as her mother had with her. She also instilled in her children a love of languages. During some of William's absences, his unmarried sisters came to help Grace with the house and children. This gave her the time to work on her own research, studies, and writing and allowed her time to travel with William on some of his many trips abroad.

In 1905 Young published her own book on geometry that included patterns for folding paper into three-dimensional geometric figures. Many of these patterns are used even today in geometry and mathematics classes. In 1906 Grace and William published *The Theory of Sets and Points*, the first published book that provided comprehensive applications of set theory and problems in mathematical analysis. Although Young had received her doctorate, had raised six children, and had written scholarly books and articles, she continued studying and learning. One of her unfulfilled dreams was to become a doctor of medicine. She did take all the necessary courses to be a doctor but never completed the required internship.

Grace Chisholm Young was a powerful role model and an inspiration to her children and grandchildren, as well as to girls and women born more than one hundred years later. Of her six children, one daughter, Rosalind (Cecily) Tanner, became a mathematician and historian; another daughter, Janet Michael, became a medical doctor, thereby fulfilling her mother's dream; and Grace's youngest daughter, Helen Canu, took her graduate studies in mathematics. Two of her sons also continued her interests in mathematics and science. Lawrence became a mathematician and Patrick became a chemist. Her eldest son, Francis, was killed in World War I. Lawrence's daughter—Grace's granddaughter, **Sylvia Wiegand**—earned a Ph.D. in mathematics and is professor of mathematics at the University of Nebraska. In a time when the study of mathematics seemed out of reach to most women, the women in Grace's family seemed to think it was natural to study mathematics. Having such a role model as Grace must have provided a strong sense that mathematics was certainly within reach.

The onset of World War II started a series of tragedies in the Young family. In 1940 Grace took two of her grandchildren to England. William was supposed to follow a couple of days later. However, France was under siege. This prevented William from leaving Switzerland for England. Being isolated and separated from his family, he became depressed and senile. He never saw Grace again, and in 1942 he died. Grace stayed in England. In 1944, just two years after William's death, Grace had a heart attack and died. She was 76 years old.

Selected Works by Grace Chisholm Young

(1905). *Beginner's Book of Geometry*. London. (Reprinted: New York: Chelsea, 1970.)

(1905). On the Form of a Certain Jordan Curve. *Quarterly Journal of Pure and Applied Mathematics* 37, pp. 87–91.

(1906). *The Theory of Sets and Points* (with William H. Young). Cambridge, England. (Reprinted: New York: Chelsea, 1972.)

(1916). On the Derives of a Function. *Proceedings of the London Mathematical Society* 2(15), pp. 360–84.

(1924). On the Solution of a Pair of Simultaneous Diophantine Equations Connected with the Nuptial Number of Plato. *Proceedings of the London Mathematical Society* 2(23), pp. 27–44.

(1929). On Functions Possessing Differentials. *Fundamenta Mathematicae* 14, pp. 61–94.

Selected Works about Grace Chisholm Young

Grattan-Guinness, I. (1972). A Mathematical Union: William Henry and Grace Chisholm Young. *Annals of Science* 29(2), pp. 107–51.

Perl, Teri. (1978). *Math Equals: Biographies of Women Mathematicians and Related Activities* (pp. 149–71). Menlo Park, CA: Addison-Wesley.

Smith, Sanderson M. (1996). *Agnesi to Zeno: Over 100 Vignettes from the History of Math* (pp. 159–60). Berkeley, CA: Key Curriculum Press.

Weigand, Sylvia M. (1987). Grace Chisholm Young. In Louise S. Grinstein and Paul J. Campbell, Eds., *Women of Mathematics* (pp. 247–54). Westport, CT: Greenwood Press.

LAURA COFFIN KOCH

APPENDIX I: DATES OF BIRTH

c. 360–415	Hypatia
1706–1749	Emilie Du Chatelet
1718–1799	Maria Agnesi
1776–1831	Sophie Germain
1780–1872	Mary Somerville
1815–1852	Ada Lovelace
1847–1930	Christine Ladd-Franklin
1850–1891	Sofya Kovalevskaya
1858–1931	Charlotte Angas Scott
1860–1940	Alicia Boole Stott
1868–1944	Grace Chisholm Young
1882–1935	Emmy Noether
1885–1967	Pauline Sperry
1900–1986	Ida Rhodes
1902–	Mina Rees
1906–	Emma Lehmer
1906–1992	Grace Hopper
1906–1995	Olga Taussky-Todd
1908–	Herta Taussig Freitag
1914–1979	Marjorie Lee Browne
1915–	Alice Schafer
1919–1985	Julia Robinson

1922–	Anneli Lax
1923–	Cathleen Morawetz
1924–	Evelyn Boyd Granville
1924–	Mary Ellen Rudin
1928–	Elizabeth Fennema
1928–	Marion Walter
c. 1931–	Etta Falconer
1932–1995	Vivienne Malone-Mayes
1935–	Gloria Hewitt
1936–	Leone Burton
1939–	Mary Gray
1939–	Doris Schattschneider
1939–	Marjorie Senechal
1940–	Cora Sadosky
c. 1940–	Lesley Sibner
1941–	Gilah Leder
1941–	Marie-Louise Michelsohn
1942–	Lenore Blum
1942–	Nancy Kopell
1942–	Harriet Pollatsek
1942–	Karen Uhlenbeck
1944–	Mary Beth Ruskai
1944–	Jean Taylor
1945–	Joan Hutchinson
1945–	Dusa McDuff
1945–	Judith Roitman
1945–	Sylvia Wiegand
1947–	Sylvia Bozeman
1947–	Rhonda Hughes
1948–	Cheryl Praeger
1949–	Fan Chung
1949–	Chuu-Lian Terng
1954–	Ingrid Daubechies
1955–	Karen Parshall
1955–	Bernadette Perrin-Riou
1958–	Joan Feigenbaum
1965–	Andrea Bertozzi

APPENDIX II: COUNTRIES OF EMPLOYMENT AND ORIGIN

Note that "Country of Employment" refers to the country or countries in which the biographee did the majority of her postgraduate work, excluding time-limited positions such as visiting professorships or postdoctoral fellowships.

Country of Employment	Name	Country of Origin
Argentina	Cora Sadosky	Argentina
Australia	Gilah Leder	The Netherlands
	Cheryl Praeger	Australia
Austria	Olga Taussky-Todd	Czechoslovakia
Belgium	Ingrid Daubechies	Belgium
Egypt	Hypatia	Egypt
England	Leone Burton	Australia
	Ada Lovelace	England
	Dusa McDuff	Scotland
	Charlotte Angas Scott	England
	Mary Somerville	Scotland
	Alicia Boole Stott	Ireland
	Olga Taussky-Todd	Czechoslovakia
	Grace Chisholm Young	England

Country of Employment	Name	Country of Origin
France	Emilie Du Chatelet	France
	Sophie Germain	France
	Sofya Kovalevskaya	Russia
	Bernadette Perrin-Riou	France
Germany	Sofya Kovalevskaya	Russia
	Emmy Noether	Germany
	Olga Taussky-Todd	Czechoslovakia
Italy	Maria Agnesi	Italy
Russia	Sofya Kovalevskaya	Russia
Sweden	Sofya Kovalevskaya	Russia
Switzerland	Grace Chisholm Young	England
United States	Andrea Bertozzi	United States
	Lenore Blum	United States
	Sylvia Bozeman	United States
	Marjorie Lee Browne	United States
	Fan Chung	Taiwan
	Ingrid Daubechies	Belgium
	Etta Falconer	United States
	Joan Feigenbaum	United States
	Elizabeth Fennema	United States
	Herta Taussig Freitag	Austria
	Evelyn Boyd Granville	United States
	Mary Gray	United States
	Gloria Hewitt	United States
	Grace Hopper	United States
	Rhonda Hughes	United States
	Joan Hutchinson	United States
	Nancy Kopell	United States
	Christine Ladd-Franklin	United States
	Anneli Lax	Upper Silesia

Country of Employment	Name	Country of Origin
	Emma Lehmer	Russia
	Vivienne Malone-Mayes	United States
	Dusa McDuff	Scotland
	Marie-Louise Michelsohn	United States
	Cathleen Morawetz	Canada
	Emmy Noether	Germany
	Karen Parshall	United States
	Harriet Pollatsek	United States
	Mina Rees	United States
	Ida Rhodes	Ukraine
	Julia Robinson	United States
	Judith Roitman	United States
	Mary Ellen Rudin	United States
	Mary Beth Ruskai	United States
	Cora Sadosky	Argentina
	Alice Schafer	United States
	Doris Schattschneider	United States
	Charlotte Angas Scott	England
	Marjorie Senechal	United States
	Lesley Sibner	United States
	Pauline Sperry	United States
	Olga Taussky-Todd	Czechoslovakia
	Jean Taylor	United States
	Chuu-Lian Terng	Taiwan
	Karen Uhlenbeck	United States
	Marion Walter	Germany
	Sylvia Wiegand	South Africa
Venezuela	Cora Sadosky	Argentina

INDEX

Page numbers in **bold** refer to main entries.

ABOUT THE EDITORS AND CONTRIBUTORS

EDITORS

CHARLENE MORROW earned her Ph.D. in clinical psychology from Florida State University. She worked for many years in community mental health and taught psychology before coming to Mount Holyoke College, where she currently co-directs SummerMath, a six-week program for high school women. Dr. Morrow investigates effective learning approaches and educational environments for girls and women and has presented and written extensively on this topic. She is a past president and current co-executive director of Women and Mathematics Education, which actively promotes women's participation in mathematics. She is current chair of the Comprehensive Mathematics Education for Every Child Committee of the National Council of Teachers of Mathematics.

TERI PERL is the author of two highly acclaimed books on women and mathematics: *Math Equals* (1978) and *Women and Numbers* (1993). Other educational books and materials she has written include *Patches* and *Alphagrams*, teacher activity books for Relationshapes, a manipulative material developed by Cuisenaire Company of America. She is also coauthor of *A Sourcebook for Substitutes* (1974). Dr. Perl has been an educational consultant and software designer since 1975; she received her Ph.D. in mathematics education from Stanford University in 1979. As a co-founder of The Learning Company, Dr. Perl helped create several award-winning software packages in mathematics education. She continues to be involved in teacher development, both at the preservice and in-service levels.

CONTRIBUTORS

SUSAN BEAL, Ph.D., has been a professor of mathematics and mathematics education at Saint Xavier University in Chicago, Illinois, for the past nineteen years. She has taught students from kindergarten through graduate school. Her research interests include the mathematical understanding of preservice teachers. She has also written materials for teachers on the use of manipulatives in the teaching of mathematics. She has given workshops and presentations at the local, state, and national levels.

LYNN BENANDER coordinates Mount Holyoke College's Teaching for Understanding Project for urban teachers and middle-school youth and directs leadership training and education programs for cooperative businesses in the northeastern United States. She has completed graduate work in mathematics and holds a master's degree in education. She is interested in gender and class issues in schools and businesses.

REGINA BARON BRUNNER, Ph.D., is an associate professor of mathematics and computer science at Cedar Crest College in Allentown, Pennsylvania. Her research interests include gender equity issues, collaborative learning, and mathematics-science integration at K–12 and college levels. Since 1988 she has served as project director of MathConn, a mathematics awareness day for seventh and eighth grade girls and their teachers.

FLORENCE FASANELLI is director of SUMMA (Strengthening Underrepresented Minority Mathematics Achievement) Intervention Programs at the Mathematical Association of America. Formerly chair of the International Study Group on the Relation between the History and Pedagogy of Mathematics, she focuses her research on the visualization of mathematics throughout history.

HELEN J. FORGASZ, Ph.D., is a postdoctoral research fellow at La Trobe University in Melbourne, Australia. Before working in academia she taught mathematics, physics, and computer studies at the secondary school level. Her research interests in education include gender equity issues, mature-age students of mathematics, and affect and context factors that relate to mathematics learning. She has published widely in these and other areas.

HANNIA GONZALEZ is a graduate student in mathematics at the University of Massachusetts at Amherst. She has taught for several years at the University as well as in the SummerMath program at Mount Holyoke College. She has worked as a mathematics education consultant in Washington, D.C., and New York. Her main professional interest is in teaching math to minorities who are underrepresented in the field.

LOUISE ROSLANSKY GROSSLEIN holds B.A. and M.S. degrees in biology. She is a biology lab instructor and assistant director of laboratories at Mount Holyoke College in South Hadley, Massachusetts. For the past twelve years she has taught computer programming, biology, and math at SummerMath, a national program for teenage women at Mount Holyoke College. Previously she worked in environmental education at the elementary school level at the Hitchcock Center in Amherst, Massachusetts.

DENISE GÜRER, Ph.D., is a computer scientist who works in the areas of education and artificial intelligence, cognitive modeling, and the history of women in computing. Since joining Stanford Research Institute International in Menlo Park, California, she has led many technology-related projects and has received numerous awards for her work in the development of computer environments and mentorship for girls through the use of technology.

KATHERINE HANSON is the director of the Women's Educational Equity Act Resource Center at Education Development Center in Newton, Massachusetts. She conducts research and writes extensively about the sociological and educational implications of gender. She is a national presenter on equity and diversity, and she provides professional development workshops to hundreds of teachers each year, focusing on creating more equitable classrooms.

PATRICIA CLARK KENSCHAFT, Ph.D., is a professor of mathematics at Montclair State University, where she has taught for twenty-three years. She has written widely on women, blacks, and careers in mathematics. She edited the book *Winning Women into Mathematics*, published in 1991 by the Mathematical Association of America, and is now writing a book for parents *Math Power for Your Child*.

LAURA COFFIN KOCH, Ph.D., is an associate professor at the University of Minnesota. In her research she explores how girls, women, and minority students come to know mathematics. With a grant from the National Science Foundation she is developing a mathematics, science, and technology program for girls in grades 4–8 who have disabilities.

She has given presentations and published articles related to gender and cultural issues in the learning of mathematics.

EDITH KORT is the director of the Math, Science and Computer Camp for Girls, a summer day camp for girls ages 8–12. She is completing her doctoral work in mathematics education at the University of Rochester, New York, and is interested in innovative teaching in mathematics and in gender issues. She has also been a computer project leader for Mobil Corporation and a manager and computer specialist for various government agencies.

GREER LLEAUD holds a B.F.A. in bookmaking. She has written articles on women's issues and the arts for the *Tenderloin Times,* a San Francisco community newspaper. Currently she is chief copy editor at Key Curriculum Press in Emeryville, California, and editor of Key Curriculum's *Agnesi to Zeno: Over 100 Vignettes from the History of Math* (1996).

CAROL E. MALLOY, Ph.D., is an assistant professor of education at the University of North Carolina at Chapel Hill, where she teaches preservice secondary-level mathematics teachers. Previously she taught for twenty years at the middle and secondary school levels. Her research interests include the effects of culture on learning mathematics, student resiliency and responsibility for mathematics learning, and mathematical problem solving. Currently she is president of the Benjamin Banneker Association.

JUNE MARK is a project director at Education Development Center, a nonprofit research and development organization in Newton, Massachusetts. Her work includes a wide range of materials development and qualitative research activities in mathematics education, community technology access, and the professional development of teachers. Currently she is editing a bibliography on gender equity in mathematics education for the Women and Mathematics Education organization.

MARGARET R. MEYER, Ph.D., is a faculty associate in the Department of Curriculum and Instruction at the University of Wisconsin, Madison, where she teaches in the secondary mathematics certification program. She is also an associate researcher at the National Center for Mathematical Sciences Education, where she is involved in the development of a new middle-school mathematics curriculum.

JAMES MORROW, who holds a Ph.D. in mathematics from Florida State University, currently directs Mount Holyoke College's SummerMath program along with his colleague and companion, Charlene Morrow. He is working on ways in which computer technology, combined with reflection on problem solving, can be used to make sense of mathematics. He actively promotes women's participation in mathematics.

JUDITH OLSON holds an Ed.D. in curriculum and instruction. She is currently a professor of mathematics at Western Illinois University, where she teaches mathematics and mathematics education courses and actively promotes the importance of mathematics for all—especially women and traditionally underrepresented groups. She directed a National Science Foundation project, Connecting the Past with the Future: Women in Mathematics and Science, and has coauthored articles about multicultural education.

MELFRIED OLSON, who holds an Ed.D. in curriculum and instruction, secondary mathematics, is a professor of mathematics and mathematics education at Western Illinois University, where he works with precollege teachers of mathematics. He has obtained funding for several school-based projects that have focused on equity in education. He has written mathematics materials for the project known as Connecting the Past with the Future: Women in Mathematics and Science, and he has coauthored two articles about multicultural education.

ULRICA WILSON PARKER did her undergraduate work in mathematics at Spelman College in Atlanta, Georgia. She earned an M.S. in mathematics at the University of Massachusetts, Amherst. Parker takes every opportunity to surround herself with young people who are interested in the challenges that mathematics can bring.

CASSONDRA MCDANIEL POWERS earned a B.S. in science from Oakland University in Michigan. She taught at the elementary school level in Pontiac, Michigan, where she developed several science games. Currently she divides her time between mothering her two children, freelance writing, and working toward her M.S. in curriculum instruction and leadership at Oakland University.

JOAN ROSS is a mathematics consultant based in Ann Arbor, Michigan. She did her graduate work at the University of Wisconsin. She has designed Family Math Nights, mathematical exhibits, and classes for the Ann Arbor Hands-On Museum. She has consulted with numerous organizations ranging from the Instructional Gaming Group at the University of Michigan to software companies. She has taught math at the college and precollege levels, and she has published articles on mathematical topics.

FAYE NISONOFF RUOPP is a project director at the Education Development Center in Newton, Massachusetts, where she directs mathematics teacher enhancement projects. Previously she taught mathematics for twenty years at Lincoln-Sudbury Regional High School. Her professional interests also include cooperative learning, equity in K–12 mathematics education, curriculum development, and school-business partnerships.

AYSE A. SAHIN, Ph.D., is an assistant professor of mathematics at North Dakota State University in Fargo. She received her undergraduate degree from Mount Holyoke College in South Hadley, Massachusetts, in 1988. She went on to do graduate work at the University of Maryland in College Park, earning her doctorate in 1994. Her research is in the area of measurable dynamical systems with multidimensional time parameters.

LYNAE E. SAKSHAUG, who holds a Ph.D. in mathematics education, is an assistant professor of mathematics at Western Illinois University. She teaches mathematics and mathematics education courses for pre-service and in-service elementary and middle-school teachers. She is a strong advocate of diversity in mathematics and admires the women who have gone before her in the field.

JEAN SCHMITTAU, Ph.D., is an associate professor at the State University of New York at Binghamton, where she teaches master's and doctoral courses in the psychology of learning and mathematics education. She has done research in Russia and has published articles on Vygotskian psychology, cognitive development, and mathematics learning. She is editor of the international journal *Focus on Learning Problems in Mathematics*.

SANDERSON M. SMITH, Ed.D., is a mathematics teacher at the Cate School in Carpenteria, California. The author of numerous books and articles relating to mathematics and its history, he is a frequent speaker at mathematics conferences. He is the recipient of teaching awards, including the California Presidential Award in Mathematics. Currently he serves on the Educational Material Committee of the National Council of Teachers of Mathematics.

HOMER STAVELY, Ph.D., is a professor of psychology and director of multicultural programs at Keene State College in Keene, New Hampshire, where he teaches a wide variety of courses. He also teaches computer programming in Mount Holyoke College's SummerMath program. His interests include the information revolution, educational uses of computers, and multicultural issues. For several years he wrote a column on computers for the bimonthly magazine *Education Australia*.

KATHLEEN SULLIVAN, Ph.D., is an associate professor of mathematics at Seattle University. Before beginning her doctoral studies she taught in grade school and secondary school. She directs Science Splash, a program designed to interest middle-school girls in mathematics and science by giving them an opportunity to be taught and mentored by professional volunteers, university faculty, and college students. Science Splash is supported by government, foundation, and corporate grants.

LYN TAYLOR, Ph.D., is an associate professor of mathematics education at the University of Colorado, Denver, where she works with preservice and in-service teachers. Her research interests include mathematical life histories and attitudes, Vygotskian theory, and gender- and culture-fair materials and environments for learning mathematics. She has given talks in Hungary, Australia, and Russia, as well as doing many presentations and workshops in the United States. She is a past president of Women and Mathematics Education.

BARBARA TERMAAT did her undergraduate work in geological oceanography and holds an M.Ed. in mathematics and science education from Harvard University. She has interwoven teaching, mathematics, science, and computer skills in public and private schools with corporate technical writing and training positions. Currently she is a technical trainer in San Jose, California. Her career interest is in making abstract and technical concepts accessible to any audience through curriculum development.

DYANNE M. TRACY, Ph.D., is an associate professor of curriculum instruction and leadership at Oakland University in Rochester, Michigan. She enjoys team teaching mathematics with first- through eighth-grade teachers to develop an innovative curriculum that promotes effective mathematics instruction. Her research interests include gender socialization in schools, and the effects of mathematics education innovations on teaching and assessment. Dr. Tracy gives presentations and has authored many articles related to her interests.

PATRICIA S. WILSON is a professor at the University of Georgia, where she works with high school mathematics teachers and students who are becoming mathematics teachers. Her research interests include teacher development and culture-inclusive mathematics. She is an active member and former officer of Women and Mathematics Education and of other professional organizations that promote equity in mathematics education.

KAY A. WOHLHUTER, who holds a Ph.D. in mathematics education from Oregon State University, is an assistant professor of mathematics education at Western Illinois University. She teaches mathematics and mathematics education courses for preservice and in-service elementary and middle-school teachers. She is interested in providing all individuals equal access to mathematics.

BONNIE S. WOOD, Ph.D., is an associate professor of biology at the University of Maine, Presque Isle, where she teaches biology and genetics. She earned a B.A. in biology from Wellesley College and a Ph.D. in medical sciences from Cornell University Medical College. Her current research interest is gender equity in mathematics and science education.

SUSAN ZACHARKIW holds an M.B.A. from the University of Colorado and is currently pursuing a master's degree in curriculum and instruction. She taught fourth- and fifth-grade mathematics at the Challenge School in Denver, Colorado, and will continue to teach and develop gender-equitable math curricula in Pennsylvania, where she currently lives. Her interests include gender equity in the teaching of mathematics, and the empowering of girls at the elementary school level.